# WRITING CENTERS

Recent Titles in
Bibliographies and Indexes in Education

# WRITING CENTERS

*An Annotated Bibliography*

*Compiled by*
Christina Murphy,
Joe Law,
and Steve Sherwood

*Bibliographies and Indexes in Education, Number 17*

**GREENWOOD PRESS**
Westport, Connecticut • London

**Library of Congress Cataloging-in-Publication Data**

Murphy, Christina.
  Writing centers : an annotated bibliography / compiled by
Christina Murphy, Joe Law, and Steve Sherwood.
    p.    cm.—(Bibliographies and indexes in education, ISSN
0742–6917 : no. 17)
  Includes indexes.
  ISBN 0–313–29831–9 (alk. paper)
  1. English language—Rhetoric—Study and teaching—Bibliography.
2. English language—Composition and exercises—Study and teaching—
Bibliography.  3. Resource programs (Education)—Management—
Bibliography.  4. Tutors and tutoring—Bibliography.  5. Writing
centers—Bibliography.    I. Law, Joe.  II. Sherwood, Steve.
III. Title.  IV. Series.
Z5818.E5M87  1996
[PE1404]
016.808′042′07—dc20          96–18521

British Library Cataloguing in Publication Data is available.

Library of Congress Catalog Card Number: 96–18521
ISBN: 0–313–29831–9
ISSN: 0742–6917

First published in 1996

Greenwood Press, 88 Post Road West, Westport, CT 06881

Printed in the United States of America

The paper used in this book complies with the
Permanent Paper Standard issued by the National
Information Standards Organization (Z39.48–1984).

P

# Contents

# Preface

### Rationale

This annotated bibliography introduces the reader to almost a century of writing center scholarship and provides an overview of the history, educational philosophies, and day-to-day practices that define the writing center field.

An annotated bibliography on writing centers is especially apt at this point in American educational history because writing centers have been one of the most significant educational innovations of this century. Today it is a rare high school, community college, college or university that does not have a writing center, and the impact of writing centers upon the way writing is taught has been both revolutionary and lasting. The collaborative, interactive model of writing center tutorials based upon individualized instruction has called into question much of the traditional theory and practice of classroom instruction. Consequently, the paradigm shift initiated by this model has moved writing instruction away from knowledge transfer to knowledge construction, with students operating as active participants in their own learning.

Such an important movement deserves a full historical accounting, but specific scholarship on writing centers has been difficult to find in its entirety—an obstacle this volume seeks to address. Because early writing center practice was carried out much more by networking than by historical record, many early documents are located in a variety of sources not easy to chronicle. In a similar vein, many of the outlets for the publication of writing center scholarship did not appear until several decades after the writing center movement came to prominence. Even with the presence of such important venues as *Writing Lab Newsletter* and *The Writing Center Journal*, complete sets of these two publications are not common in many libraries or archives. As a consequence, writing center researchers often have trouble knowing what the issues contain and thus what directions writing center scholarship suggests for investigation.

Since the writing center field is a nexus of many disciplines, ranging from educational psychology to psychoanalytic theory and from small group dynamics to management theory, much writing center scholarship has been published in a range of journals that might not readily suggest themselves to the researcher. Further complicating this picture is the fact that writing centers themselves span the whole realm of academics, from elementary school writing centers to those that serve graduate students and faculty in professional fields. Again, locating all the scholarship on such a diverse range of activities and educational philosophies proves an enormous challenge. However, a guide such as this annotated bibliography makes clear the scholarship on writing centers, the fields that have converged to define this field, and the areas of inquiry that still need to be pursued.

### Organization

We have divided this bibliography into sections that reflect the central concerns of the entries in each grouping. We would like to feel that the complexity of writing center theory and practice—and even the entries in each section—divided so neatly, but obviously they do not. Only conceptually can writing center administration be separated out from writing center theory or theory separated from ethics. In a similar vein, many of the entries themselves have multiple points of investigation and inquiry and could justify inclusion in several sections.

To address this very real dilemma, we have grouped the entries by what we consider to be the main focus, and we have provided an extensive subject index with cross-referencing so that subtopics within the entries in each section can be traced.

### Reference Style

We have used the documentation style of the *MLA Handbook*, 4th edition, in this bibliography. This style is the most common for the humanities and also for the journals in which most writing center scholarship is published. It is generally, too, the one that scholars in the humanities are most familiar with and able to apply easily in their own research on writing centers.

## STRUCTURE

### History, Program Descriptions, and Professional Concerns

Since the structure of this annotated bibliography reflects the dominant

areas of inquiry and practice defining writing centers as a discipline, some of
the major divisions suggest themselves logically as starting points—such as the
history of the writing center movement, the program descriptions of early
writing centers as they were established in high schools and universities across
the country, and the professional concerns of those working in writing centers
as they sought to establish an identity for their work and means for validating
their achievements and contributions. Therefore, the first section focuses on
clarifying the early record and also revealing the enthusiasms and frustrations
writing center professionals experienced as they established a new practice and
developed innovative responses to the myriad of institutional configurations and
philosophies they faced.

### Writing Center Theory

As educational history proves, theory tends to emerge from practice, and
certainly the writing center field proves no exception to the truth of this maxim.
Scholars and researchers sought to define the discipline and to seek
commonalities of practice that could identify both a movement and its
philosophies. Within the theory section, the scholarly record indicates an
alliance between writing center theory and pedagogy and the theory and
pedagogy of composition studies. Clearly, the documents in this section reflect
the major movements that shaped composition pedagogy during this century,
from current-traditional rhetoric with a focus on the stylistic correctness of the
text, to the emphasis upon the individual writer in process pedagogy, to the
focus on cultural and historical forces in the shaping of the writer's personal
and social identity.

Evident in this section, too, is the theory-practice dichotomy that informs
much writing center scholarship as it seeks to establish conceptual models of the
writing center and of its place in literacy education. So much of the writing
center experience seems to be grounded in practice as day-to-day management
and in the shepherding of scarce resources that there is a sense that theory
should address practical issues and provide models of management,
organization, and interdisciplinarity. To this end, a large portion of writing
center theory suggests the following sections on administration, writing across
the curriculum, and educational technology as the center point in defining the
writing center's mission within the academy.

### Administration, Writing Across the Curriculum, and Educational Technology

The section on administration, like the program designs section preceding
it, is imbued with a mix of history, individual narratives of writing centers
responding to educational demands and seeking institutional validation, and

efforts to establish some common principles or guidelines of management theory. The focus on networking returns, as mentoring becomes a major theme of the documents in this section. The mentoring model emerges from many of the theoretical and practical concerns articulated in the theory section. The concept of apprenticeship learning defines many articles in this section as writing center directors learn from the most successful program directors and seek to apply similar strategies in structuring their own centers.

A prominent theme, too, is the effort to establish program links with other academic constituencies, most especially the academic departments on campus. Writing across the curriculum and educational technology offer the writing center centripetal energy for connecting with these units and for serving the needs of the campus. As a result, a substantial number of entries address the relationship of writing centers to writing across the curriculum programs, most especially in considering to what extent each program drives the other and how beneficial alliances shall be established.

With educational technology, writing centers move through a series of administrative paradigms that are described in this section. In the earliest phase, writing centers had an uneasy union with educational technology because so much of what was available was primitive in its applications and value to instruction. The focus on computer-driven grammar instruction through drill is apparent as well as the efforts of writing center personnel to develop more meaningful applications of this technology and more enriching instructional materials to offer students.

As educational technology advanced beyond grammar drills, the opportunities computers and electronic discourse communities offered to explore students' learning styles and composing strategies seemed vast, and many of the entries address this phenomenon in detail. The technology offered, too, virtually unlimited opportunities for outreach—not only to other academic units on campus but to the community and to society as a whole.

### Tutoring Theory, Tutor Training, Tutoring, and Ethics

Clearly, administration and educational technology come together in the central rationale and activity of writing centers—tutoring. Like the writing center itself, tutoring is defined by both theory and practice, and so the first introduction to this activity is based on a theoretical overview of tutoring as an instructional practice grounded in the humanistic tradition's appreciation for interpersonal dynamics and for individual learning styles. Many of the entries in this section endeavor to define tutoring's special qualities and effects in relation to other fields, especially those drawn from the healing arts like psychology and counseling. There are efforts, too, to define roles for tutors and to see their work within professional contexts.

These emphases extend logically to a discussion of tutor training and also as to what shape tutor training programs will take. Entries focus on training tutors in particular styles that emphasize collaborative interactions with those being tutored and also consider the ways in which the tutor should or should not intervene directly in the invention and revision processes of the writer.

The section on tutoring considers not only strategies and techniques but also the types of interactions tutors have in responding to writers with different socioeconomic and ethnic backgrounds, differing levels of ability, and different attitudes toward the writing process itself. The qualities of good tutors and good tutoring also are investigated, together with a consideration of what tutoring as an instructional method adds to a writer's learning process. A number of entries investigate tutoring as an example of collaborative, nonhierarchical learning within a traditionally hierarchical academy, or they examine the processes from poststructuralist and postmodern perspectives. Many of the entries call for further investigation of tutoring and its relationship to a cultural studies model.

### Research

All of the sections of this bibliography share a common interest in urging that more research be conducted on writing centers and their contributions to literacy education. The research section picks up this theme and also focuses on the writing center as a research site and the applicability of research findings to pedagogy. A substantial number of the entries also report on local, regional, or national surveys of writing center operations or personnel or assess faculty, student, and administrative attitudes about writing center services and benefits. There are considerations, too, of future trends in writing center research and scholarship as well as commentary on the numerous types of research that can be conducted in writing centers, from investigations of the learning styles of preschoolers to models for teaching training and education.

## CONCLUSION

We believe this annotated bibliography accomplishes several important goals. First, it reflects both the present and the historical state of writing center theory, practice, and administration. Second, it provides a comprehensive single-reference resource on all the major dimensions of writing center scholarship. Third, it offers information on this scholarship of relevance to those in related disciplines, such as composition studies, cultural studies, education, and educational technology, whose work parallels or is influenced by writing center praxis. Finally, an extensive bibliography of this type shows the themes that recur—the unresolved issues—and also suggests new issues and research agendas that merit further investigation. One thing is certain, as this bibliography indicates, the research on writing centers is vast and far-reaching, and it will continue to find meaningful avenues of investigation and commentary.

# Acknowledgments

Many kind and supportive colleagues have assisted us in completing this annotated bibliography by providing items from archives or from their personal collections. We especially thank Muriel Harris and Mary Jo Turley of *Writing Lab Newsletter* and Purdue University for making available to us copies of the earliest issues of the newsletter. We thank Muriel Harris, too, for her encouragement and friendship and also for her immeasurable contributions to the writing center profession. Muriel Harris has helped to define writing center work and scholarship, and her presence is demonstrated throughout this book.

Dave Healy of *The Writing Center Journal* and the University of Minnesota sent us copies of the earliest journals and answered questions and provided insights that helped us define our approach. We thank him for sharing his knowledge of writing center scholarship and for his collegiality in making time in a busy schedule to help so promptly.

Eric H. Hobson of Eastern Illinois University also sent us issues of *Writing Lab Newsletter* from his collection and indicated new sources for locating information. We value his enthusiasm for our project and his assistance.

Peter Carino of Indiana State University kindly sent us a photocopy of one of the earliest historical documents on writing centers that we would have had great difficulty in locating. We appreciate Peter for his willingness to help and also for his excellent contributions to the study of writing center history.

Stephen M. North of the State University of New York at Albany went out of his way to locate information on his dissertation and to respond by E-mail to several inquiries about his scholarship. We thank him for his kind efforts on our behalf and for his important place in writing center theory.

Donna Dunbar-Odom of East Texas State University photocopied documents for us that were difficult to locate and did so during the busiest part of her semester. We thank her for help and her friendship.

At the time we compiled this bibliography, all three of us were members of the staff of the William L. Adams Writing Center at Texas Christian

University. We thank the Interlibrary Loan department of the Texas Christian University Library for their speedy and patient responses to our numerous requests for materials.

We thank, too, our colleagues and friends in the William L. Adams Writing Center at TCU who encouraged us. And we thank our families and friends for believing in us as we worked on this extensive project. Steve Sherwood especially thanks his wife Mary and his sons Evan and Scott for the sacrifices they made during the time work was a primary focus. Christina Murphy thanks Amy Whitten, Pamela Evans, and Steve Yarbrough for lifetime friendships and for the pleasure of sharing this book with them.

# Anthologies

0001. **Farrell, Pamela B., ed.** *The High School Writing Center: Establishing and Maintaining One.* **Urbana: NCTE, 1989.** Collection of 21 brief essays devoted to setting up, operating, and staffing high school writing centers. Includes bibliography and selective high school writing center directory. See entries 0325, 0379, 0380, 0390, 0392, 0396, 0453, 0508, 0514, 0578, 0579, 0590, 0608, 0617, 0692, 0750, 0753, 0761, 0946, 1039, and 1072.

0002. **Flynn, Thomas, and Mary King, eds.** *Dynamics of the Writing Conference: Social and Cognitive Interaction.* **Urbana: NCTE, 1993.** Collection of 11 essays selected from the first 10 conferences of the East Central Writing Centers Association. All focus on the questions of how writing conferences foster growth in writing skills and activate higher-order thinking. See entries 0792, 0802, 0803, 0838, 0849, 0923, 0930, 1178, 1263, 1294, and 1416.

0003. **Harris, Muriel, ed.** *Tutoring Writing: A Sourcebook for Writing Labs.* **Glenview: Scott, Foresman, 1982.** A collection of 28 essays addressing most aspects of writing center operation, providing information on the theories and research supporting tutoring practices, training tutors, employing educational technology, maintaining links with other parts of the campus, and keeping useful records. See entries 0106, 0118, 0318, 0384, 0386, 0387, 0438, 0468, 0486, 0509, 0532, 0577, 0725, 0726, 0764, 0800, 0805, 0816, 0823, 0886, 0984, 0988, 1068, 1075, 1182, 1241, 1286, and 1300.

0004. **Hawkins, Thom, and Phyllis Brooks, eds.** *Improving Writing Skills.* **New Directions for College Learning Assistance 3. San Francisco: Jossey-Bass, 1981.** A collection of 11 essays focusing on the writing center as a collaboration between academic departments and student services as one response to "the national decline in the writing abilities of college students." See entries 0257, 0284, 0293, 0365, 0497, 0766, 0767, 0850, 0938, 1073, and 1284.

0005. **Kinkead, Joyce A., and Jeanette G. Harris, eds.** *Writing Centers in Context: Twelve Case Studies.* **Urbana: NCTE, 1993.** Detailed profiles of twelve writing center programs, describing contexts in which they operate, services offered, tutor selection and training methods, and physical layout. Schools featured are Purdue University (by Muriel Harris), Medgar Evers College, City University of New York (Brenda M. Greene), University of Toledo (Joan A. Mullin and Luanne Momenee), Lehigh University (Edward Lotto), University of Southern California (Irene L. Clark), Harvard University (Linda Simon), University of Puget Sound (Julie Neff), Johnson County Community College (Ellen Mohr), University of Washington (Gail Y. Okawa), two programs at Utah State University (Joyce A. Kinkead), and Colorado State University (Dawn Rodrigues and Kathleen Kiefer). Concludes with a bibliographic essay surveying major themes in writing center scholarship.

0006. **Maxwell, Martha, ed.** *When Tutor Meets Student.* **2nd ed. Ann Arbor: U of Michigan P, 1994.** Collection of 57 vignettes, divided into six categories: "The Tutor's Role," "The Tutor as Writer and Reader," "Increasing Confidence," "Cultural Diversity," "Check Your Assumptions at the Door," and "Tutors Learn from Tutoring Too." Discussion questions follow each essay. Includes extensive appendix of materials from the Student Learning Center's Peer Tutoring in Writing Program at the University of California—Berkeley. Originally published in a shorter version (with only 19 vignettes) as *When Tutor Meets Student: Experiences in Collaborative Learning* (Kensington: MM Associates, 1990). The following entries also appeared in *Writing Lab Newsletter*: 1079, 1128, 1129, 1167, 1225, 1240, 1246, 1297, 1342, 1350, and 1352.

0007. **Murphy, Christina, and Joe Law, eds.** *Landmark Essays on Writing Centers.* **Davis: Hermagoras, 1995.** Collection of 21 essays important in shaping writing center theory and practice; divided into sections on historical perspectives, theoretical foundations, and writing center praxis. See entries 0037, 0052, 0070, 0150, 0238, 0242, 0243, 0261, 0269, 0277, 0287, 0302, 0330, 0341, 0345, 0375, 0645, 0666, 0782, 0845, and 1109.

**0008. Murphy, Christina, and Steve Sherwood.** *The St. Martin's Sourcebook for Writing Tutors.* **New York: St. Martin's, 1995.** Introduction presents paradigms and stages of tutoring process; central section collects 11 essays providing information about theoretical constructs, interpersonal dynamics, ways of responding to texts, and ways of affirming diversity; final section describes additional resources. See entries 0330, 0345, 0469, 0781, 0880, 0892, 0915, 1109, 1137, 1201, and 1357.

**0009. Mullin, Joan A., and Ray Wallace, eds.** *Intersections: Theory-Practice in the Writing Center.* **Urbana: NCTE, 1994.** A collection of 15 essays that examine the theoretical bases of writing center practice. See entries 0013, 0247, 0281, 0312, 0331, 0339, 0340, 0344, 0371, 0801, 0806, 0817, 0852, 1254, and 1366.

**0010. Olson, Gary A., ed.** *Writing Centers: Theory and Administration.* **Urbana: NCTE, 1984.** Collects 19 essays under three headings: "Writing Center Theory," "Writing Center Administration," and "Special Concerns," which addresses attitudinal issues, ESL students, professionalism, and expanding writing center services. See entries 0253, 0350, 0372, 0412, 0464, 0483, 0542, 0571, 0623, 0782, 0882, 0919, 0929, 0954, 0991, 1089, 1135, 1402, and 1428.

**0011. Stay, Byron L., Christina Murphy, and Eric H. Hobson, eds.** *Writing Center Perspectives.* **Emmitsburg: NWCA Press, 1995.** Contains 18 essays on a range of topics related to writing center history and theory, writing across the curriculum, administrative concerns, tutoring, and conducting research in the writing center. See entries 0212, 0235, 0275, 0303, 0359, 0560, 0565, 0634, 0640, 0804, 0912, 0973, 1038, 1190, 1277, 1279, 1364, and 1409.

**0012. Wallace, Ray, and Jeanne Simpson, eds.** *The Writing Center: New Directions.* **New York: Garland, 1991.** A collection of 18 essays reflecting new developments in writing centers, such as new roles, evolving clientele and staff, and changing conditions affecting writing centers. See entries 0023, 0078, 0124, 0147, 0341, 0357, 0488, 0567, 0598, 0613, 0635, 0636, 0642, 0657, 0668, 0680, 0903, and 0964.

# History

**0013. Adams, Katherine H., and John L. Adams. "The Creative Writing Workshop and the Writing Center."** *Intersections: Theory-Practice in the Writing Center.* **Ed. Joan A. Mullin and Ray Wallace. Urbana: NCTE, 1994. 19-24.** Traces the history of the creative writing workshop and points out its impact on writing centers, particularly commending the tutor's role as facilitator rather than authority.

**0014. Almasy, Rudolph. "Special Interest Session on Writing Labs at the 4C's."** *Writing Lab Newsletter* **2.7 (1978): 1.** Lists the discussion topics for the special interest session at the 1978 CCCC, ranging from "Setting Up a Writing Lab—Various Models, Various Problems" to "Moving the Writing Lab Beyond Freshman English: What Are the Possibilities?"

**0015. Almasy, Rudolph. "Writing Lab Session at 1978 4C's."** *Writing Lab Newsletter* **2.4 (1977): 1.** Discusses the efforts to establish a special interest session at the 1978 CCCC in Denver for writing lab directors. The session is to focus on "the sharing of information and solving of problems."

**0016. Arkin, Marian. "A Tutoring Retrospective."** *Writing Lab Newsletter* **14.10 (1990): 1-6, 15.** Traces the history and development of writing centers from the 1970s to the 1990s, taking a wide-ranging look at such issues as tutor training, computers, collaborative learning, and multiculturalism.

**0017. Bates, Patricia. "See You at CCCC."** *Writing Lab Newsletter* **6.6 (1982): 6.** Describes the special sessions on writing centers planned for the 1982 CCCC meeting. Topics include the use of heuristics, strategies for training tutors, writing center outreach, bridging the gap between writing centers and academic departments, ensuring the success of new centers, building cognitive skills in basic writers, and developing spelling skills.

0018. **Bell, Jim. "What Are We Talking About? A Content Analysis of the** *Writing Lab Newsletter*, **April 1985 to October 1988."** *Writing Lab Newsletter* **13.7 (1989): 1-5.** Finds that popular article topics include methods of tutoring, computers, special student populations, high school writing labs, promoting writing center services, and general descriptions of specific writing centers. Topics seldom discussed include evaluation, research, adult students, and neo-Marxist theory.

0019. **Brannon, Lil. "A 4C's Report: Materials Development."** *Writing Lab Newsletter* **2.10 (1978): 1-2.** Discussions of materials development for writing labs focused on (1) an autotutorial approach, (2) a two-year college approach, and (3) a university-wide approach.

0020. **Brannon, Lil. "Report of the 1979 Special Interest Session Discussion Group on Training Tutors."** *Writing Lab Newsletter* **3.10 (1979): 3.** Argues that tutors often are knowledgeable about content areas but lack interpersonal skills or have excellent interpersonal skills but lack knowledge of content areas. Thus, tutors need to be trained "on both the cognitive and affective levels."

0021. **Brannon, Lil, and Stephen North. "From the Editors."** *The Writing Center Journal* **1.2 (1981): 1-6.** Repeats type of articles and subject matter initially requested for the journal: primarily theoretical, theory into practice, and experience that can be generalized. Evaluates articles submitted to journal, pointing out research issues still needing to be addressed.

0022. **Buck, Philo Melvyn, Jr. "Laboratory Method in English Composition."** *National Education Association Journal of Proceedings and Addresses of the 43rd Annual Meeting. St. Louis, 27 June-1 July 1904.* **Winona: National Education Association, 1905.** Suggests that writing instruction is more effective when students are asked to write in class and then share the responsibility of editing and revising those compositions, while the teacher works with individual writers who are having difficulty.

0023. **Bushman, Donald E. "Past Accomplishments and Current Trends in Writing Center Research: A Bibliographic Essay."** *The Writing Center: New Directions.* **Ed. Ray Wallace and Jeanne Simpson. New**

York: Garland, 1991. 27-38. Surveys trends in 20 years of writing center scholarship, identifying key topics (writing center identity, peer tutoring, research possibilities). Notes compatibility of emerging social constructionist thought and opportunities for ethnographic studies in writing centers. Urges making writing center the center of writing research on campus.

0024. Cady, Frank W. "The Laboratory Method at Middlebury College." *English Journal* 4.2 (1915): 124-25. Describes the "laboratory method" in use at Middlebury College (VT), which asks students to analyze an essay, evaluate it according to specific guidelines, and then write out the results of that investigation. Claims that this approach offers opportunities to "guide and correct the thought-processes of the student."

0025. Campbell, Elizabeth. "The Evolution of a Writing Laboratory." *College English* 3 (1941-42): 399-403. Describes transfer of writing laboratory from freshman composition to a freshman humanities survey after freshman composition class discontinued at Park College (MO). Details approach of English teachers working with students writing on a variety of topics in the humanities.

0026. Carino, Peter. "Early Writing Centers: Toward a History." *The Writing Center Journal* 15.2 (1995): 103-15. Critiques historical research into writing labs as fitting too neatly into the theoretical constructs of researchers. Suggests that early writing labs were more complex and more sensitive to individual student differences than many scholars believe. Contends that such labs differed in key ways from modern writing centers yet foreshadowed the collaborative learning model now in use.

0027. Cozzo, Joyce R. "Clinics for Writing." *English Journal* 51 (1962): 26-32, 43. Describes special one-day writing clinics for junior high and high school students for which students submit papers; on day of clinic, groups of 10 students, headed by a teacher, read, analyze, and correct those papers.

0028. Dewey, Evelyn. *The Dalton Laboratory Plan.* New York: Dutton, 1922. Offers a favorable critique of Helen Parkhurst's the Dalton Plan of classroom and laboratory instruction, a system that played an important role in the development of writing laboratories. See entry 0060.

0029. Dominguez, Delma Diane. "Writing Labs: A Comparative Study and an Analysis of Their Effectiveness." Thesis. Texas A & I U, 1990.

*MAI* 29-01 (1990): 0012. Presents a brief overview of the history of writing labs, discusses the development of the Del Mar College Learning Lab, and evaluates the efficacy of one-to-one tutorials as a method of composition instruction.

0030. Douglas, Lucile. "Teaching English on the Dalton Plan." *English Journal* 13 (1924): 335-40. Describes the philosophy and methods of the Dalton Laboratory Plan as developed in England and recently making its way into American education. Advocates acceptance of the Dalton Plan for teaching writing and for restructuring traditional classroom instruction as a series of small-group and individual conferences.

0031. Durkin, Margaret. "The Teaching of English in England and Under the Dalton Plan." *English Journal* 15 (1926): 256-66. Discusses the Dalton Plan's instructional principles of freedom, cooperation, and individual work and considers how these can be applied effectively in composition instruction and in the study of literature.

0032. Edwards, June. "To Teach Responsibly, Bring Back the Dalton Plan." *Phi Delta Kappan* 72 (1991): 398-401. Discusses the Dalton Plan and its relationship to educational innovation and reform.

0033. Garay, M.S. "'Writing Labs: Boon or Boondoggle': Report of a Debate at the 1980 Freshman English Session of SCMLA." *Writing Lab Newsletter* 7.3 (1982): 5-6. Reports that panelists at a special session discussed the history of writing labs, emphasizing current diversity of programs and offerings; debated whether labs were necessary versus extra help from the classroom teacher; discussed the cost effectiveness of labs; and considered whether labs worked best as extensions of the composition classroom.

0034. Hargrave, Mary. "The Dalton Plan in Practice." *English Journal* 17 (1928): 372-80. Describes how the author's high school implemented the Dalton Plan as an alternative to the traditional five-period-a-week classroom recitations. Concludes that individual instruction and small-group work lead to major educational gains for students.

0035. Harris, Jeanette. "Report of Workshop Given at 4C's 1980 Special Interest Session for Writing Lab Directors." *Writing Lab Newsletter* 4.10 (1980): 3. Discusses how grants are an effective means for funding writing labs—particularly grants that support writing instruction across the curriculum and faculty development programs.

0036. Harris, Muriel. "We Are Launched!" *Writing Lab Newsletter* 1.1 (1977): 1. Rpt. in *Writing Lab Newsletter* 16.8 (1992): 11. Announces the creation of the *Writing Lab Newsletter* and requests announcements, news, and suggestions for publication.

0037. Harris, Muriel. "What's Up and What's In: Trends and Traditions in Writing Centers." *The Writing Center Journal* 11.1 (1990): 15-25. Rpt. in 0007. Examines the traditions of writing centers, including a sharing information, being misunderstood and undervalued, embracing collaborative learning, enhancing the personal enrichment of tutors and students alike, and being people-oriented. Identifies and discusses trends toward greater professionalism, more growth in high school writing centers, more integration with classrooms, more contact with nontraditional students, and less remediation.

0038. Hill, James S. "A 4C's Report: The Writing Lab as a Supplement to Freshman English." *Writing Lab Newsletter* 2.9 (1978): 1. Topics of discussion at the CCCC special session ranged from the psychological implications of the lab as a place of learning rather than for "bad" students to the importance of having a rhetorician in the English department who can oversee and organize the format of the lab.

0039. Hocks, Elaine. "Conference Report." *Writing Lab Newsletter* 8.1 (1983): 8. Reports on the meeting of the first annual conference of the Midwest Writing Center Association held at the University of Missouri.

0040. Holcomb, Esther Lolita. "The English Laboratory." *English Journal* 17 (1928): 50-52. Calls for changes in classroom design that would allow freedom of grouping so that teacher can work with groups of students and students can work at their own pace.

0041. Holt, Mara. "Dewey and the 'Cult of Efficiency': Competing Ideologies in Collaborative Pedagogies of the 1920s." *Journal of Advanced Composition* 14.1 (1994): 73-92. Offers a historical overview of the development of theories of collaboration during the 1920s by contrasting John Dewey's advocacy of the Project Method with Helen Parkhurst's of the Dalton Plan, the philosophy from which much writing center practice has derived. See entry 0060.

0042. Horner, Warren B. "The Economy of the Laboratory Method." *English Journal* 18 (1929): 214-21. Describes the findings of an experiment conducted at Roosevelt-Wilson High School (WV) designed to compare the efficacy of the laboratory method of teaching English

composition with the recitation method. Concludes that, in comparison
to the laboratory method, the recitation method is wasteful of students'
time and energy and may have harmful effects upon the formation of
good study habits.

0043. **Horton, Sherry, and William L. Stull. "New England Writing
Centers Association Joins National Network."** *Writing Lab Newsletter*
**10.1 (1985): 8.** Describes the first meeting of the New England Writing
Centers Association. Sessions focused on such issues as training tutors,
tutoring ESL students and students with special needs, promoting writing
across the curriculum, using computers in the writing center, and
motivating students to use the writing center.

0044. **Jonz, Jon, and Kathleen Yancey. "Report of the 1979 Special Interest
Session Discussion Group on Serving ESL Students in the Writing
Lab."** *Writing Lab Newsletter* **4.2 (1979): 1-2.** Discusses methods of
diagnosing and responding to the writing problems of ESL students from
error frequency counts to devising individualized plans of study.

0045. **Kail, Harvey. "The Third Annual Conference on Writing and Peer
Tutoring: A Review."** *Writing Lab Newsletter* **11.6 (1987): 8-9.**
Discusses the issues examined at this conference, including whether to
refer to peer tutors as *writing consultants*, *writing assistants*, or *writing
fellows*; how much authority peers have; whether the best tutoring venue
is the drop-in writing center or the classroom; and how race, class, and
tutoring are related.

0046. **Kinkead, Joyce, and Jan Ugan. "A Report on the 1983 CCCC
Special Session for Writing Lab Directors."** *Writing Lab Newsletter*
**7.10 (1983): 5-6.** Workshop topics at this special session focused on "the
liberatory qualities of writing labs," "the tutor as writer," designing and
operating the high school writing lab, and "reaching a tough
constituency"—convincing colleagues in English departments of the lab's
value, and programs of instruction offered by writing labs.

0047. **Kinkead, Joyce, and Jeanette Harris. "An Interview with the
Founding Editors of** *The Writing Center Journal.***"** *The Writing
Center Journal* **11.1 (1990) 3-14.** An extended interview with Stephen
M. North and Lil Brannon about the origins of *The Writing Center
Journal*. Provides information on the historical and philosophical
contexts of the writing center movement.

0048. **Leahy, Richard. "Rocky Mountain Diary."** *Writing Lab Newsletter* **13.8 (1989): 1-3, 8.** Uses diary of events at a Rocky Mountain Writing Centers Association conference to reflect on issues ranging from tutor training to writing across the curriculum programs for secondary schools.

0049. **Maize, Ray C. "A Writing Laboratory for Retarded Students."** *College English* **16 (1954-55): 44-48.** Reports results of experiment comparing progress of two classes of remedial freshman composition, one taught by grammar workbook drill, one by "laboratory method" involving group work among students and individual consultation with teacher.

0050. **McCracken, Nancy. "News from the National WCA."** *Writing Lab Newsletter* **8.1 (1983): 6.** Tells of establishing the National Writing Centers Association (NWCA) as an affiliate of the National Council of Teachers of English (NCTE). The NWCA was created to "foster communication among writing centers and to provide a forum for their concerns."

0051. **McCracken, Nancy. "News from the Regions."** *Writing Lab Newsletter* **8.1 (1983): 7.** Lists the regional writing center associations offering annual conferences and states that "with the exception of the Pacific Coast, all regions of the country have now established regionals or are in the process of doing so."

0052. **Moore, Robert H. "The Writing Clinic and the Writing Laboratory."** *College English* **11 (1950): 388-93. Rpt. in 0007.** Reports on a survey concerning the use of writing clinics and writing laboratories, indicating that about 70% of the schools responding use or are considering these methods for remediation. Distinguishes between services of clinics and laboratories and indicates variety of configurations across the country.

0053. **Morrison, Elizabeth, and Robin Tatu. "Frags to Riches: Writing Centers Grow Up."** *A Guide to Writing Programs: Writing Centers, Peer Tutoring Programs, and Writing Across the Curriculum.* **Ed. Tori Haring-Smith, Nathaniel Hawkins, Elizabeth Morrison, Lise Stern, and Robin Tatu. Glenview: Scott, Foresman, 1985. 1-6.** Traces history of writing centers from the early 1970s, when many were established as remediation centers. After a period of redefinition (1974-79), writing centers moved toward a more general mission, serving all disciplines. With the growth of the process model of composition at the end of the 1970s, writing centers became still more general in their approach, sometimes becoming part of larger study skills approach.

0054. **Mullin, Joan. "An Interview with Muriel Harris."** *Composition Studies* **23.1 (1995): 37-53.** In-depth interview covers Harris's academic career and her work as the founding editor of *Writing Lab Newsletter*. Offers insights into her philosophy of writing center theory and practice as well as discussions of her major publications and contributions to the field.

0055. **Naugle, Helen. "Report of the 1979 CCCC Special Interest Session Discussion Group on Expanded Uses of the Lab."** *Writing Lab Newsletter* **4.1 (1979): 1-2.** Discusses such expanded uses of the writing lab as training graduate teaching assistants, conducting interdisciplinary programs and courses, helping students to pass state-mandated competency tests, and offering minicourses on vocabulary building, interpreting literature, and writing resumes and letters of application.

0056. **Nash, Thomas. "Report of a 1981 CCCC Special Interest Session on Prewriting Strategies in the Writing Lab."** *Writing Lab Newsletter* **5.10 (1981): 4-5.** Discusses the value of using heuristics for discovery and invention in tutorials. Focuses, in particular, on Aristotle's *topoi*, Kenneth Burke's pentad, prewriting, and tagmemics.

0057. **Olson, Gary A. "Unity and the Future of the Writing Center."** *Writing Lab Newsletter* **5.10 (1981): 5-7.** Reports on the enthusiasm and high attendance at the Southeastern Writing Center Conference in Alabama as a means to argue that the time has come to establish regional organizations and a national writing centers association as a way to show the growth and the professional unity of the writing center movement.

0058. **"The Organization and Use of the Writing Laboratory: The Report of Workshop No. 9A."** *College Composition and Communication* **1.2 (1950): 31-32.** Identifies five typical writing laboratory approaches: remedial laboratories required for some students; mandatory laboratories associated with composition classes; optional laboratories associated with composition classes; optional laboratories available to all students; laboratories available to help students pass a standardized test in lieu of formal composition courses.

0059. **Osterholm, Kathy. "Separation of NWCA and WCA: East Central."** *Writing Lab Newsletter* **8.7 (1984): 9.** Tells of the initial process of creating the National Writing Centers Association by a separation from the East Central regional group.

0060. **Parkhurst, Helen.** *Education on The Dalton Plan.* **New York: Dutton, 1922.** Describes a method of instruction based upon classroom and laboratory instruction. The laboratories for each class would provide student-centered, self-paced learning that appealed to students' interests and supported students' autonomy. The central text and philosophy from which much writing center theory and practice derive.

0061. **Report of Workshop 11. "Skills Laboratories for Any Student."** *College Composition and Communication* **7.3 (1956): 143-44.** Discusses the functions of a laboratory course in helping students improve beyond minimal competence in the skill areas of reading and writing.

0062. **Royster, Jacqueline Jones. "On Writing Centers: Reflections of a Wanderer about Time, Space, and Variable Fortune."** *Focuses* **7.1 (1994): 18-26.** Surveys past decade of writing center scholarship, pointing out its increasing sophistication and suggesting that writing centers improve the quality of learning, skills acquisition, and academic life as a whole.

0063. **Ruoff, James E. "The English Clinic at Flounder College."** *College English* **19 (1957-58): 348-51.** Tongue-in-cheek description of an imaginary college at which individual consultations dealing with grammatical errors are modeled on medical examinations and diagnosis.

0064. **Scanlon, Leone, and Mildred Steele. "A 4C's Report: Writing Lab Possibilities at the Small College/University."** *Writing Lab Newsletter* **2.10 (1978): 2.** Topics of discussion include motivating students, bringing services to students and student centers as a way of drawing them to the writing lab, funding writing labs, and the use of computer-assisted instruction.

0065. **"Shall 'Laboratory Work' in Composition Be Given Up?"** *English Journal* **1 (1912): 48.** Argues that laboratory principles in composition should be given an adequate test before teachers and administrators conclude that instruction in English composition has been a "hopeless failure" and should be given up.

0066. **Sheridan, Marion C. "An Evaluation of the Dalton Plan."** *English Journal* **15 (1926): 507-14.** Discusses the merits and weaknesses of the Dalton Plan as a method of instruction. Argues that the plan is effective for individual instruction in grammar and mechanics but does not provide sufficient social stimulus for the teaching of reading, creative writing, or literary appreciation.

0067. Sherwood, Phyllis, and Kathy Osterholm. "A 4C's Report: Setting
Up a Writing Lab." *Writing Lab Newsletter* 2.10 (1978): 5-6.
Acknowledges that labs differ in purpose, staff, clientele, and institution,
but finds four constants: writing center personnel must do extensive
public relations work with the faculty and administration, a stable budget
is required, the lab must meet the needs of students, and accurate record
keeping is essential.

0068. Simpson, Jeanne. "Growing Interest in Secondary School Writing
Centers Presents New Problems to NWCA." *Writing Lab Newsletter*
10.7 (1986): 5. Discusses the challenges of bringing the high school
writing center movement, ten years behind the university movement, up
to speed. Urges other writing center people to look for ways to help.

0069. Spear, Karen I. "Toward a Comprehensive Language Curriculum."
*The Writing Center Journal* 2.1 (1982): 34-47. Surveys historical
educational forces impinging on writing centers to confine their activity
to remediation. Argues that flexible centers can begin to move away
from the skills model and toward an individualized, process-oriented
approach.

0070. Summerfield, Judith. "Writing Centers: A Long View." *The Writing
Center Journal* 8.2 (1988): 3-9. Rpt. in 0007. Traces the evolution of
the writing center from remedial grammar clinic through expressivism
and the beginnings of social constructionism. Reviews reasons why the
writing center's revolutionary nature often threatens the status quo of the
university community (and is therefore vulnerable to budget cuts). Warns
that trends toward computers and standardized testing may harken back
to the grammar clinic days and threaten the existence of modern writing
centers.

0071. Thomas, Sharon. "The Michigan Writing Centers Association."
*Writing Lab Newsletter* 20.2 (1995): 10. Announces the inauguration of
the Michigan Writing Centers Association, formed to address "the
concerns of professional and tutorial staff in writing centers and writing
support programs within Michigan."

0072. Trimmer, Joseph F. "Story Time: All About Writing Centers."
*Focuses* 1.2 (1988): 27-35. Offers an imaginative narrative "history" of
writing centers from the writing workshop (circa 1960), the writing
laboratory (circa 1965), the writing clinic (circa 1970), the writing center
(circa 1975), the learning center (circa 1985), to the culture club (circa

1990). Relates each phase of this "history" to prevailing composition theories and social philosophies of the times.

0073. Ugan, Jan. **"1984 CCC Special Interest Session on Writing Labs."** *Writing Lab Newsletter* **8.5 (1984): 5.** Reports on the topics for the session, which ranged from setting up a writing lab, to the use of microcomputers in the lab, to extending the lab's influence across the curriculum.

0074. Wagner, Lilya. *Peer Teaching: Historical Perspectives.* **Contributions to the Study of Education 5. Westport: Greenwood, 1982.** Traces the development of peer teaching throughout Western history from the first century to the present and concentrates on such issues as defining peer tutoring's multiple functions, describing how social and economic conditions influence the idea and use of peer teaching, and twentieth-century developments in the theory and practice of peer teaching in the United States.

0075. Wykoff, George S. **"Current Solutions for Teaching Maximum Numbers with Limited Faculty."** *College Composition and Communication* **9.2 (1958): 76-80.** Discusses the writing laboratory as one means to address the issue of large classes with limited numbers of instructors by offering a tutorial method in which "students write continuously with the teacher moving from student to student and offering on-the-spot advice."

0076. Yahner, William, and William Murdick. **"The Evolution of a Writing Center: 1972-1990."** *The Writing Center Journal* **11.2 (1991): 13-28.** Offers lessons learned from the start-up and 18-year development of a writing center at California University of Pennsylvania. Explores various institutional models the writing center embraced, each mirroring the contemporary theories governing English studies (from conservative to progressive). Concludes that the center's experience reflected national, not local, trends.

0077. Ziegler, Carl W. **"Laboratory Method in English Teaching."** *English Journal* **8 (1919): 143-53.** Describes the author's visit to an English class at Osceola City High School (no state given), organized and conducted as a laboratory for individualized instruction and self-paced learning. Lauds the results achieved in student motivation and comprehension.

# Program Descriptions

0078. Addison, Jim, and Henry L. Wilson. "From Writing Lab to Writing Center: Reinventing, Advancing, and Expanding." *The Writing Center: New Directions*. Ed. Ray Wallace and Jeanne Simpson. New York: Garland, 1991. 56-72. Uses the history of the writing center at Western Carolina University to demonstrate the changing nature of writing center work, tracing its evolution from the remedial "lab," with its emphasis on defective text, to the "center," with its focus on the writer.

0079. Arkin, Marian. "Special Projects in LaGuardia's Writing Center." *Writing Lab Newsletter* 3.2 (1978): 3. Discusses programs offered in the writing center at LaGuardia Community College (NY) that respond to the needs of second language learners, basic writers, and creative writers.

0080. Baltrinic, Barb. "In the Beginning There Was Confusion." *Writing Lab Newsletter* 11.6 (1987): 13-14. Describes the creation of a writing center at Ellet High School (Akron, OH) designed to prepare students to take a statewide writing competency exam. Traces the center's development, from staff training to student usage.

0081. Bator, Paul G. "Proficiency Exam Assistance in Wayne State's Writing Workshop." *Writing Lab Newsletter* 2.5 (1978): 1. Discusses the implications of a proficiency exam that requires those who fail to register for a writing workshop offered by the writing center at Wayne State University (MI).

0082. Bauso, Jean. "Bringing in Business." *Writing Lab Newsletter* 7.3 (1982): 5-6. Discusses how the Writing Assistance Program in the School of Engineering at North Carolina State University increased student drop-in use by giving presentations on writing to engineering classes and by conducting a six-session writing workshop for international graduate students.

0083. **Beck, Paula. "The Writing Skills Workshop: Not a Laboratory."** *Teaching English in the Two-Year College* **2.2 (1976): 99-100.** Describes the peer-tutor method of writing instruction at Nassau Community College (NY), stressing its collaborative approach.

0084. **Beck, Paula, Thom Hawkins, and Marcie Silver. "Training and Using Peer Tutors."** *College English* **40 (1978): 443-49.** Text of peer tutoring session at 1977 meeting of National Council of Teachers of English. Includes introduction by Kenneth Bruffee, descriptions of training programs at Brooklyn College (NY), Nassau Community College (NY), and University of California—Berkeley, and transcript of discussion that followed.

0085. **Behm, Richard. "Establishing Writing Centers Throughout a School District."** *Writing Lab Newsletter* **12.6 (1988): 1-5.** Describes the process the New London (WI) school district went through to set up and staff writing centers in every elementary, middle, and high school in the district. Cites commitment by the administration and professional development of the writing centers' staff members as keys to success.

0086. **Benedict, Michael A. "From Wrestling to Writing: The Genesis of a Writing Center."** *Writing Lab Newsletter* **11.3 (1986): 3-5.** Recounts the start-up and first semester of service of a high school writing center at Fox Chapel (Pittsburgh, PA) established in what used to be a wrestling practice room.

0087. **Bhakuni, Rosa I. "Progress Report of the Kenmore High School Writing Lab."** *Writing Lab Newsletter* **10.10 (1986): 2-3.** Chronicles the first 49 days of operation of the Kenmore High School (Akron, OH) writing lab, which quickly became a high-use center, serving 343 students.

0088. **Bloomberg, Blanche R. "English Y and the Study Clinic."** *College English* **13 (1951): 104-06.** Discusses English Y as an ancillary composition course at Los Angeles Valley Junior College (CA) that operates as a study clinic focused on individual instruction in reading and comprehension skills.

**0089. Bonnell, Marilyn F. "'The Best Thing Going!'"** *Writing Lab Newsletter* **11.1 (1986): 4-5.** Describes mandated weekly tutorials at the writing center at for members of a composition class at Salem State College (MA). Contends that students made significant progress in their writing ability. A survey indicates students responded favorably to the required visits.

**0090. Bordwell, C.B. "The Writing Tutorial Across Campus."** *College English* **26 (1964-65): 562-64.** Describes a one-hour-credit writing tutorial offered by the English department at the University of Oregon but available in conjunction with courses in various disciplines. Outlines tutors' strategies for learning writing conventions of other disciplines.

**0091. Bowers, Kim Silveira. "The Evolution of a Writing Center."** *Writing Lab Newsletter* **12.1 (1987): 12-14.** Describes the formation from scratch of a successful writing center at the University of the Pacific (CA), despite faculty ambivalence, no budget, and other challenges. Offers lessons learned from the first semester of operation, during which the center began by serving only English students and ended by opening its doors to all disciplines.

**0092. Brannon, Lil. "Tutors and Materials Development at East Texas State University."** *Writing Lab Newsletter* **2.4 (1977): 4.** Discusses the establishment and procedures of the East Texas State University Writing Center, which serves the entire campus and "not just the remedial program."

**0093. Brooks, Barbara. "A High School Writing Center Grows—and Grows."** *Writing Lab Newsletter* **12.8 (1988): 9-10.** Traces the growth of the award-winning writing center at Pattonville High School (St. Louis, MO).

**0094. Brown, Alan. "The High School Writing Center: Surviving Our Mistakes."** *Writing Lab Newsletter* **9.10 (1985): 4-5.** Discusses the mistakes a first-time writing center director made at Griffin High School (no state given) and how he overcame initial difficulties.

**0095. Bruffee, Kenneth A. "The Brooklyn Plan: Attaining Intellectual Growth Through Peer-Group Tutoring."** *Liberal Education* **64 (1978): 447-68.** Describes the Brooklyn Tutoring Plan at the Brooklyn College Writing Center (NY). Students collaboratively learn and practice judgment through a progressive set of analytical and evaluative tasks applied to each other's writing in a context that fosters self-esteem.

0096. **Campman, M. Sue. "UT Austin Freshman Lab: Big as Texas."** *Writing Lab Newsletter* **7.5 (1983): 1-3.** Describes the difficulties involved in getting the word out to over 5,400 freshmen at the University of Texas on the writing lab designed to reinforce and supplement the one-year freshman sequence. Discusses promotional efforts and liaison efforts with the English department.

0097. **Candelaria, Frederick. "Of Courses and Tutorials at Oregon."** *College English* **25 (1963-64): 620.** Briefly describes a three-semester honors program at the University of Oregon, in which students write essays in consultation with tutors other than the professors who assigned those essays. Notes that tutorial system is being moved beyond the honors program.

0098. **Carnicelli, Thomas A. "The Writing Conference: A One-to-One Conversation."** *Eight Approaches to Teaching Composition.* **Ed. Timothy R. Donovan and Ben W. McClelland. Urbana: NCTE, 1980. 101-31.** Describes varieties of individual conferences instituted as required part of composition course at the University of New Hampshire. Often cited in writing center literature, though not specifically about writing center conferences.

0099. **Castelucci, Maryann F. "Some Thoughts and Reminiscences on How a Faculty-Centered Skills Center Became a Peer Tutoring Program."** *Writing Lab Newsletter* **8.3 (1983): 1-2.** Tells of how a fiscal crunch, the demands of open admissions, and increasing numbers of underprepared students led to the development of the Reading, Writing, and English as a Second Language Skills Center at the College of Staten Island, City University of New York, staffed exclusively by peer tutors.

0100. **Centner, Marilyn. "Good News from Alabama! Improved Preparation and Innovation."** *Writing Lab Newsletter* **8.6 (1984): 4-5.** Discusses the successes of the Learning Lab at Lurleen B. Wallace State Junior College (AL) in which developmental students were enrolled for workshops in the lab rather than being enrolled in traditional basic writing classes.

0101. **Charleston, Carmen. "Inner-City Writing Centers in St. Louis Public Schools."** *Writing Lab Newsletter* **15.5 (1991): 10-11.** Discusses the purpose and services of writing enrichment labs, sixty of which were established in 1980 to serve predominantly or all African-American schools in St. Louis (MO). Portrays the labs' primary purpose as giving students experience writing in a variety of genres and formats.

0102. **Coggin, William, and June Fenning. "The Writing Workshop at Miami—Middletown."** *Writing Lab Newsletter* 5.8 (1981): 2-3. Discusses the establishment of the Writing Workshop at Miami University—Middletown, a two-year branch of Miami University of Ohio, with particular emphasis upon a one-hour credit course for underprepared learners.

0103. **Colby, Elbridge. "'Laboratory Work' in English."** *College English* 2 (1940-41): 67-69. Enumerates advantages of procedure at George Washington University (Washington, DC) in which a student brings an outline or partial draft for a general consultation and then completes the draft in the laboratory before submitting the paper at the regular class time. Laboratory open to students in all classes.

0104. **Cole, Marlene. "A Dual Purpose Writing Lab."** *Writing Lab Newsletter* 6.6 (1982): 4. Describes two purposes of the writing lab at Broward Community College (FL): to "refresh" the memories of older, nontraditional students on grammar issues and reinforce the classroom learning of all students enrolled in the college.

0105. **Coleman, Shirley L. "Establishment of UAPB Writing Center."** *Writing Lab Newsletter* 5.7 (1981): 8. Describes the set-up, organization, and procedures of the Writing Center Program at the University of Arkansas—Pine Bluff.

0106. **Collins, James, and Charles Moran. "The Secondary-Level Writing Laboratory: A Report from the Field."** *Tutoring Writing: A Sourcebook for Writing Labs.* **Ed. Muriel Harris. Glenview: Scott, Foresman, 1982. 196-204.** Describes a sophomore writing class at Springfield Technical High School (MA) in which students meet daily in the writing lab and write throughout the period, conferring briefly with the teacher on occasion. Examines work of individual student to illustrate effectiveness of program.

0107. **Cooper, Marilyn M., and Cynthia L. Selfe. "Computer Conferences and Learning: Authority, Resistance, and Internally Persuasive Discourse."** *College English* 52 (1990): 847-69. Describes the nontraditional discourse forum created in the Center for Computer-Assisted Language Instruction (Michigan Technological University) where students take part in discussions via computer log. Contends this approach complements classroom instruction by expanding beyond the teaching of conventions and that students exercise more autonomy and control in this forum.

0108. Covington, David H., Ann E. Brown, and Gary B. Blank. "An Alternative Approach to Writing Across the Curriculum: The Writing Assistance Program at North Carolina State University's School of Engineering." *WPA: Writing Program Administration* 8.3 (1983): 15-23. Describes a discipline-specific writing center, including its general methods of operation and staff. Notes similar writing center in Forest Resources and suggests general guidelines for developing such writing assistance programs.

0109. Davis, Kevin. "The Davis and Elkins Academic Resource Center." *Writing Lab Newsletter* 9.5 (1985): 7. Discusses the organization and physical set-up of the Academic Resource Center at Davis and Elkins College (WV).

0110. Day, Ellen, Mary Foster, and Pat Naranjo. "Tulane Workshop Stresses Student Responsibility." *Writing Lab Newsletter* 4.7 (1980): 5-6. Describes the establishment of a "stop-gap" writing workshop set up without specialized facilities to meet the growing need among Freshman English students for remedial instruction.

0111. DeCiccio, Albert. "Merrimack College Writing Center." *Writing Lab Newsletter* 10.1 (1985): 11. Describes the operations of a writing center at Merrimack College (MA), a small liberal arts college. Center offers one-to-one tutorials to students, gives presentations to classes, and hosts a series of brown-bag seminars on aspects of composition.

0112. Desjardins, Margaret M. "Center for Assessment & Skills Development." *Writing Lab Newsletter* 11.3 (1986): 9-10. Describes the start-up and first year of operation of an interdisciplinary learning center at Manatee Community College (FL).

0113. Dille, Ralph G. "Teaching Communication Skills in Southern Colorado's Lab." *Writing Lab Newsletter* 2.3 (1977): 1. Describes the University of Southern Colorado's Basic Communications Department's learning laboratory for reading and composition.

0114. Doggett, Joseph M. "English Laboratory at the University of Houston." *College English* 26 (1964-65): 50-51. Announces opening of a laboratory to which students with writing problems can be referred by instructors from all departments of the university.

0115. Dugger, Ronnie. "Cooperative Learning in a Writing Community." *Change: The Magazine of Higher Learning* July 1976: 30-33. Profiles the writing center established at Brooklyn College (NY) in response to open admissions policy. Outlines philosophy of its founder, Kenneth Bruffee, highlighting his sensitivity to issues of authority and power relations. Describes several tutor training classes and tutoring sessions.

0116. **Einerson, Allen. "Writing Center Workshops for High Risk Students."** *Writing Lab Newsletter* **13.6 (1989): 1-5.** Describes three workshops sponsored by the writing center at the University of Wisconsin—Whitewater to increase the survival potential of high-risk students. The workshops focus on specific strategies for solving math word problems, engaging in critical thinking, and writing more effective essay exams.

0117. **Epes, Mary. "The COMP-LAB Project at York College of the City University of New York."** *Writing Lab Newsletter* **2.7 (1978): 1-3.** Describes the development of a laboratory-centered basic writing course in which reduced classroom hours are coordinated with a flexible schedule of autotutorial work in a writing laboratory.

0118. **Epes, Mary, Carolyn Kirkpatrick, and Michael G. Southwell. "The Autotutorial Writing Lab: Discovering Its Latent Power."** *Tutoring Writing: A Sourcebook for Writing Labs.* **Ed. Muriel Harris. Glenview: Scott, Foresman, 1982. 132-46.** Traces evolution of a full-scale, self-teaching facility at York College, City University of New York, pointing out its effectiveness for some kinds of instruction and suggesting its possible suitability for some writing center applications.

0119. **Evans, Eileen B. "Western Michigan University's Writing Lab."** *Writing Lab Newsletter* **10.2 (1985): 17-18.** Describes the functions and policies of the Western Michigan University's writing lab that, at the time, had served 17,000 students, faculty, and staff for 12 years.

0120. **Ewing, Noreen J. "Small Really Is Beautiful: The Success of a Writing Center."** *Writing Lab Newsletter* **10.1 (1985): 1-3.** Describes the successful first three years of the writing center at Southern Technical Institute (no state given), offers advice on how to start such a center on a small budget, and discusses the need for effective public relations.

0121. **Feeman, Jeffrey. "The High School Writing Center: A Place Where Writing Is Fun!"** *Thrust for Educational Leadership* **16.5 (1987): 21-22.** Describes the writing center at Central-Hower High School (OH), including its purpose and goals, its computer hardware and software, and its strategies for training teachers and students to use the computer system.

0122. **Fishbain, Janet. "Write with Confidence: A Writing Lab Workshop for Returning Adult Students."** *Writing Lab Newsletter* **13.9 (1989): 1-4, 10.** Describes a brief, noncredit writing course offered at the University of Wisconsin to boost returning adult students' confidence and update their skills.

0123. **Fishman, Judith. "The Tutor as Messenger."** *The Writing Center Journal* **1.2 (1981): 7-12.** Reports on the two-year Queens English Project, an articulation program between Queens College, City University of New York, and five high schools in New York City. The program put up to 40 college student tutors into newly formed high school tutoring centers. Shows effectiveness of young tutors still familiar with environment and examines the impact of the program on tutors, students, and teachers.

0124. **Fitzgerald, Sallyanne, Peggy Mulvihill, and Ruth Dobson. "Meeting the Needs of Graduate Students: Writing Support Groups in the Center."** *The Writing Center: New Directions.* **Ed. Ray Wallace and Jeanne Simpson. New York: Garland, 1991. 133-44.** Extends practice of collaborative learning to groups of graduate students led by faculty facilitators in the writing center at the University of Missouri—St. Louis. Outlines benefits of such programs, especially for ESL students, and offers practical guidelines for setting up such groups.

0125. **Gengler, Barb, and Cindy Johanek. "Munchkin Madness: Creating a Real Discourse Community."** *Writing Lab Newsletter* **14.4 (1989): 3-6.** Tells how the writing center at St. Cloud State University (MN) created a discourse community among executives of a fictitious plastics corporation to make writing more relevant to reluctant writing students. Claims the writing center is an ideal place to test such methods.

0126. **Giles, Ronald. "The Applied Writing Lab at Auburn University."** *Writing Lab Newsletter* **5.6 (1981): 7-8.** Describes the Business and Technical Writing Lab at Auburn University (AL) that offers tutorial assistance as well as supplementary audiovisual materials, programmed tape recorders, library reference sheets catalogued by discipline, and a reading library of sample reports and resumes.

0127. **Gills, Paula. "Lab Troubleshooter."** *Writing Lab Newsletter* **13.4 (1988): 7-8.** Profiles five writing centers to illustrate how some directors operate viable tutoring programs on limited budgets. Schools include Austin College (TX), St. Mary's University (TX), Cameron University (OK), Oklahoma Christian College, and Oklahoma State University.

0128. **Glassman, Susan. "The English Department Connection."** *Writing Lab Newsletter* **12.6 (1988): 9-10.** Describes how the writing center at Southeastern Massachusetts University integrated its services into the basic writing program and formed closer bonds with the English department.

0129. **Glassman, Susan. "Southeastern Mass. Writing Lab Offers Multiple Services."** *Writing Lab Newsletter* **3.3 (1978): 4.** The writing lab at Southeastern Massachusetts University, as part of the Cooperative Learning Center, offers tutoring in reading, math, science, and writing; counseling and supportive services; and programming and materials for international students and learning disabled students.

0130. **Goldenberg, Myrna. "The Evolution of a Writing Lab."** *Writing Lab Newsletter* **4.1 (1979): 2-4.** Discusses the progression of a writing center at Montgomery College—Rockville (MD), an open-admission, urban community college from start-up, dealing with issues of public relations and promotion, staffing, record keeping, and the creation of style sheets for courses across the disciplines.

0131. **Goldsmith, James. "Re-Inventing the Wheel: Very Quickly."** *Writing Lab Newsletter* **9.10 (1985): 1-3.** Tells of the dilemmas and challenges the writing lab director at Lewis-Clark State College (ID) faced when four sections of developmental English were cancelled and students were assigned to work in the lab instead.

0132. **Goodson, F. Todd. "Opening a High School Writing Center: Three Easy Lessons."** *Writing Lab Newsletter* **16.1 (1991): 4-6.** Discusses lessons learned in the process of starting a writing center at Blue Valley North High School (Overland Park, KS), including the need to attract students, involve teachers, and avoid getting bogged down in paperwork.

0133. **Grandy, Adah G. "A Writing Laboratory."** *English Journal* **25 (1936): 372-76.** Describes the establishment of a writing laboratory at the University of Minnesota in 1934 and considers the merits of the laboratory method for composition instruction.

0134. **Greenawalt, Sister Vinnetia. "The Learning Proficiency Center."** *Writing Lab Newsletter* **4.9 (1980): 8.** Describes the set-up and operation of the Learning Proficiency Center at St. Mary of the Plains College (KS).

0135. **Griebel, Garitt. "The Writing Lab Program at USAO."** *Writing Lab Newsletter* **5.9 (1981): 2-4.** Describes the philosophy and operating procedures of the Writing Lab Program at the University of Science and Arts of Oklahoma, a small liberal arts college. Lists the lab's primary activities as remediation, one-on-one conferencing, minicourses, and answering faculty members' questions about grammatical correctness.

0136. **Grout, Donna M. "Lincoln University's New Writing Program: An Interlocked Package with a Writing Center."** *Writing Lab Newsletter* **5.3 (1980): 7-9.** Describes the writing center's role in three interlocked courses in remedial English and freshman composition at Lincoln University (no state given). All courses are competency-based, so the writing center offers tutorials that respond to the courses' requirements.

0137. **Haas, Teri. "Profiles: An Interview with Dr. Myra Kogen, Director of the Brooklyn College Writing Center."** *Writing Lab Newsletter* **13.8 (1989): 11-15.** Discusses the training of staff, master, and peer tutors in the writing center at Brooklyn College (NY). Examines an undergraduate tutor training class, methods of evaluating tutors, research, and funding.

0138. **Hague, Angela, and Betty W. Meers. "Enrichment Activities and the Writing Lab."** *Writing Lab Newsletter* **7.6 (1983): 6-8.** Discusses the Academic Enrichment and Skills Center at the University of North Florida, which serves only upper-division and graduate students. Describes the enrichment programs developed to respond to these students' needs, such as workshops on anxiety and stress, independent studies, and "The Second Time Around" group for nontraditional students.

0139. **Haring-Smith, Tori, Nathaniel Hawkins, Elizabeth Morrison, Lise Stern, and Robin Tatu.** *A Guide to Writing Programs: Writing Centers, Peer Tutoring Programs, and Writing-Across-the-Curriculum.* **Glenview: Scott, Foresman, 1985.** Bulk of text describes 230 programs in outline form. Brief introductory essays trace histories of writing centers (entry 0053) and peer tutoring (entry 0821).

0140. **Harrington, John P. "The Idea of a Center for Writing and Speaking."** *Writing Lab Newsletter* **12.10 (1988): 1-3.** Discusses the role of the writing center at The Cooper Union (NY) in helping students prepare for oral presentations. Sees close link between the strategies used in helping students develop speeches and write essays.

0141. **Haviland, Carol P. "Taking the Lab to the Non-English Class."** *Writing Lab Newsletter* **6.8 (1982): 9.** Describes a program developed at the University of Montana in which writing center instructors work with classroom teachers in physics, ceramics, nursing, business, and pre-medical sciences to design and test writing components for their courses and to assist students with their writing processes.

0142. **Hawkins, Thom. "Joining Hands."** *Writing Lab Newsletter* **18.6 (1994): 5, 16.** Describes the successful efforts of the Student Learning Center at the University of California—Berkeley to meet the needs of a culturally diverse student body.

0143. **Hicks, Joyce. "Beginning a Writing Center at Valparaiso."** *Writing Lab Newsletter* **2.4 (1977): 4.** Discusses the rationale, organization, and staffing of the writing center at Valparaiso University (IN).

0144. **Hildebrand, Veta. "The Writing Lab: From Fantasy to Fact."** *Writing Lab Newsletter* **12.2 (1987): 12-14.** Describes the creation, growth, and services of a writing center at North Tama County High School (IA), including a step-by-step list on how to establish such a center.

0145. **Hodgdon, David G. "The Evolution of a Writing Center."** *Writing Lab Newsletter* **13.3 (1988): 5-6.** Discusses the director's involvement in developing writing centers at Somersworth High School (no location given) and Pembroke Academy (NH) intended to serve students and teachers from all disciplines and to encourage collaboration, research, and publication by students and teachers.

0146. **Howard, Kathy. "Writing Centers: The Hong Kong Experience."** *Writing Lab Newsletter* **18.8 (1994): 10-11.** Recounts the challenges faced in setting up two writing centers in Hong Kong colleges (Hong Kong Baptist College and The Chinese University of Hong Kong), including correcting common misconceptions about how such centers operate. Also offers advice on the tutoring of ESL students.

0147. **Jacoby, Jay, and Stan Patten. "Changing the Ways We Teach: The Role of the Writing Center in Professional Development; or, the Virtue of Selfishness."** *The Writing Center: New Directions.* **Ed. Ray Wallace and Jeanne Simpson. New York: Garland, 1991. 157-68.**

Discusses three groups that staff the writing center at the University of North Carolina—Charlotte: faculty who teach composition, graduate students who will teach that course, and undergraduates who will teach in public schools. Considers the impact of tutoring on subsequent classroom practice.

0148. **Jonz, Jon. "Freshman Foundation Program at West Virginia State College."** *Writing Lab Newsletter* **2.9 (1978): 3.** Describes how the lab at West Virginia State College responded to two principal barriers underprepared students encounter in acquiring literacy skills: (1) the lack of contextualization of skills-acquisition activities and (2) the general lack of acknowledgement by professors of the "personness" of students.

0149. **Kelly, Dorothy. "A High-School Writing Laboratory."** *English Journal* **30.8 (1941): 660-62.** Describes the writing laboratory in Elkhart High School (Elkhart, IN), where students write papers for all their classes under the supervision of a teacher. Lab approach combines lecture and drill with individual work with students. Notes that this system has been in place at the University of Minnesota for six years and at many high schools and junior colleges.

0150. **Kelly, Lou. "One-on-One, Iowa City Style: Fifty Years of Individualized Instruction in Writing."** *The Writing Center Journal* **1.1 (1980): 4-19. Rpt. in 0007.** Describes origins of the writing lab in the 1930s at the University of Iowa and provides overview of the current model, stressing ways of helping individual writers overcome their fears of failure in writing.

0151. **King, Mary. "A Writing Lab Profile."** *Writing Lab Newsletter* **6.8 (1982): 6-8.** Presents the results of a survey of 50 writing centers in Ohio and neighboring states that sought information on the place of writing centers within their institutions and on the professional status of writing center directors and their staffs. Attempts to use information from the survey to sketch an outline of the writing center profession itself.

0152. **Kirby, John Dillingham. "Make-up English at Northwestern."** *English Journal* **20 (1931): 829-31.** Describes the development of "make-up" classes in English composition at Northwestern University (IL) as a form of "private tutoring" that is systematized and fitted into the English curriculum of the university. Discusses the benefits, for both students and teachers, of individual instruction and additional attention to deficiencies.

**0153. Kirzner, Laurie. "The Instant Writing Workshop."** *Writing Lab Newsletter* **2.6 (1978): 1.** Describes the establishment of the writing workshop at the Philadelphia College of Pharmacy (PA) created in response to "increasingly frequent questions about writing problems from students and faculty at all levels of competence."

**0154. Kovich, Charles. "Writing Competency and the Writing Lab: Methods of Evaluation at Northern Iowa."** *Writing Lab Newsletter* **5.2 (1980): 7-8.** Discusses the criteria used in the program at the University of Northern Iowa to determine competency in writing, based upon an analysis of 1,200 student themes for patterns of error. Considers how these criteria can be of value to tutors working with students who must pass the Writing Competency Essay test.

**0155. Kurak, Vernelle.** *At Large: The General College Reading/Writing Skills Center and Its Satellites, 1974-75.* **General College Studies 11.4. Minneapolis: University of Minnesota, 1975.** Pamphlet tracing the history of the General College Reading/Writing Skills Center at the University of Minnesota since its establishment (1972). Describes its expansion into several satellite centers on and off campus, including community agencies and the state correctional system, and provides tables indicating the number of students served and faculty employed by each center.

**0156. Lee, Eleanor. "The Writing Center at Troy State University: A Multi-Service Learning Center."** *Writing Lab Newsletter* **13.2 (1988): 1-4.** Describes the structure, services, tutor-training program, equipment, and relationship of the writing center to the writing across the curriculum program at Troy State University (AL).

**0157. Lefelt, Carol. "One High School Writing Center: Looking Back After the First Year."** *Writing Lab Newsletter* **10.10 (1986): 11-13.** Relates the ups and downs of the first year of operation of the writing center at Highland Park High School (Highland Park, NJ). Contends that, despite unfavorable commentary in the school's yearbook and a lack of faculty support, the center had a successful year, recording 185 sessions.

**0158. Leibowitz, Ivy. "Long Beach High School English Department Writing Lab."** *Writing Lab Newsletter* **7.8 (1983): 3-5.** Describes the establishment of an open lab at Long Beach High School (NY) to provide concentrated and individual work in the language arts. Lab participants were identified through teacher recommendation or volunteered to participate in the programs on reading, writing, and speaking.

0159. **Leonard, Bob. "The Huntington High School Writing Center: A Process Oriented Model of Peer Tutoring."** *Writing Lab Newsletter* **6.5 (1982): 5-6.** Discusses the development of a course at Huntington High School (Huntington, NY) on "Advanced Methods of Composition: Theory and Practicum" to train students to become peer tutors.

0160. **Linden, Myra J. "Joliet Junior College Academic Skills Center."** *Writing Lab Newsletter* **3.2 (1978): 1-2.** Describes the operations of the center in terms of the individualized courses offered in developmental reading, speed reading, developmental writing, and composition. Also discusses funding of the center through Illinois State aid, the Illinois Community College Board, and student tuition.

0161. **Loris, Michelle Carbone. "The Workshop Skills Center: A Cross Disciplinary Full Language Development Center."** *Writing Lab Newsletter* **9.4 (1984): 6-8.** Argues that writing centers should expand their missions by emphasizing "languaging"—the language processes of listening, speaking, reading, and writing. Describes the implementation of this philosophy in the Workshop Skills Center at Sacred Heart University (CT).

0162. **Lovejoy, K.B. "Beginning the Writing Lab at William Woods College."** *Writing Lab Newsletter* **3.1 (1978): 4-5.** Describes the establishment of the writing lab at William Woods College (MO), with a particular focus on responding to the implications of a required statewide test of student abilities—the Basic Essential Skills Test (BEST).

0163. **Loxterman, Alan. "Interdisciplinary Writing at Richmond."** *Writing Lab Newsletter* **2.1 (1977): 1-2.** Discusses the proposal at the University of Richmond (VA) to encourage widespread faculty and student involvement in an interdisciplinary writing center designed to help junior and senior students.

0164. **Luban, Nina, Ann Matsuhashi, and Tom Reigstad. "One-to-One to Write: Establishing an Individual-Conference Writing Place."** *English Journal* **67.8 (1978): 30-35.** Describes sequence of planning activities to establish a writing center in East High School (Buffalo, NY), emphasizing operational concerns (physical setting and materials, scheduling tutors and clients, record keeping, and advertising).

0165. **Magaha, Ann. "Technical Writing and Tutor Training."** *Writing Lab Newsletter* **12.4 (1987): 11-12.** Describes a program instituted at Embry-Riddle Aeronautical University (FL) to link peer tutor training to the university's technical writing course. Results included better training for tutors and technical writers and the production of a handbook for technical writing students.

0166. **Markline, Judy. "Peer Tutors in the Community College."** *Writing Lab Newsletter* **10.4 (1985): 11-12.** Describes the tutor recruitment and training program of the writing center at Allan Hancock College (CA).

0167. **Martin, Kathy. "Perry Meridian High School's Writing Lab."** *Writing Lab Newsletter* **8.9 (1984): 5-6.** Discusses the organizational model of the writing lab at Perry Meridian High School (IN).

0168. **McCloskey, Frank H., and Lillian Herlands Hornstein. "Subfreshman Composition—a New Solution."** *College English* **11 (1949-50): 331-39.** Describes the establishment of the "Booster System" of individual and group tutoring at Washington Square College of Arts and Sciences of New York University as a means of correcting deficiencies in students' writing and of creating a positive and supportive atmosphere for enhancing student morale. Favors this approach over the remedial English class.

0169. **McCullough, Jean. "The Writing Lab at St. Petersburg Jr. College (Clearwater Campus)."** *Writing Lab Newsletter* **5.8 (1981): 2-3.** Describes the writing lab at St. Petersburg Junior College (FL), with a particular focus on a program of self-directed learning.

0170. **McDonald, Robert E. "Gallaudet College's New Writing Center."** *Writing Lab Newsletter* **9.9 (1985): 9.** Tells of the opening of the writing center at Gallaudet College in Washington, D.C., a liberal arts college for the severely hearing impaired.

0171. **McKeague, Patricia M., and Elizabeth Reis. "Serving Student Needs Through Writing Centers."** *Community/Junior College Quarterly of Research and Practice.* **16.2 (1992): 199-206.** Describes 13 community college writing centers and the services they provide. Examines these centers' staffing, facilities, clientele, budget, program evaluation, and plans for expansion.

0172. **McMillan, Peter. "Tadpoles and Topic Sentences: A Writing Center in Asia."** *Writing Lab Newsletter* **11.3 (1986): 1-3.** Discusses the start-up of what the author contends is the first Asian writing center, on Yokota Air Base in Japan. Describes the challenges of serving a diverse clientele and characterizes the center as place where discussions of writing, philosophy, and literature converge.

0173. **Melko, James. "The Miami University Spelling Skills Center."** *Writing Lab Newsletter* **6.10 (1982): 1-2.** Describes how the Writing Skills Center at Miami University of Ohio set up a Spelling Skills Center as a "sub-operation" that represented "a concentrated attack upon the problems inherent in teaching spelling."

0174. **Meyers, Douglas, and Susan Kleiman. "The University of Maryland's Junior Writing Center."** *Writing Lab Newsletter* **6.5 (1982): 9.** Describes the operations and philosophy of a writing center set up to offer supplementary assistance through individualized tutoring sessions for advanced composition and technical writing students.

0175. **Miller, Toni. "Carleton Tutors in the Business World."** *Writing Lab Newsletter* **10.10 (1986): 1-2.** Describes courses the Carleton College (MN) writing center offers to writers in the business world, such as lawyers, engineers, and administrative assistants. Contends such a program not only broadens writing center services but provides employment opportunities for tutors.

0176. **Miller, William V. "Now and Later at Ball State."** *Writing Lab Newsletter* **6.6 (1982): 1-2.** Describes the projected growth of the writing clinic at Ball State University (IN) in terms of a fantasy from its real origins as a small facility in the basement of a three-bedroom bungalow to its idealized future as a large, well-funded, state-of-the-art facility.

0177. **Mink, JoAnna Stephens. "Developing a Writing Center Identity."** *Writing Lab Newsletter* **13.6 (1989): 5-6.** Discusses the importance of establishing an identity for the writing center as a "special place" on campus. Describes how the writing center at Atlantic Christian College (NC) sought out help from campus specialists in art and graphic design in developing its own logo.

0178. **Miron, Louis. "The Writing Laboratory at William Carey College: A Tutorial Approach."** *Writing Lab Newsletter* **3.7 (1979): 3-4.** Describes how the Department of Special Programs in conjunction with the English department at William Carey College (MS) established a writing laboratory to meet the needs of underprepared students.

0179. **Munro, John M. "New Writing Laboratory in the University of Toronto."** *College English* **26 (1964-65): 50.** Briefly describes laboratory available on a voluntary basis to all students for assistance in grammar and composition. Intended to be "something other than a convalescent home for the semiliterate, the usual fate of English programs which function outside the regular curriculum."

0180. **Naugle, Helen. "How Georgia Tech's Lab Prepares Students for the Georgia Mandated Proficiency Examination."** *Writing Lab Newsletter* **5.4 (1980): 5-6.** Discusses how the writing lab's program of individualized instruction and a workshop on the requirements of the proficiency exam reduced Georgia Tech University's failure rate on the exam. Offers general suggestions on how writing centers can respond to state-mandated testing.

0181. **Nelson, Betty Palmer. "Course Offerings at Volunteer State's Writing Lab."** *Writing Lab Newsletter* **2.3 (1977): 2-3.** Describes three courses offered by the writing lab at Volunteer State Community College (TN). Two preparatory courses diagnose writing problems and assign "individual auto-instructional work" on the problems; a support course for freshman composition gives "auto-instructional and tutorial help on rhetorical problems."

0182. **Neuleib, Janice. "Training Potential English Teachers in the Writing Center."** *Writing Lab Newsletter* **3.2 (1978): 2-3.** Discusses the contributions the writing center at Illinois State University makes to the training of graduate students enrolled in the Doctor of Arts program in community college teaching. Argues that these students receive an alternative model of instruction to complement traditional classroom instruction.

0183. **Nigliazzo, Marc A. "Building a Comprehensive English Learning Center at Del Mar College."** *Writing Lab Newsletter* **3.8 (1979): 2-3.** Discusses the organization and administration of the learning center at Del Mar College (TX) in terms of equipment, materials, scope, courses offered, and the promotion of services.

0184. **Norton, Don. "The Writing Lab at Brigham Young University."** *Writing Lab Newsletter* **2.6 (1978): 3.** Discusses the writing lab—a part of the Learning Services Center that offers tutoring in math, reading, writing, effective study, and communication skills—and its relationship to the General Education program.

0185. Olson, Ann, and Nancy V. Wood. "Peer Tutors Staff Writing Room at the University of Texas at El Paso." *Writing Lab Newsletter* 4.6 (1980): 1-2. Describes the operations of the writing room in terms of set-up and procedures, with particular emphasis on the role of peer tutors in the staffing and daily operations.

0186. Opitz, Jane Z. "Saint John's WRITING WORKSHOP: A Summary of the First Semester Report." *Writing Lab Newsletter* 2.9 (1978): 2-3. Describes a system of record keeping at St. John's University (MN) for tracing staffing and time utilization, clients, and evaluation of services.

0187. Perkins, Lorraine. "The Writing Clinic at St. Cloud." *Writing Lab Newsletter* 2.2 (1977): 1-2. Discusses the establishment, set-up, operating procedures, and evaluation of the writing clinic at St. Cloud State University (MN).

0188. Puma, Vincent. "The Write Staff: Identifying and Training Tutor-Candidates." *Writing Lab Newsletter* 14.2 (1989): 1-4. Describes the writing center at Flagler College (FL), emphasizing its screening and training program for tutors.

0189. Quinn, Helen, and Carole Flint. "The Technical Communication Resource Center and Writing Lab: Special Services for Basic, Technical, and Learning Disabled Writers." *Writing Lab Newsletter* 14.9 (1990): 10-14. Discusses policies and procedures of the writing center at the University of Wisconsin—Stout for assisting basic writers, technical writing students, and students with learning disabilities.

0190. Rhyan, Donald K. "Credit Courses in the KCKCC Learning-Skills Center." *Writing Lab Newsletter* 2.6 (1978): 4. Describes the basic skills, study skills, and spelling courses offered by the learning-skills center at Kansas City Kansas Community College.

0191. Rochelle, Larry. "The 'Just Pretend' Room: The Writing Center." *Clearing House* 52.3 (1978): 115-18. A fantasy description of an innovative approach to learning in which elementary school teachers and volunteers turn a schoolroom into a writing center where elementary students can work on their writing with the assistance of secondary school tutors.

0192. Salerno, Grace Foley. "An English Laboratory in Action." *English Journal* 52 (1963): 37-41. Describes an experimental program set up at Barringer High School (Newark, NJ) to provide tutoring in fundamentals of reading, writing, and speaking to limited number of students, including not only ESL students and at-risk students but college-bound students as well. Limited to five to eight students per period, five periods per day (five different English teachers staff lab).

0193. **Schulte, Richard J. "The Individualized Learning Center at P.C.C."** *Writing Lab Newsletter* 2.9 (1978): 4-6. At Parkersburg Community College (WV), instructors found that individualizing instruction to fit a student's needs was effective in mathematics and extended this method to include college-level composition, technical writing, business writing, and literature courses.

0194. **Sherwood, Phyllis A. "The Rise and Fall of Basic English and the Writing Lab."** *Writing Lab Newsletter* 7.1 (1982): 1-3. Discusses administrators' plans to study the effectiveness of the writing lab at Raymond Walters College of the University of Cincinnati in Ohio and restructure its offerings after basic English courses and a proficiency exam in English were discontinued.

0195. **Simpson, Jeanne. "Voyages of Discovery in a New Writing Center."** *Writing Lab Newsletter* 7.1 (1982): 9. Discusses how the writing center at Eastern Illinois University "commandeered" posters from staff offices and apartments for decorative use in the writing center and also how the center used cassette recorders in tutorial work with ESL students.

0196. **Skerl, Jennie. "The Writing Center at RPI."** *Writing Lab Newsletter* 2.4 (1977): 5-6. Discusses the establishment of the writing center at Rensselaer Polytechnic Institute (NY) as part of "a general program to encourage the improvement of writing in coursework throughout the Institute, thus providing a back-up resource for faculty and students."

0197. **Skerl, Jennie. "A Writing Center for Engineering Students."** *Engineering Education* 70 (1980): 752-55. Describes the program designed to assist students with technical writing at Rensselaer Polytechnic Institute (NY) and outlines the principles underlying the tutorial services offered there.

0198. **Southwell, Michael G. "Computer-Assisted Instruction in the COMP-LAB at York College/CUNY."** *Writing Lab Newsletter* 7.8 (1983): 1-2. Discusses the development of the COMP-LAB, an autotutorial writing lab, and the philosophy behind the introduction of technology into tutoring. Basic writing students receive classroom instruction and then work in the lab on modules of self-teaching exercises, each dealing with a grammatical or syntactical problem.

0199. **Stauffenberg, Henry J. "The Scranton Approach."** *Writing Lab Newsletter* **4.8 (1980): 3-5.** Describes the set-up, administration, services, and philosophy of the writing lab at the University of Scranton (PA), with particular reference to the writing lab's connection to the freshman composition program.

0200. **Steward, Joyce S. "To Like to Have Written: Learning the Laboratory Way."** *ADE Bulletin 6* **(1975): 32-43.** Discusses the writing lab at the University of Wisconsin and the kinds of problems students have, approaches taken to them, methods of recording students' progress, selection and training of staff, and measures of effectiveness of the laboratory.

0201. **Stoddart, Pat. "Computers as Tools for Writing at Logan High School."** *Writing Lab Newsletter* **9.9 (1985): 5-6.** Discusses the use of computers in the "Writing Room" at Logan High School (Logan, UT). Text-analysis and word-processing software enable students to spend a fourth of their class time in the lab working on their assignments.

0202. **Stone, Virginia. "ELC at Del Mar College."** *Writing Lab Newsletter* **2.8 (1978): 5.** Describes the development of the English Learning Center at Del Mar College (TX). Focuses, in particular, on the center's system of faculty referrals.

0203. **Stone, Virginia. "Phase Two in the Competency Program at Del Mar College."** *Writing Lab Newsletter* **4.10 (1980): 8.** Describes the establishment of two remedial courses emphasizing the process and techniques of composition to be offered through the Competency Program and the English Learning Center at Del Mar College (TX).

0204. **Stroud, William Banks. "The Remediation of Written Discourse in Rochester, New York." Diss. U of Rochester, 1990.** *DAI* **51-02A (1990): 0402.** Examines the relationship between the New York State Education Department guidelines for a writing remediation program and the actual practices of the writing remediation program and writing lab at the secondary level in the Rochester City School District. Found the district's program met or exceeded the state guidelines in all areas except the documentation of services provided each student.

**0205. Stull, William. "The Hartford Sentence-Combining Laboratory: From Theory to Program."** *The Writing Center Journal* **1.1 (1980): 20-33.** Describes a sentence-combining laboratory at the University of Hartford (CT) that is part of the Learning Skills Center and forms a third element of the first-year writing program (along with two composition courses). Reviews research supporting sentence-combining approach and evaluates success of program.

**0206. Stull, William L. "A Sentence-Combining Laboratory for Basic-Writing Students."** *Writing Lab Newsletter* **5.5 (1981): 1-3.** Describes the establishment of a two-hour sentence-combining laboratory at the University of Hartford (CT) required of all students enrolled in the basic writing sections of freshman composition. Offered by the learning skills center, this laboratory on "error-centered instruction" proved a success with students and faculty.

**0207. Tanner, Marva. "The Seminole Community College Writing Center."** *Writing Lab Newsletter* **9.7 (1985): 4.** Discusses the development and expansion of the writing center at Seminole Community College (FL), especially in terms of expanded computer offerings.

**0208. Thomas, Gordon K. "Remedial English for Upper-Division Students at the Church College of Hawaii."** *College English* **28 (1966-67): 326-27.** Reports effectiveness of a writing lab recently added to the remedial course for students who fail the school's proficiency exam. Writing lab staff mark papers written for teacher of course and then consult individually with students.

**0209. Thornbury, Charles. "St. John's Adds Writing Requirements to Colloquium."** *Writing Lab Newsletter* **2.2 (1977): 2.** Discusses the establishment and set-up of the writing lab/workshop at St. John's University (MN). The lab/workshop is to be open to all students enrolled in a required colloquium; however, services will be limited to basic writers if the facility becomes "overrun."

**0210. Upton, James. "We Hold These Truths to be Sometimes Not So Self-Evident."** *Writing Lab Newsletter* **17.8 (1993): 5, 8.** Reveals the underlying philosophy of a high school communication resource center at Burlington High School (Burlington, IA), including working to help students become independent writers, offering no guarantees for success, keeping up on the latest professional developments, and striving to make writing to learn a goal of all classes.

0211. **Vick, Richard D. "The Western Illinois University Writing Center."** *Writing Lab Newsletter* **9.3 (1984): 7-9.** Discusses the development of this writing center by emphasizing philosophy and objectives, staff training, tutoring procedures, materials, and future plans.

0212. **Waldo, Mark L., Jacob Blumner, and Mary Webb. "Writing Centers and Writing Assessment: A Discipline-Based Approach."** *Writing Center Perspectives.* **Ed. Byron L. Stay, Christina Murphy, and Eric H. Hobson. Emmitsburg: NWCA Press, 1995. 38-47.** Describes pilot program at the University of Nevada—Reno to help disciplines establish criteria for evaluating writing and avoid imposing standards of some other field.

0213. **Walker, Francis Ingold. "The Laboratory System in English."** *English Journal* **6 (1917): 445-53.** Describes a laboratory system of instruction the author developed for a high school English class at New Trier Township High School (Kenilworth, IL). Concludes that administrators and teachers do not regard English as a laboratory subject but should do so because of the exceptional results such an approach achieves.

0214. **Warters, Susan. "Mount Royal College."** *Writing Lab Newsletter* **5.7 (1981): 6-7.** Describes the courses in basic writing and reading skills offered by the Learning Skills Program at Mount Royal College, a two-year, open admissions community college in Canada.

0215. **Welch, George W. "Organizing a Reading and Writing Lab in Which Students Teach."** *College Composition and Communication* **25 (1974): 437-39.** Discusses the Reading and Writing Workroom at Miami-Dade Community College—South Campus (FL). Drop rates in freshman English classes were lowered when students used the lab. The lab functioned as a model of an "academic community." Tutors were students themselves, and faculty served as resource persons.

0216. **Werdin, Mark. "A Summer Exercise in Wholeness: ESL Teaching as Cooperative Cultural Exchange."** *Writing Lab Newsletter* **18.10 (1994): 10-11.** Describes the goals and achievements of the English Language Institute at Pepperdine University (CA). Concludes that writing center instructors should see their teaching relationships with international students as cooperative learning relationships.

0217. **Wess, Robert C. "Making Connections: The Writing Lab at PSU."** *Writing Lab Newsletter* **6.7 (1982): 4-5.** Describes a course instituted by the writing lab at Pembroke State University (NC) to train peer tutors. The course provides English majors first-hand experience in working with students who need help and also enables the writing lab to create connections with the English department.

0218. **Whitson, Lynn. "Experimental Program at Odessa College."** *Writing Lab Newsletter* **2.10 (1978): 7.** Describes the writing lab at Odessa College (TX) with special emphasis on its system of formalized instruction through a series of one-hour lab courses.

0219. **Whitted, Dorothy. "A Tutorial Program for Remedial Students."** *College Composition and Communication* **18.1 (1967): 40-43.** Describes the four-year, all-campus English Proficiency Program at Ohio Wesleyan University in which writing tutors work with remedial students who are designated for the program by instructors across the disciplines who do not find the students' writing "of sufficient clarity or organizational skills."

0220. **Wilson, Paula. "A Jr. High Lab Takes Shape."** *Writing Lab Newsletter* **6.6 (1982): 7.** Recounts the set-up, administration, philosophy, and offerings of the writing lab at Wainwright Junior High School (IN), with a particular focus on the difficulties of securing funding and arranging class schedules.

0221. **Winter, Frances. "The Research Paper Tutorial Project at Mass. Bay C.C."** *Writing Lab Newsletter* **4.9 (1980): 7.** Describes the operations at Massachusetts Bay Community College of a "mini-writing lab" that is part of a learning resources center and offers tutorial instruction solely on writing the research paper.

0222. **Wise, J. Hooper. "A Comprehensive Freshman English Course in Operation."** *English Journal* **28 (1939): 450-60. Appears in college edition only.** Describes a five-hour freshman composition course at the University of Florida, two hours of which are devoted to laboratory work. There the student may consult with an instructor while working on any sort of writing task (not limited to composition course).

0223. **Woodward, Pauline. "The Writing Center Community: Getting It Together."** *Writing Lab Newsletter* **8.8 (1984): 5-8.** Discusses the establishment of the Writing Skills Center at Lesley College (MA) and the center's efforts to serve students, faculty, and staff as an "academic community."

0224. Word, Joan. "TSU Surveys Campus Writing/Learning Practices." *Writing Lab Newsletter* 14.6 (1990): 14-16. Gives the results of a survey at Troy State University (AL) to determine a university's specific needs in writing instruction. Results indicated a need for writing-to-learn courses and assignments, which the university instituted.

0225. Wright, Anne. "Beyond Tutoring: The Writing Lab as the Write Place." *Writing Lab Newsletter* 11.8 (1987): 13-14. Describes how the writing center at Hazelwood High School (Hazelwood, MO) moved into realms other than tutoring, including encouraging students to enter writing contests, sponsoring a writing club, furnishing computers for student use, and maintaining a library of books about writing.

0226. Wright, Anne. "Terminal Writing in the Writing Lab." *The Writing Center Journal* 8.1 (1987): 21-28. Describes experience in starting and staffing a computer lab in the writing center at Hazelwood High School (Hazelwood, MO). Discusses how composition classes used the computers, how computer-assisted writing instruction benefited students, how to use computers to teach revising skills, and how to use computers to keep records. Offers advice on designing a computer lab and choosing equipment.

0227. Young, Ginger. "CMSU's Most Valuable Lab Resource." *Writing Lab Newsletter* 9.6 (1985): 8. Discusses handouts on grammar provided by the Central Missouri State University writing lab to prepare students for the rigors of composition courses, sustaining their fragile egos, and aiding student retention.

# Professional Concerns

**0228. Balester, Valerie. "Revising the 'Statement': On the Work of Writing Centers."** *College Composition and Communication* 43 (1992): 167-71. Part of "Symposium on the 1991 'Progress Report from the CCC Committee on Professional Standards.'" Points out that the "Statement" perpetuates the view of writing centers as supplemental to the English department curriculum and fails to acknowledge writing centers as places where research takes place and teaching unrelated to the classroom occurs.

**0229. Cobb, Loretta. "Addressing Professional Concerns."** *Writing Lab Newsletter* 13.7 (1989): 11-12. Urges writing center specialists to speak out about their concerns involving faculty status and stable funding for centers. Sees signs of support from the National Council of Teachers of English and the National Writing Centers Association as particularly encouraging.

**0230. Davis, Kevin. "Homemade Pasta, Writing Centers and the Evolution of Approach: A Call for Research."** *Writing Lab Newsletter* 13.1 (1988): 5-6. Calls on writing center practitioners to support their efforts with solid research that shows how and why tutoring works.

**0231. Devet, Bonnie. "National Certification for a Writing Lab."** *Writing Lab Newsletter* 17.2 (1992): 12-13. Describes the standards of the College Reading and Learning Association for certifying tutor training programs in academic skills centers. Questions whether a writing lab should be certified by a reading and study skills association. Also discusses the process The College of Charleston (SC) went through to win certification.

0232. **Elliott, M.A. "Writing Center Directors: Why Faculty Status Fits."** *Writing Lab Newsletter* **14.7 (1990): 1-4.** Argues that the teaching, administrative, and research obligations assigned to writing center directors merit faculty status. Discusses the implications of a failed attempt to upgrade the status of the writing center director at one community college.

0233. **Endicott, Phyllis Stevens, and Carol Peterson Haviland. "Empowering Writing Center Staff: Martyrs or Models?"** *Writing Lab Newsletter* **16.8 (1992): 1-6.** Argues that negative attitudes of faculty who see writing centers as little more than stopgap grammar clinics too often infect writing center personnel with poor self-esteem. Offers advice on improving the writing center's image and raising tutors' self-esteem.

0234. **Healy, Dave. "Writing Center Directors: An Emerging Portrait of the Profession."** *WPA: Writing Program Administration* **18.3 (1995): 26-43.** Detailed report of demographic and attitudinal information obtained from a national survey of directors and assistant directors of writing centers. Results indicate that directors are disproportionately female, perceive themselves as working long hours for low pay and dealing with inadequate resources; directors also report taking great satisfaction in working with writing center clients and staff.

0235. **Law, Joe. "Accreditation and the Writing Center: A Proposal for Action."** *Writing Center Perspectives.* **Ed. Byron L. Stay, Christina Murphy, and Eric H. Hobson. Emmitsburg: NWCA Press, 1995. 155-61.** Proposes that the National Writing Centers Association establish an accrediting agency that would evaluate writing centers and certify that they meet a nationally recognized standard at one of several levels.

0236. **Murray, Patricia Y., and Linda Bannister. "The Status and Responsibilities of Writing Lab Directors: A Survey."** *Writing Lab Newsletter* **9.6 (1985): 10-11.** Discusses the results of a survey of 298 writing lab directors to determine the scope of their responsibilities, ranging from administration, promotion, and tutor training, to sponsoring activities for returning adults and creating and supervising computer-assisted instruction.

0237. **North, Steve. "Us 'N Howie: The Shape of Our Ignorance."** *Writing Lab Newsletter* **6.1 (1981):3-7.** Uses a narrative about Howie, a talented high school basketball player unaware of the fundamentals and the rules of the game, to argue that writing center professionals need a greater understanding of the writing process and composition theories.

0238. **Olson, Gary, and Evelyn Ashton-Jones. "Writing Center Directors: The Search for Professional Status."** *WPA: Writing Program Administration* **12.1-2 (1988): 19-28. Rpt. in 0007.** National survey of directors of freshman English indicates that most consider the writing center director more an administrator than a teacher, scholar, or writing specialist. Briefly suggests ways to change this perception and increase professional status.

0239. **Perdue, Virginia. "Writing-Center Faculty in Academia: Another Look at Our Institutional Status."** *WPA: Writing Program Administration* **15.1-2 (1991): 13-24.** Examines why administrators and professors undervalue writing center faculty. Cautions writing center faculty seeking higher status not to rely exclusively on numerical data reflecting writing center usage. Suggests writing center faculty also demonstrate their effectiveness as teachers and tutors by citing student progress reports and case histories.

0240. **Peterson, Linda. "The WPAs Progress: A Survey, Story, and Commentary on the Career Patterns of Writing Program Administrators."** *WPA: Writing Program Administration* **10.3 (1987): 11-18.** Survey of writing program administrators indicates that 64% directed (or were responsible for) writing centers, 46% supervised peer-tutor training, and 50% judged their workload as higher than that of their colleagues.

0241. **Simpson, Jeanne. "A Reader Responds ... So Demanding a Job."** *Writing Lab Newsletter* **9.5 (1985): 5-6.** Discusses professional concerns that writing center directors face in addition to their heavy workloads, such as faculty status with provisions for retention, tenure, and promotion; release time; clerical help; and the advocacy and support of a strong national organization.

0242. **Simpson, Jeanne. "What Lies Ahead for Writing Centers: Position Statement on Professional Concerns."** *The Writing Center Journal* **5.2/6.1 (1985): 35-39. Rpt. in 0007.** Position statement formulated by the Executive Board and Professional Concerns Committee of the National Writing Centers Association. Recommends specific guidelines in three areas: establishing institutional working conditions when hiring directors; developing job description for directorships; and operating a writing center.

0243. Simpson, Jeanne, Steve Braye, and Beth Boquet. "War, Peace, and Writing Center Administration." *Composition Studies/Freshman English News* 22.1 (1994): 65-95. Rpt. in 0007. Transcript of an E-mail conversation on WCenter about the institutional status of writing centers, particularly the concept of writing center marginalization.

0244. Spooner, Michael. "Circles and Centers: Some Thoughts on the Writing Center and Academic Book Publishing." *Writing Lab Newsletter* 17.10 (1993): 1-3, 10. Examines, from a publisher's perspective, the market for books about writing centers. Suggests that the market for "pure" writing center books (of interest primarily to writing center practitioners and administrators) is rather small. Contends a larger market exists for books addressing issues of interest to both writing centers and the larger world of "English Studies," including such issues as tutor and TA training, multiculturalism, computers and writing, teaching English as a second language, and writing across the curriculum.

0245. Stay, Byron. "Writing Centers on the Margins: Conversing from the Edge." *Writing Lab Newsletter* 17.1 (1992): 1-4. Argues that, since the writing center mission is pivotal to the university in many ways, writing centers should find ways to avoid political and professional marginalization. Suggests writing centers begin by moving out of English departments, tapping into institutional power sources, and urging national organizations to speak out on their behalf.

0246. Steele, Mildred. "A Statement Given in Behalf of a Resolution About Writing Lab Professionals." *Writing Lab Newsletter* 5.10 (1981): 4. Writing lab professionals are involved and invested in improving student writing and in carrying out a number of academic responsibilities. Therefore, they should be provided opportunities for professional growth, funding for travel to conferences, and service on departmental and college committees.

# Writing Center Theory

0247. **Abascal-Hildebrand, Mary. "Tutor and Student Relations: Applying Gadamer's Notions of Translation."** *Intersections: Theory-Practice in the Writing Center.* **Ed. Joan A. Mullin and Ray Wallace. Urbana: NCTE, 1994. 172-83.** Uses Hans-Georg Gadamer's theories to describe the limited kind of understanding negotiated between tutor and student as they become "translators" for each other. Argues that this process moves the tutorial into an ethical realm because the conversation is based on mutual regard and respect.

0248. **Armstrong, Cherryl, and Sheryl I. Fontaine. "The Power of Naming: Names that Create and Define the Discipline."** *WPA: Writing Program Administration* **13.1-2 (1989): 5-14.** Includes a short discussion on the ramifications of naming a tutoring facility the writing "lab," "center," "clinic," or "workshop." Explores the psychological and social effects of naming on students, tutors, and faculty.

0249. **Birnbaum, Lisa C. "Toward a Gender-Balanced Staff in the Writing Center."** *Writing Lab Newsletter* **19.8 (1995): 6-7.** Argues for gender balance in the female-dominated field of writing center work. Suggests such a balance is consistent with enlightened feminism.

0250. **Boquet, Elizabeth Helen. "Writing Centers: History, Theory, and Implications." Diss. Indiana U of Pennsylvania, 1995.** *DAI* **56-05A (1995): 1671.** Presents a theoretical examination of the history of writing centers, theories of writing center practice, and the implications of two trends, ethics and cultural studies theory, on current and future writing center practice.

0251. Bosley, Deborah, and Linda Droll. "Creating Collaborative Writing Centers." *Writing Lab Newsletter* 15.8 (1991): 12-14. Sees a growing need for writing centers to offer tutoring for small groups engaged in collaborative writing projects. Argues that, while many centers embrace one-on-one collaboration, few are prepared to facilitate collaboration among members of a group working on a single project.

0252. Bottoms, Laurie, Jerilyn Carter, Finlay McQuade, James Upton, Diane Lockward, Ellen Brinkley, Susan K. Carroll, and Carol Mendenhall. "Round Table." *English Journal* 76.7 (1987): 68-70. Eight secondary teachers discuss the value of high school writing centers. Contend writing centers create changes in presentation of subject matter (no longer is the English teacher the only writing teacher), cooperation (students share ideas), and authority (the extent to which the teacher is responsible for what the student writes).

0253. Brannon, Lil, and C.H. Knoblauch. "A Philosophical Perspective on Writing Centers and the Teaching of Writing." *Writing Centers: Theory and Administration*. Ed. Gary A. Olson. Urbana: NCTE, 1984. 36-47. Finds protocol analysis preferable to traditional instruction that focuses on form and recommends this approach to both classroom and writing center instructors.

0254. Brinkley, Ellen. "The Writing Center Model at the Heart of Writing Instruction from Kindergarten to College." *Writing Lab Newsletter* 14.9 (1990): 1-4. Points out some of the potential benefits of patterning writing instruction at all levels of education after the writing center model. Suggests the model empowers students to take control of their writing and, therefore, their learning.

0255. Brinkley, Ellen H. "Writing Centers in Secondary Schools: An Idea Beyond the Puberty Stage." *Writing Lab Newsletter* 11.4 (1986): 5-7. Argues that the secondary school writing center—though a descendent of college writing centers—has matured and become distinct from its ancestor. Argues that, while secondary writing centers have embraced the individual conference, they face different challenges and obstacles and therefore have developed their own approach.

0256. Brown, Alan Norman. "Writing Centers: How They Succeed and Fail." Diss. Illinois State U, 1984. *DAI* 46-01A (1984): 0091. Examines the characteristics of successful and unsuccessful writing centers and concludes that most writing centers are shaped by "the expectations of their constituencies."

0257. **Bruffee, Kenneth A. "The Politics of Innovation: A Primer."** *Improving Writing Skills.* **Ed. Thom Hawkins and Phyllis Brooks. New Directions for College Learning Assistance 3. San Francisco: Jossey-Bass, 1981. 53-59.** Claims that all innovation involves change that must be negotiated politically. Urges writing center directors to be aware of this principle as they establish new programs and offerings. Claims well-founded plans and powerful allies are the directors' greatest assets in bringing about innovation.

0258. **Butler, Wayne M., and James L. Kinneavy. "The Electronic Discourse Community: god meet Donald Duck."** *Focuses* **4.2 (1991): 91-108.** Replaces the traditional concept of the writing center as a place where writers come to get help and be "fixed" with the idea of the writing center as an electronic discourse community where writers write to other writers via electronic conferencing.

0259. **Campbell, Hugh. "Two Memos to Colleagues."** *College Composition and Communication* **42 (1991): 368-71.** Claims a university writing program is an important component of undergraduate and graduate education and the "hub" of this program should be a "*real* writing center" where "writers of all levels can come for help, feedback, and conversation about the art and craft of writing."

0260. **Carino, Peter. "Theorizing the Writing Center: An Uneasy Task."** *Dialogue: A Journal for Writing Specialists* **2.1 (1995): 23-37.** Examines the tensions in the writing center community between practice and theory. Argues for the value of theory "as a means of establishing disciplinary and institutional respectability" for writing center work, which, historically, has not been recognized as a discipline. Establishing a theoretical framework would allow writing centers to "explain themselves" to other entities within the academy and to "the disciplines to which they are related, particularly composition studies."

0261. **Carino, Peter. "What Do We Talk About When We Talk About Our Metaphors: A Cultural Critique of Clinic, Lab, and Center."** *The Writing Center Journal* **13.1 (1992): 31-42. Rpt. in 0007.** Examines from a cultural and historical perspective the ramifications of the terms used to describe writing centers (*clinic*, *lab*, *center*). Contends that the metaphor behind each term reveals (and often affects) not only how the centers are perceived but how they operate. Urges directors and administrators to name centers carefully to avoid perpetuating stereotypes of writing centers as "remedial fix-it shops."

0262. **Chase, Geoffrey. "Small Is Beautiful: A Plan for the Decentralized Writing Center."** *Writing Lab Newsletter* **9.8 (1985): 1-4.** Claims that, when most writing center directors envision the future, they see their writing centers expanding in size, staff, and services. Argues this vision can be counterproductive because the predilection for centralization and for large organizations and structures can contribute to a sense of isolation and alienation for students and the academic community at large.

0263. **Clara, Louise. "Individualized Instruction: A Response to Errol Erickson's Article in the December, 1977 Issue of the** *WLN.*" *Writing Lab Newsletter* **2.6 (1978): 4, 3.** Supports Erickson's ideas, drawn from Benjamin Bloom, of mastery learning and its special relevance to individualized writing lab programs (see entry 0279). Cautions, though, that this concept must be employed in its entirety, which presupposes competency-based instruction in order to identify what constitutes mastery learning.

0264. **Clark, Irene. "Information Literacy and the Writing Center."** *Computers and Composition* **12 (1995): 203-09.** Stressing importance of information literacy to all areas of students' lives, argues that instruction in retrieving and evaluating electronic sources ought to be among goals of writing centers. Recommends that process and collaborative models informing writing center practice be applied in this area as well.

0265. **Clark, Irene L. "Portfolio Evaluation, Collaboration, and Writing Centers."** *College Composition and Communication* **44 (1993): 515-24.** Describes how a university-wide portfolio assessment project focused attention on four questions: the meaning of the assertion that writing centers "assist" students in becoming better writers, the ethical boundaries of collaboration, the reciprocal effect of pressure for grades and visits to the writing center, and the aspect of the writing process emphasized in writing center visits.

0266. **Clark, Irene L. "Portfolio Grading and the Writing Center."** *The Writing Center Journal* **13.2 (1993): 48-62.** Describes effects of portfolio grading on the practices and policies of writing centers. Supports portfolio grading but indicates dilemmas—practical and ethical—such a system poses to writing consultants.

0267. **Clark, Irene Lurkis. "Maintaining Chaos in the Writing Center: A Critical Perspective on Writing Center Dogma."** *The Writing Center*

*Journal* **11.1 (1990): 81-93.** Encourages writing centers, despite their becoming firmly established, to continue to "entertain multiple perspectives on critical issues," to "tolerate contradictions and contraries," and to continue to grow and evolve. Argues against formulaic rules for tutoring and rigid models for writing center design. Critiques easy assumptions (e.g., the validity of rules against editing) and terms (e.g., *collaborative learning*) as too often unexamined by practitioners.

0268. **Cooper, Marilyn. "'We Don't Belong Here, Do We?' A Response to** *Lives on the Boundary* **and** *The Violence of Literacy.***"** *The Writing Center Journal* **12.1 (1991): 48-62.** Examines the ramifications of reserving innovative literacy programs for children of the social elite, issues posed by Mike Rose's and J. Elspeth Stuckey's books. Questions society's desire to educate all of its children. Suggests writing centers can, by focusing on individual students, "help each of them learn how to use their minds and their energies to succeed." Urges changing the system to accommodate students whose social status has negatively affected their literacy.

0269. **Cooper, Marilyn M. "Really Useful Knowledge: A Cultural Studies Agenda for Writing Centers."** *The Writing Center Journal* **14.2 (1994): 97-111. Rpt. in 0007.** Discusses the tutor's role in helping students understand the cultural constraints that affect their writing. Suggests empowering students by teaching them to find autonomous spaces within restrictive writing assignments in which to address their own experiences and beliefs. Contends that writing centers themselves must make better use of such spaces within their institutions if they are to teach effectively.

0270. **Crump, Eric. "Voices from the Net: Reshaping Writing Instruction in the Writing Center Image?"** *Writing Lab Newsletter* **18.1 (1993): 8-9.** Discusses the possibility of designing composition courses on the writing center model, including doing away with freshman composition altogether and basing all writing instruction in the writing center.

0271. **Daniel, Neil, and Christina Murphy. "Correctness or Clarity? Finding Answers in the Classroom and the Professional World."** *The Place of Grammar in Writing Instruction: Past Present Future.* **Ed. Susan Hunter and Ray Wallace. Portsmouth: Boynton/Cook Heinemann, 1995. 225-42.** Claims the writing center model of individualized instruction should replace the traditional first-year composition course. Eliminating this course and expanding the role of

writing in the disciplines would "increase the role and significance of
writing teachers/consultants at many university writing centers."

0272. **Davis, Kevin. "Life Outside the Boundary: History and Direction in
the Writing Center."** *Writing Lab Newsletter* **20.2 (1995): 5-7.** Argues
that the personal histories of writing center personnel place them right
where they belong—on the boundary of the academy. Suggests writing
center personnel have a duty to be insolent, idealistic, subversive, and
creative as they balance their often conflicting duties to the institution
and the student.

0273. **DeCiccio, Albert. "Moving the Boundary: Putting the Idea of a
Writing Center to the Test."** *Writing Lab Newsletter* **17.5 (1993): 1-4.**
Challenges writing center personnel to move out of the periphery and
risk spreading their collaborative, egalitarian, student-centered pedagogy
to the mainstream of the academy.

0274. **DeCiccio, Albert C. "The Writing Center, Lyotard, and
Postmodernism."** *Writing Lab Newsletter* **20.3 (1995): 10-12.** Contends
that the questions inherent in postmodern theories of language and
literature are similar to those that have been posed in writing centers in
challenging "traditional theories and practices of language and literature."
Claims Jean-François Lyotard's ideas in *The Postmodern Condition*
provide writing centers a way to argue for the acceptance of differences
in writing.

0275. **DeCiccio, Albert C., Michael J. Rossi, and Kathleen Shine Cain.
"Walking the Tightrope: Negotiating Between the Ideal and the
Practical in the Writing Center."** *Writing Center Perspectives.* **Ed.
Byron L. Stay, Christina Murphy, and Eric H. Hobson.
Emmitsburg: NWCA Press, 1995. 26-37.** Points out the common gap
between discussions of theory and actual writing center work as both are
carried out by writing center professionals, warns against creating a false
dichotomy between theory and practice, and illustrates how the
conversations of tutors embrace these supposed contraries.

0276. **Dow, Ronald. "The Writer's Laboratory—One Approach to
Composition."** *Arizona English Bulletin* **16 (1974): 55-56.** Views the
writing laboratory as a model for the ideas developed by Herbert R.
Kohl in *The Open Classroom* that educators should abandon the
authoritarian use of power and provide workable alternatives based upon
shared authority and non-hierarchical interpersonal relationships between
teacher and student.

0277. **Ede, Lisa. "Writing as a Social Process: A Theoretical Foundation for Writing Centers?"** *The Writing Center Journal* **9.2 (1989): 3-13. Rpt. in 0007.** Attempts to ground writing center practice in social constructionist theory. Explores the concept of authorship and challenges the notion of writer as solitary creator. Urges writing center practitioners to find time to think and write about what they do in order to add to the theoretical conversation.

0278. **Eggers, Tilly. "Things Fall Apart: The Writing Center Will Hold."** *The Writing Center Journal* **1.2 (1981): 33-40.** Suggests that Kenneth Burke's theory of language as "symbolic action" can give a sense of coherence and continuity to the constant change experienced in writing centers. Also applies the notion of the "Burkean parlor" to the writing center's mission to help students see their writing in terms of a larger conversation.

0279. **Erickson, Errol. "Using Smaller Learning Packages in Labs."** *Writing Lab Newsletter* **2.4 (1977): 3.** Discusses Benjamin Bloom's research on human characteristics and school learning that indicates 80% of students can achieve mastery in nontraditional learning environments compared to 20% in traditional settings. Views the writing lab as a nontraditional approach and calls for further discussion of the writing lab's potential to enhance student learning.

0280. **Farrell, Pam. "College/High School Connections."** *Writing Lab Newsletter* **16.9-10 (1992): 1-2, 8.** Discusses college-secondary school collaborations in creating and running writing centers. Disadvantages include a misunderstanding of pedagogical roles, time constraints, and disputes over pecking order. Advantages include interactive tutor training, exchange of ideas and support, and shared expenses.

0281. **Farrell-Childers, Pamela. "A Unique Learning Environment."** *Intersections: Theory-Practice in the Writing Center.* **Ed. Joan A. Mullin and Ray Wallace. Urbana: NCTE, 1994. 111-19.** Endorses goals of affective education, which include drawing upon personal resources and fostering "authentic" behavior, empathy, and respect for the self and others; describes how typical writing center environments further those goals.

0282. **Fishman, Judith. "The Writing Center—What Is Its Center?"** *Writing Lab Newsletter* **5.1 (1980): 1-4.** Argues that, in the demands of the moment to respond to literacy crises in education, writing centers often become operative "without knowing who we are" and, once in motion, find it impossible to discover an identity because of day-to-day pressures of survival and accountability. Claims that "a sense of a community of writers" is and should be "the center of a successful writing center."

0283. Fontaine, Sheryl I. "Finding Consistency and Speculating Change: What We Can Learn About Portfolio Assessment from the Writing Center." *The Writing Center Journal* 16.1 (1995): 46-58. Discusses ways in which typical writing center practice and portfolio assessment are consistent. Suggests that, rather than anticipating the impact of portfolio assessment on writing centers, writing centers may provide useful insights to · disciplines employing this type of assessment by demonstrating how to focus on revision, make students responsible for their work, and find ways to deal with inconsistencies in responses to writing.

0284. Freedman, Aviva. "Research and the Writing Center." *Improving Writing Skills.* Ed. Thom Hawkins and Phyllis Brooks. New Directions for College Learning Assistance 3. San Francisco: Jossey-Bass, 1981. 83-93. Argues that the focus in composition research on the composing processes of writers links classroom and writing center instruction.

0285. George, Diana, and Nancy Grimm. "Expanded Roles/Expanded Responsibilities: The Changing Nature of Writing Centers Today." *The Writing Center Journal* 11.1 (1990): 59-66. Examines pitfalls writing centers face as they grow larger, more respectable, and more central to the university mission. Cautions that one-to-one instruction may suffer as a result of growth and centers may distance themselves from the students they are designed to serve. Suggests directors approach growth in careful stages, being sure to "preserve the heart of writing center work—the strong human connection."

0286. Gere, Anne Ruggles. "The Politics of Teaching Writing." *Focuses* 3.2 (1990): 89-98. Claims that writing instruction is "saturated with politics" and discusses the implications of three models of writing instruction—societal, institutional, and classroom—for the teaching and tutoring of writing.

0287. Gillam, Alice M. "Writing Center Ecology: A Bakhtinian Perspective." *The Writing Center Journal* 11.2 (1991): 3-11. Rpt. in 0007. Applies the theories of Mikhail Bakhtins to the conversations of students and tutors in the writing center. Focuses on the fruitful interplay of the centripetal force of academic language and the centrifugal force of individual voice. Argues that this interplay creates a fertile environment for discourse and should be cultivated by writing center tutors.

0288. **Ginn, Doris O. "De-Pidginization: A Rhetoric and Writing Dilemma in Cross-Cultural Communications."** *Focuses* **1.2 (1988): 41-50.** Claims classrooms and writing centers have become "sociolinguistic settings of cross-cultural communication through distinctive student populations of multilinguals, bilinguals, and bidialectals" and offers commentary on the rhetoric and writing dilemmas of "culture-specific and cross-cultural communication."

0289. **Glassman, Susan. "The Writing Center in an Identity Crisis."** *Writing Lab Newsletter* **6.4 (1981): 6-10.** Claims that the difficulty in defining exactly what a writing center is lies in the difficulty of defining the specialized instruction that takes place there. Administrative dilemmas about the jurisdictional identity of the writing center in terms of where on campus and under whose authority the writing will be placed also add to this identity crisis.

0290. **Glover, Carl W., and Byron L. Stay. "Grammar in the Writing Center: Opportunities for Discovery and Change."** *The Place of Grammar in Writing Instruction: Past Present Future.* **Ed. Susan Hunter and Ray Wallace. Portsmouth: Boynton/Cook Heinemann, 1995. 129-35.** Argues that the writing center—not the writing classroom—is the most effective site for melding instruction in grammar and writing because the individualized, process-oriented collaboration of the writing center helps students understand the relationship between grammatical choices and self-expression.

0291. **Grimm, Nancy. "Contesting 'The Idea of a Writing Center': The Politics of Writing Center Research."** *Writing Lab Newsletter* **17.1 (1992): 5-7.** Critiques aspects of the writing center philosophy put forth in Stephen M. North's 1984 essay (entry 0291). Argues that, instead of merely providing institutional support for teachers, writing center specialists should use what they learn about the deleterious effects of educational discourse to spark political and pedagogical changes that benefit disadvantaged students.

0292. **Grimm, Nancy Maloney. "Making Writing Centers Work: Literacy, Institutional Change, and Student Agency." Diss. Michigan Technological U, 1995.** *DAI* **56-05A (1995): 1693.** Argues that "writing centers are underutilized sites of research into the contact of literacies in higher education." Claims that writing centers can "contribute to theorizing about curriculum and literacy" and uses postmodern theory to develop "a tactical theory of agency for writing centers."

0293. **Harris, Muriel. "Process and Product: Dominant Models for Writing Centers."** *Improving Writing Skills.* **Ed. Thom Hawkins and Phyllis Brooks. New Directions for College Learning Assistance 3. San Francisco: Jossey-Bass, 1981. 1-8.** Discusses two models of writing centers—the lab that focuses on assistance with grammar and mechanics and the center that assists students with their writing processes. Considers the future of both models in terms of individualized instruction, supplementary instruction, and writing across the curriculum.

0294. **Harris, Muriel. "Talking in the Middle: Why Writers Need Writing Tutors."** *College English* **57.1 (1995): 27-42.** Contrasts the kind of knowledge students gain from teachers in the classroom to the types they gain from tutors, particularly in helping students learn to think and act independently, acquire rhetorical strategies, cope with emotional aspects of writing, and translate academic language. Concludes that "writing instruction without a writing center is only a partial program, lacking essential activities students need in order to grow and mature as writers."

0295. **Harris, Muriel. "Theory and Reality: The Ideal Writing Center(s)."** *Writing Center Journal* **5.2/6.1 (1985): 4-9.** Claims ideal writing centers cannot be defined by size, staff, services, or student populations but by diagnostic work in how "to look beyond symptoms to underlying causes."

0296. **Harris, Muriel. "Writing Centers."** *Encyclopedia of English Studies and Language Arts.* **Ed. Alan Purves. New York: Scholastic, 1994. 1293-95.** Defines writing centers, describes the range of configurations they may take, traces their development, discusses pedagogical-theoretical approaches and goals, and outlines some of the most pressing issues writing centers face.

0297. **Harris, Muriel. "Writing Labs: Why Bother?"** *English Quarterly* **16.2 (1983): 6-13.** States that too often writing labs are viewed and judged as only a cure-all for students' writing problems when, instead, they should be understood as an additional source of instruction for students and as a multidimensional resource for classroom teachers.

0298. **Hartwell, Patrick. "A Writing Laboratory Model."** *Basic Writing: Essays for Teachers, Researchers, and Administrators.* **Ed. Lawrence Kasden and Daniel R. Hoeber. Urbana: NCTE, 1980. 63-73.** Discusses the protocols, philosophy, and goals of a writing lab for basic writers. Views the writing lab as a "new paradigm" more valid than "a return to the basics" or drill and review for basic writers and their composition instructors.

0299. **Haynes-Burton, Cynthia. "Constructing Our Ethos: Making Writing Centers 'Convenient.'"** *Composition Studies* **20.2 (1992): 51-59.** Discusses how writing center personnel need to legitimate their activities by constructing their ethos, or moral character, based on the roles they play within institutions rather than by relying on arguments based on test scores and usage statistics.

0300. **Haynes-Burton, Cynthia. "'Hanging Your Alias on Their Scene': Writing Centers, Graffiti, and Style."** *The Writing Center Journal* **14.2 (1994): 112-24.** Portrays writing centers as mediators between the discourses of dominant and dominated cultures. Suggests that writing centers must strike a balance between subverting and cohering to the "dominant discourse" in order to preserve intellectual freedom and the vitality of student writing (and to avoid being co-opted by the dominant culture).

0301. **Hayward, Malcolm. "The Role of the Writing Center in the Student's Sense of Himself as a Writer."** *Writing Lab Newsletter* **5.8 (1981): 5-6.** Urges that writing centers shift the perspective of tutorials away from discussions of surface errors and onto the students' perceptions of themselves as writers. Each student must be understood as a "whole writer" whose morale and motivation are essential to writing improvement.

0302. **Healy, Dave. "A Defense of Dualism: The Writing Center and the Classroom."** *The Writing Center Journal* **14.1 (1993): 16-29. Rpt. in 0007.** Discusses the different aims and levels of authority of classroom teachers and writing center tutors. Focuses on the "semi-autonomous" spaces writing centers provide to students, with an emphasis on the democratic sharing of authority between student and tutor.

0303. **Healy, Dave. "In the Temple of the Familiar: The Writing Center as Church."** *Writing Center Perspectives.* **Ed. Byron L. Stay, Christina Murphy, and Eric H. Hobson. Emmitsburg: NWCA Press, 1995. 12-15.** Argues that metaphors commonly used to describe writing centers fail to account for institutional diversity and conflicting views of the roles of writing center personnel; offers the church, with its various denominations, functions, and debates over the nature of its workers, as a more illuminating metaphor.

0304. Healy, Dave. "Specialists vs. Generalists: Managing the Writing Center-Learning Center Connection." *Writing Lab Newsletter* 15.9 (1991): 11-16. Discusses the advantages and disadvantages of a marriage between university writing centers and learning centers. Notes that the urge to professionalize writing center work by separating writing centers from study skills centers is not always in the best interest of students.

0305. Healy, Dave, and Susan Bosher. "ESL Tutoring: Bridging the Gap Between Curriculum-Based and Writing Center Models of Peer Tutoring." *College ESL* 2.2 (1992): 25-32. Discusses the pros and cons of integrating ESL tutors into the classroom versus writing center tutoring and advocates the classroom or curriculum-based model.

0306. Hemmeter, Thomas. "The 'Smack of Difference': The Language of Writing Center Discourse." *The Writing Center Journal* 11.1 (1990): 35-48. Analyzes the language of writing center theorists, pointing out a number of apparent contradictions (e.g., cries for independence couched in the language of dependency). Challenges common assumptions and suggests that the dualistic discourse of theorists explains the "current failure of efforts to define the writing center." Calls upon theorists to choose their words more carefully.

0307. Hemmeter, Tom, and Carolyn Mee. "The Writing Center as Ethnographic Space." *Writing Lab Newsletter* 18.3 (1993): 4-5. Defines the writing center as an ethnographic space in which writing consultants and clients interact, all parties bringing with them their connections to broader discourse communities. Further divides the ethnographic space into interpersonal, textual, intertextual, environmental, and writing community spaces.

0308. Henderson, Maurice Melvin. "A Study of the Structure of the Writing Laboratory Programs in Two-year Community Colleges." Diss. Indiana U of Pennsylvania, 1980. *DAI* 41-09A (1981): 3924. Provides an overview of the typical structure of the writing laboratory program in the two-year community college nationwide and examines regional differences.

0309. **Hill, James. "The Writing Lab: An Anecdote."** *Writing Lab Newsletter* 2.7 (1978): 3. Cautions that programs in writing centers must not become so rigid that they fail to respond sensitively to "human beings who are often very confused and unsure of their ability to work, to achieve, and to succeed in an academic subject."

0310. **Hobson, Eric. "Where Do College Students Come From? School/University Articulation in Writing Theory."** *Freshman English News* 19.3 (1991): 26-28. Aligns writing center practice with principles of the whole language movement and urges college writing teachers to examine its application in elementary and secondary schools. Argues that the growing number of elementary, middle, and secondary school writing centers has helped college writing centers avoid being viewed as remedial.

0311. **Hobson, Eric H. "Maintaining Our Balance: Walking the Tightrope of Competing Epistemologies."** *The Writing Center Journal* **13.1 (1992): 65-75.** Attempts to reconcile three primary schools of thought that influence writing center practice: positivism, expressionism, and social constructionism. Defines the theoretical camps into which most writing center personnel settle. Argues for a serviceable mix of the best qualities of each.

0312. **Hobson, Eric H. "Writing Center Practice Often Counters Its Theory. So What?"** *Intersections: Theory-Practice in the Writing Center.* **Ed. Joan A. Mullin and Ray Wallace. Urbana: NCTE, 1994. 1-10.** Acknowledges that theories articulated to describe writing center practice and the practice itself are often contradictory. Draws on poststructuralist critiques of disciplinarity and totalizing paradigms to urge that writing center professionals accept no single theory but reshape theory to fit their needs in light of practitioner lore.

0313. **Hobson, Eric Hughes. "Where Theory and Practice Collide: Beyond Essentialist Descriptions of the Writing Center."** **Diss. U of Tennessee, 1992.** *DAI* **53-11A (1993): 3828.** Explores definitions frequently applied to the writing center from within and without the writing center community. Argues that a strong strain of essentialist thought underlies the predominant discussions about the theoretical and practical nature of the writing center, providing only the most generic introductions to and critiques of theory and practice. Considers ways to move beyond the limits of epistemologically influenced descriptions of writing center theory and practice and understand the writing center as "postdisciplinary."

0314. Horner, Winifred Bryan. "Dialectic as Invention: Dialogue in the Writing Center." *Focuses* 1.1 (1988): 11-19. Explores the role of dialogue in the creative processes of writers. Argues that the kind of dialogue that goes on between writer and tutor in the writing center makes invention a social, rather than a solitary, act—an act of "'mutual discovery and mutual refutation.'" Traces dialectic to classical rhetoric and examines more recent scholarship on the social aspects of composition.

0315. Hughes, Bradley T. "Institutional and Intimate Contexts: A Review of Recent Writing Center Scholarship." *The Writing Center Journal* 14.2 (1994): 172-82. Uses recent publication of *Writing Centers in Context: Twelve Case Studies* (entry 0005) and *Dynamics of the Writing Conference: Social and Cognitive Interaction* (entry 0002) as an occasion to examine recent writing center scholarship. Provides an in-depth look at each volume, endorsing both.

0316. Hunt, Barbara Jean. "Establishing and Implementing a Writing Center on the College Level." Diss. U of Michigan, 1980. *DAI* 41-05A (1980): 2083. Examines 17 writing centers to develop a profile of writing center philosophies, administration, services, and use rates.

0317. Kail, Harvey. "The Best of Both Worlds." *Writing Lab Newsletter* 9.4 (1984): 1-5. Addresses the question of whether the writing lab is a viable, long-term educational strategy by focusing on its major activity, one-to-one tutoring. Argues that one-to-one tutoring is labor intensive, reinforces the idea of writing labs as supplemental instruction, and isolates students from each other. Claims that writing labs need to stake out more viable and pertinent territory than tutoring by offering credit-bearing courses, placing ongoing groups of student writers in the lab, and developing a pedagogy of group work.

0318. Kail, Harvey, and Kay Allen. "Conducting Research in the Writing Lab." *Tutoring Writing: A Sourcebook for Writing Labs.* Ed. Muriel Harris. Glenview: Scott, Foresman, 1982. 233-45. Argues that research component ought to be built into writing lab both to improve instruction and to supply data for administration. Among projects recommended are the case study, the survey, and experimental research.

0319. Keil, Marjorie, and Debra Johanyak. "The Writing Center: An Idea Beyond Containment." *Writing Lab Newsletter* 20.2 (1995): 1-4. Describes an outreach seminar in which writing center tutors helped senior citizens write their autobiographies. Argues that such programs take the center's mission and jurisdiction beyond the restrictions of the university setting, though acknowledging that "institutional baggage" cannot be left behind.

0320. **Kostelnick, Charles, Richard C. Freed, and Thomas Kent. "Centers for Applied Writing: A Conceptual Model."** *Technical Writing Teacher* **17.2 (1990): 136-49.** Proposes a conceptual model of a Center for Applied Writing that would simultaneously provide practice in business and technical communication and explore varied approaches to writing. Would combine elements of both the writing across the curriculum and developmental models to bring together academic and professional writing.

0321. **Lauer, Janice M. "Instructional Practices: Toward an Integration."** *Focuses* **1.1 (1988): 3-10.** Argues that writing centers and writing classrooms must integrate two instructional practices—teaching writing as an art and nurturing natural writing processes—if they are to help students develop as writers. Suggests that such an integration requires tutors and teachers to adopt a creative pedagogy suitable to all parties and cites historical precedent for this approach.

0322. **Leahy, Richard. "Of Writing Centers, Centeredness, and Centrism."** *The Writing Center Journal* **13.1 (1992): 43-52.** Critiques writing center theorists' condemnation of the term *lab* and glorification of the term *center*. Implies that, while the concept of *centeredness* brings with it positive images of an integrated community, the concept of *centrism* brings unfortunate connotations of "monopoly and self-importance." Argues that centrism could work against interdepartmental collaboration and writing across the curriculum goals.

0323. **Leahy, Richard. "On Being There: Reflections on Visits to Other Writing Centers."** *Writing Lab Newsletter* **15.8 (1991): 1-6.** Examines the lessons a writing center director learned after visiting 20 writing centers during a sabbatical. Reflects on various issues, including the need to embrace flexibility and contradiction in writing center practice, replace *tutor* with *writing assistant*, and build a sense of community with other writing centers.

0324. **Leahy, Rick, and Roy Fox. "Seven Myth-Understandings About the Writing Center."** *Writing Lab Newsletter* **14.1 (1989): 7-8.** Debunks many of the common misconceptions about the writing center's mission, including the idea that it is remedial, primarily concerned with competency exams, only for students in English classes, does students' work for them, and helps only with essays and term papers.

0325. **Levin, Amy K. "Goals and Philosophies of High School Writing Centers."** *The High School Writing Center: Establishing and Maintaining One.* **Ed. Pamela B. Farrell. Urbana: NCTE, 1989. 23-29.** Describes goals common to high school writing centers, whether staffed by peer tutors or adults. In addition to dealing in remediation and preparation for state competency tests, high school writing centers also model relationships among students and between students and adults.

0326. **Lochman, Daniel T. "'A Dialogue of One': Orality and Literacy in the Writing Center."** *The Writing Center Journal* **10.1 (1989): 19-29.** Discusses the value of the writing center in forming a "bridge between orality and academic literacy" for students. Contends the dialogue of student and tutor can strengthen connections and interactions among five levels of oral and literate speech (pre-reflexive discourse, inner speech, reflective discourse, analysis, and evaluation). Links this process to student creativity, empowerment, and increasing sophistication of language use.

0327. **Lochman, Daniel T. "Play and Game: Implications For the Writing Center."** *The Writing Center Journal* **7.1 (1986): 11-18.** Discusses Theodore Roszak's research on play to argue that fun and playfulness have a place in the writing center. Connects playfulness to the theories of Peter Elbow, Ken Macrorie, and Donald Murray. Suggests that the writing center is an arena in which students can learn to play with words and master the "'game' of academic writing."

0328. **Lowenstein, Sharyn. "Let's Have a Different Conversation!"** *Writing Lab Newsletter* **19.6 (1995): 9-12.** Contends that *dependence* is too ambiguous a term to define easily, much less use, in reference to diverse student writers. Argues, instead, for the concept of student "misuse" of writing center personnel and resources and concludes that to address such misuse, scholars need to examine the institutional ecology that encourages it.

0329. **Luckett, Clinton. "Adapting a Conventional Writing Lab to the Berthoff Approach."** *Writing Center Journal* **5.2/6.1 (1985): 21-24.** Discusses the move in the Marquette University (WI) writing center from a traditional approach to tutoring composition based on grammar and form to Ann E. Berthoff's more philosophical emphasis on how individual minds create meaning.

0330. **Lunsford, Andrea. "Collaboration, Control, and the Idea of a Writing Center."** *The Writing Center Journal* **12.1 (1991): 3-10. Rpt. in** *Writing Lab Newsletter* **16.4-5 (1992): 1-6. Rpt. in 0007 and 0008.** Offers three models of writing centers: the "storehouses" of current-traditional rhetoric, the "garrets" of expressivism, and the "Burkean parlors" of social constructionism. Reviews the evolution of social constructionism to establish a theoretical context for writing center work. Contends that "Burkean parlor" writing centers pose "a threat as well as a challenge to the status quo in higher education" and urges writing centers to embrace the challenge.

0331. **MacLennan, Tom. "Buberian Currents in the Collaborative Center."** *Intersections: Theory-Practice in the Writing Center.* **Ed. Joan A. Mullin and Ray Wallace. Urbana: NCTE, 1994. 120-31.** Uses concepts drawn from Martin Buber (I-It, I-Thou, the narrow ridge, relation is reciprocity, and encounter) to characterize writing center development and to illuminate collaborative theory and practice.

0332. **MacLennan, Tom. "Martin Buber and a Collaborative Learning Ethos."** *Writing Lab Newsletter* **14.6 (1990): 6-8.** Relates Martin Buber's insights on reciprocal relationships to writing center philosophy and practice. Sees Buber's I/Thou concept as particularly important in establishing a collaboration in which the tutor is open and supportive.

0333. **Mayher, John S. "***Uncommon Sense* **in the Writing Center."** *Journal of Basic Writing* **11.1 (1992): 47-57.** Suggests harm done by underlying "commonsense" metaphors of skill and remediation often associated with writing centers; argues for metaphors that reflect a constructionist, transactional, holistic view of learning.

0334. **McAndrew, Donald A. "From Writing Center to Center for Writing: A Heuristic for Development."** *Writing Lab Newsletter* **9.5 (1985): 1-5.** Claims that writing centers lack a model for expanding services to the whole of the institution. Offers such a model based upon the possibilities for development that exist in four areas: clients, clients' roles, services provided to these clients, the location where the services will be provided.

0335. **McDonald, James C. "Rethinking the Research Paper in the Writing Center."** *The Writing Center Journal* **14.2 (1994): 125-35.** Characterizes the writing center as a threat to the idyllic isolation of the university classroom. Attempts to explain why professors sometimes view writing center tutors as intruders in the relationship between student and teacher. Shows how writing center pedagogy clashes with classroom pedagogy, particularly when it involves the research paper. Suggests more effective ways to aid students in writing.

0336. **Mitchell, Margaret. "Initiated into the Fraternity of Powerful Knowers: How Collaborative Technology Has Ethically Legitimized Writing Centers."** *Writing Lab Newsletter* **19.7 (1995): 11-13.** Contends that the inception of the computerized composition classroom has helped legitimize the student-centered, collaborative learning pedagogy of writing centers. Observes that E-mail collaboration by students in such classes has led to more time spent writing, more peer teaching, and less control on the part of the teacher—"exactly the things that writing centers had been promoting."

0337. **Moseley, Ann. "From Factory to Workshop: Revising the Writing Center."** *Writing Center Journal* **4.2 (1984): 31-38.** Cautions directors against a total focus on numbers and data that can change the writing center's mission from a workshop in which apprentice writers learn their craft to a factory in which "harassed and overworked tutors" generate data and rush students through.

0338. **Mullin, Joan A. "Empowering Ourselves: New Directions for the Nineties."** *Writing Lab Newsletter* **14.10 (1990): 11-13.** Acknowledges the increasing status of writing centers as they have expanded into writing across the curriculum, faculty development, curricular reform, and teacher-training programs. Laments accompanying infighting with English departments, a tendency to saddle writing centers with remedial skills programs, and the increasing administrative duties of directors.

0339. **Mullin, Joan A. "Literacy and the Technology of Writing: Examining Assumptions, Changing Practices."** *Intersections: Theory-Practice in the Writing Center.* **Ed. Joan A. Mullin and Ray Wallace. Urbana: NCTE, 1994. 161-71.** Surveys recent critiques of literacy definitions, pointing out that unexamined views of literacy may well perpetuate the rigid, hierarchical approach ("literacy as technology") that collaborative pedagogy seeks to overcome.

0340. **Murphy, Christina. "The Writing Center and Social Constructionist Theory."** *Intersections: Theory-Practice in the Writing Center.* **Ed. Joan A. Mullin and Ray Wallace. Urbana: NCTE, 1994. 25-38.** Cautions against an unexamined adoption of social constructionist theory as an exclusive paradigm for writing center theory and practice. Uses the communication-based social theories of such writers as Wilhelm Dilthey,

Sigmund Freud, Karl Marx, and Jürgen Habermas to broaden the critique. Acknowledges value of social constructionism but points out its limitations, among them its drive toward technocracy and its tendency to value consensus at the expense of individual difference.

0341. **Murphy, Christina. "Writing Centers in Context: Responding to Current Educational Theory."** *The Writing Center: New Directions.* **Ed. Ray Wallace and Jeanne Simpson. New York: Garland, 1991. 276-88. Rpt. in 0007.** Identifies the conflicting ideologies from which writing centers emerged, distinguishing three prevailing views (conservative, liberal, and radical) that make most writing centers into "instructional hybrids." Argues that the role of the writing center needs to be understood within the matrix of these views.

0342. **Nash, Thomas. "New Directions for Writing Labs."** *Writing Lab Newsletter* **9.1 (1984): 2-7.** Claims that the complex history of writing labs has led to the "Eureka Syndrome," or a frenetic search for one way to structure a lab. Argues that this focus has been limiting and contends that writing labs must be reinvented and reconceptualized in a number of new directions, including as a resource center, a training center, a community learning center, and a resource area for special interest groups.

0343. **Nash, Thomas. "The Writing Center: Life on the Frontier."** *Journal of Developmental and Remedial Education* **7.1 (1983): 3-5.** Discusses several writing center models including the campus support service and the research, training, and resource center. Also discusses and counters common misconceptions about the writing center and its practices.

0344. **Neuleib, Janice Witherspoon, and Maurice A. Scharton. "Writing Others, Writing Ourselves: Ethnography and the Writing Center."** *Intersections: Theory-Practice in the Writing Center.* **Ed. Joan A. Mullin and Ray Wallace. Urbana: NCTE, 1994. 54-67.** Recommends using ethnographic rather than positivistic research methods in writing centers and uses triangulation to model an example of ethnomethodology.

0345. **North, Stephen M. "The Idea of a Writing Center."** *College English* **46 (1984): 433-46. Rpt. in 0007 and 0008.** Points out that a writing center is frequently misunderstood as "the grammar and drill center, the fix-it shop, the first aid station." Suggests that paradigm shift has occurred in writing centers (as in writing classrooms) so that centers now focus on writers rather than just on their texts; calls for writing centers to continue to expand and publicize these changes.

0346. North, Stephen M. "Revisiting 'The Idea of a Writing Center.'" *The Writing Center Journal* 15.1 (1994): 7-19. Suggests that his own frequently cited essay (entry 0345) has, in some respects, outlived its usefulness. Highlights three relationships (tutor-writer, tutor-teacher, tutor-institution) to identify oversimplifications perpetuated by that essay and describes ways his own writing center at the State University of New York—Albany has evolved to meet local institutional needs.

0347. North, Stephen Michael. "Writing Centers: A Sourcebook." Diss. State U of New York at Albany, 1979. *DAI* 40-02A (1979): 0816. A study based on two complementary strands of inquiry: North's visits to 35 writing centers in 1977-78 and his work in the State University of New York—Albany's fledgling writing lab during its first two years. Provides an overview of writing center/writing lab practices in the late 1970s and a theoretical framework for how such places could be understood to operate in a composition program based on the idea of composing as a process.

0348. Nugent, Susan Monroe. "One Woman's Ways of Knowing." *The Writing Center Journal* 10.2 (1990): 17-29. Relates lessons from *Women's Ways of Knowing* (Mary Field Belenky et al., 1986) to tutoring in the writing center. Traces one woman's progress through five stages of intellectual development—silence, received knowledge, subjective knowledge, procedural knowledge, and connected knowledge. Contends an awareness of these stages can help writing centers assist students in developing a "voice" and continuing their intellectual growth.

0349. Olson, Gary A. "Attitudinal Problems and the Writing Center." *Liberal Education* 67.4 (1981): 310-18. Contends that the attitudes of teachers referring students to the writing center for mandatory instruction may diminish the writing center's ability to help students who need it most. Also claims that encouraging tutors to provide a pleasant learning environment can increase the center's effectiveness.

0350. Olson, Gary A. "The Problems of Attitudes in Writing Center Relationships." *Writing Centers: Theory and Administration.* Ed. Gary A. Olson. Urbana: NCTE, 1984. 155-69. Examines attitudinal problems generated by the way instructors refer students to the writing center and discusses the impact of those attitudes on writing center tutorials.

Includes a report based on a survey of referral methods at the University of Alabama.

0351. **Olson, Gary A. "Reaffirming: Research, the Humanistic Tradition, and the Modern Writing Center."** *ĆEA Forum* **12.3 (1982): 8-9.** Puts contemporary writing centers in the tradition of tutorial teaching, stressing that no stigma need attach to students or writing center staff.

0352. **Pedersen, Elray L. "Writing Labs Are More Than Remediation Centers."** *Writing Lab Newsletter* **10.7 (1986): 3-5.** Reviews ways in which writing center assistance goes beyond remediation. Argues that expectations of writing center services depend on one's definition of "writing." Examines five definitions of writing—as penmanship, copying, correctness, crafting, and authoring—and suggests that good writing centers provide services based on the last two definitions.

0353. **Pemberton, Michael A. "The Prison, the Hospital, and the Madhouse: Redefining Metaphors for the Writing Center."** *Writing Lab Newsletter* **17.1 (1992): 11-16.** Attempts to debunk common metaphors that distort and undermine the writing center's collaborative, student-centered approach to learning. Rather than accept the images of writing center as correctional facility, hospital, or asylum for the "linguistically insane," urges the profession to embrace and emphasize the metaphors of creative workshop or gathering place.

0354. **Perdue, Virginia. "Writing Center Pedagogy: Developing Authority in Student Writers."** *Writing Lab Newsletter* **11.8 (1987): 9-11.** Argues that the writing center is an effective place to improve student writing precisely because authority (in terms of self-motivation and control over text, learning, and focus) reside in the student (and in the discourse community) rather than the teacher. Discusses the social aspects of writing and making meaning, demonstrating how the writing center fits into this process.

0355. **Pezzulich, Evelyn. "The Journal as an Instrument in Learning and Writing." Diss. Catholic U of America, 1986.** *DAI* **47-04A (1986): 1225.** Discusses the journal as a tool for promoting learning and improving writing at the college level. Gives a brief historical sketch of the pedagogical uses of the journal since the 1960s and offers a rationale for the journal as a form of expressive writing in a liberal education. Focuses on the value of the journal in the writing center, across the disciplines, and in the classroom and also on the ways the journal can lead to transactional writing.

0356. Pobo, Kenneth. "Creative Writing and the Writing Center." *Writing Lab Newsletter* 15.6 (1991): 5-7. Examines how writing centers can help poets, fiction writers, and playwrights hone their craft. Emphasizes that writing center instructors are adept at providing sensitive yet honest feedback and guiding revisions. Recommends forming a closer link between university writing centers and creative writing programs.

0357. **Ricker, Curtis E. "Creating a Learning Center to Assist Developmental Studies Students Across the Curriculum."** *The Writing Center: New Directions.* **Ed. Ray Wallace and Jeanne Simpson. New York: Garland, 1991. 263-75.** Discusses the rationale for a learning resources center that goes beyond traditional remediation for educationally disadvantaged students. Presents an overview of theories of developmental studies and describes one such program in operation at Georgia Southern University.

0358. **Riley, Terrance. "The Unpromising Future of Writing Centers."** *The Writing Center Journal* **15.1 (1994): 20-34.** Cautions that the increasing respectability and stability of writing centers jeopardizes their ability to effect changes in academe. Cites similar reform movements in English departments (American literature, literary theory, and composition studies), which lost momentum as they became elitist. Urges writing center practitioners to avoid the pitfalls of professionalism.

0359. **Saling, Joseph. "Centering: What Writing Centers Need to Do."** *Writing Center Perspectives.* **Ed. Byron L. Stay, Christina Murphy, and Eric H. Hobson. Emmitsburg: NWCA Press, 1995. 146-54.** Claims writing centers can be at the center of educational reform but must first transform three areas of their own practice: become more informed and more willing to discuss the theory supporting writing center work; develop more inclusive programs that go beyond traditional limits; and avoid falling into self-satisfied orthodoxy.

0360. **Severino, Carol. "Rhetorically Analyzing Collaboration(s)."** *The Writing Center Journal* **13.1 (1992): 53-64.** Attempts to define types of collaboration that occur in writing centers "without creating reductive stereotypes or rigid dichotomies." Divides collaboration into two major categories: hierarchical (directive) and dialogic (nondirective). Shows that the types of collaborative structures used often depend on the age, gender, personality, ethnicity, motivational, and other characteristics of writer and respondent.

0361. **Severino, Carol. "Writers Writing."** *Writing Lab Newsletter* **17.6 (1993): 11-14.** Describes an alternative model for one-on-one teaching, in which writing lab "teachers" act as mentors for the writers with whom they work. Suggests several advantages of this method over drop-in, peer-tutoring centers, including long-term relationships between mentors and writers, the ability to offer voluntary writing assignments, and an immersion in an environment filled with working writers.

0362. **Severino, Carol. "Writing Centers as Linguistic Contact Zones and Borderlands."** *Writing Lab Newsletter* **19.4 (1994): 1-5.** Characterizes the writing center as a linguistic borderland, where competing voices, dialects, cultures, and metaphors clash and compromises are negotiated. Explores the potential of such "contact zones" for stimulating creativity and fostering learning in students from other cultures or subcultures.

0363. **Simpson, Jeanne. "The Challenge of Innovation: Putting New Approaches into Practice."** *Writing Lab Newsletter* **18.1 (1993): 1-3.** Calls on writing center personnel to embrace the challenges of responding to the public's demands for improved education and greater accountability by developing innovative policies and practices. Suggests writing center directors must accept the risks of acting as agents for positive change in education.

0364. **Simpson, Jeanne Hubbard. "A Rhetorical Defense of the Writing Center." Diss. Illinois State U, 1982.** *DAI* **44-03A (1982): 0693.** Presents rhetorical strategies for defending the writing center against institutional pressures. Focuses on classical and modern theories of rhetoric, especially the source of moral values in rhetoric, rhetorical choices within rhetorical situations, and audience analysis. Identifies department chairs, deans, and presidents as major audiences for writing centers.

0365. **Solinger, Rickie. "Starting Small and Thinking Big: An Administrator's Viewpoint."** *Improving Writing Skills.* **Ed. Thom Hawkins and Phyllis Brooks. New Directions for College Learning Assistance 3. San Francisco: Jossey-Bass, 1981. 61-68.** Acknowledges that writing centers face "diminished financial support and institutional ambivalence about support services on the campus." Contends, however, that literacy crises and the additional instructional requirements of nontraditional students make writing centers "extremely useful and even indispensable facilities."

0366. **Stull, William L. "The Writing Lab's Three Constituencies."** *Writing Lab Newsletter* **6.5 (1982): 1-4.** Presents an overview of the writing lab's theoretical and historical development in order to speculate on future trends. Argues that, as writing labs move beyond the realm of remediation, there lies both promise and peril in responding to the constituencies of students, administrators, and the writing center profession itself.

0367. **Tackach, James. "Theory Z Management and the College Writing Center."** *Writing Center Journal* **4.2 (1984): 1-8.** Describes the principles of William Ouchi's Theory Z management, which fosters trust between management and employees and values the quality of relationships over bureaucratic rules. Argues that writing center directors need to know this theory.

0368. **Terry, Patricia. "Things Your Mentor Never Told You: Discovering Writing Lab Identity in the Institutional Environment."** *Writing Lab Newsletter* **18.7 (1994): 1-3, 5.** Discusses how writing lab directors can best understand their responsibilities within their institutions and describes a three-stage process of accepting what the writing lab is not, analyzing how the institution's characteristics affect the writing lab, and developing the writing lab's assets.

0369. **Trachsel, Mary. "Nurturant Ethics and Academic Ideals: Convergence in the Writing Center."** *The Writing Center Journal* **16.1 (1995): 24-45.** Examines writing centers as a "feminized" site of learning and, while acknowledging the many drawbacks and disadvantages associated with that situation, argues that the maternal figure embodies a powerful educational ideal. Calls for reexamination of cultural beliefs that motherhood is a "self-obliterating role" and that "maternal nurture is essentially an emotional function"; calls for writing center scholars to personalize their inquiry along the lines urged by feminist critics and thus to challenge prevailing academic myth of the autonomous self and ultimately the divisions that separate writing centers from the rest of the academy.

0370. **Trimbur, John. "Cultural Studies and Teaching Writing."** *Focuses* **1.2 (1988): 5-18.** Argues that literacy cannot be adequately understood as a measurable set of abilities but must be viewed, instead, as "ideologically charged." The teaching of writing, therefore, cannot be reduced to techniques and methods but must be "located historically at the critical intersection where student subjectivities and cultural forms meet—in classrooms and writing centers."

0371. **Wallace, Ray. "Text Linguistics: External Entries into 'Our' Community."** *Intersections: Theory-Practice in the Writing Center.* **Ed. Joan A. Mullin and Ray Wallace. Urbana: NCTE, 1994. 68-80.** Presents a case study of writing center personnel going from the field of composition to that of text linguistics to provide a more suitable model of the composing process and thus to improve one-on-one tutoring.

0372. **Warnock, Tilly, and John Warnock. "Liberatory Writing Centers: Restoring Authority to Writers."** *Writing Centers: Theory and Administration.* **Ed. Gary A. Olson. Urbana: NCTE, 1984. 16-23.** Urges a shift from a liberal to a liberatory pedagogy, in which students are responsible for their own learning; the resulting critical consciousness will allow students to revise not only their writing but their relationship to learning and eventually their approach to the world.

0373. **Welch, Nancy. "From Silence to Noise: The Writing Center as Critical Exile."** *The Writing Center Journal* **14.1 (1993): 1-15.** Redefines *collaboration* to include "writing with and against one's many internalized voices." Characterizes the writing center as a place of metaphoric exile, where senses of language, self, and social conventions can be examined, critiqued, reassessed, and expressed. Includes a detailed case study of a student writer making meaning through writing.

0374. **Welch, Nancy. "Migrant Rationalities: Graduate Students and the Idea of Authority in the Writing Center."** *The Writing Center Journal* **16.1 (1995): 5-23.** Applies work of philosopher and feminist critic Michele Le Doeuff, particularly her concepts of "reverie" and "migrant rationality," to suggest ways writing centers can help graduate students come to terms with conflicting needs to accommodate and resist the conventions of their discipline. Employs brief stories of graduate students in four disciplines to show how writing centers might offer other solutions by dialogizing the conflict.

0375. **Woolbright, Meg. "The Politics of Tutoring: Feminism Within the Patriarchy."** *The Writing Center Journal* **13.1 (1992): 16-30. Rpt. in 0007.** Contends a hidden curriculum privileges those who surrender to patriarchal values in the academy. Compares writing center and feminist pedagogies and finds similarities in their egalitarian agendas, interactive teaching methods, emphasis on the personal, and conflicts with the patriarchy over the distribution of power. Contends good tutoring requires openly acknowledging and confronting the hidden curriculum.

0376. **Woolbright, Meg. "A Response to 'Contesting "The Idea of a Writing Center": The Politics of Writing Center Research.'"** *Writing Lab Newsletter* **17.5 (1993): 11-13.** Takes issue with Nancy Grimm's critique (entry 0291) of Stephen M. North's essay (entry 0345). Suggests the critique indicts North's 1984 article based on philosophical and political developments he could not have anticipated. Also argues that Grimm takes an idealistic view of the role of the writing center that disregards political realities.

0377. **Young, Art. "College Culture and the Challenge of Collaboration."** *The Writing Center Journal* **13.1 (1992): 3-15.** Takes issue with philosophies in the writing center that do not account for both the expressionistic and the social constructionist theories of making meaning. Helps put writing centers into historical and philosophical context and attempts to reconcile theory with tutors' everyday experience. Explores the benefits of collaboration and reproaches administrators and others who view collaborative writing, tutoring, or teaching with suspicion.

# Administration

0378. Ackley, Elizabeth. "Beginning and Maintaining a Peer-Tutor Based Writing Center in the Secondary School." *Writing Lab Newsletter* 12.3 (1987): 3-4. Discusses hurdles a director faced in designing and building a high school writing center from scratch.

0379. Ackley, Elizabeth. "Supervising." *The High School Writing Center: Establishing and Maintaining One.* Ed. Pamela B. Farrell. Urbana: NCTE, 1989. 89-91. Suggests ways to avoid common problems in writing centers staffed by students, particularly helping student tutors avoid doing the work of the client.

0380. Allen, Richard, and Pamela B. Farrell. "Finding a Space." *The High School Writing Center: Establishing and Maintaining One.* Ed. Pamela B. Farrell. Urbana: NCTE, 1989. 31-37. Illustrates physical arrangement of five high school writing centers, briefly indicating the rationale for the designs.

0381. Almasy, Rudolph. "Instructional Materials for the Writing Laboratory." *College Composition and Communication* 27 (1976): 400-03. Argues that commercially available remediation materials are unsatisfactory; urges that writing centers determine students' problem areas and design individual materials to meet those particular needs.

0382. Almasy, Rudolph. "The Writing Laboratory and the Graduate Student." *Writing Lab Newsletter* 2.4 (1977): 3. Considers ways in which writing centers can extend their services "beyond the English Department and Freshman remedial writers." Describes year-long tutorial offerings to nine graduate students taking an educational psychology class.

0383. **Amato, Katya. "Making Bricks Without Straw: The Fate of One Writing Center."** *Writing Lab Newsletter* **17.10 (1993): 4-7.** Recounts the frustrating efforts of a writing center director to save her writing center from budget cuts. Cautions that making do with few resources hurts programs and, ultimately, the profession.

0384. **Arfken, Deborah. "A Peer-Tutor Staff: Four Crucial Aspects."** *Tutoring Writing: A Sourcebook for Writing Labs.* **Ed. Muriel Harris. Glenview: Scott, Foresman, 1982. 111-22.** Provides practical guidance for recruiting, selecting, training, and evaluating peer tutors, including sample documents.

0385. **Baltrinic, Barb. "Extending the Writing Center."** *Writing Lab Newsletter* **13.1 (1988): 7-8.** Suggests that writing centers extend beyond the English department by encouraging writing across the curriculum, serving as a depository of texts and other resources on writing, sponsoring writing contests, and reaching out to the community.

0386. **Bamberg, Betty. "The Writing Lab and the Composition Class: A Fruitful Collaboration."** *Tutoring Writing: A Sourcebook for Writing Labs.* **Ed. Muriel Harris. Glenview: Scott, Foresman, 1982. 179-85.** Surveys the variety of supplementary instruction in writing available through writing centers, describing three individual programs in New York, Wisconsin, and California in more detail.

0387. **Bates, Patricia Teel. "The Public-Relations Circle."** *Tutoring Writing: A Sourcebook for Writing Labs.* **Ed. Muriel Harris. Glenview: Scott, Foresman, 1982. 206-15.** Discusses ways daily operations affect attitudes of tutors, students, faculty, administration, and larger community. Describes ways of finding opportunities for positive publicity and stresses importance of feedback and evaluation.

0388. **Benson, Kirsten F. "Who Will Staff the Center."** *Writing Lab Newsletter* **14.2 (1989): 13-16.** Explores ways to staff writing centers when university funding falls short. Advice includes establishing writing center assistantships for graduate students, funded by departments that heavily use the center, and offering noncredit workshop courses.

0389. **Bergman, Jill. "Tutor Selection: Assessing Applicants Through Group Interviews."** *Writing Lab Newsletter* **15.5 (1991): 1-6.** Suggests the traditional individual interview often fails to reveal whether a candidate possesses key traits of a good tutor. Contends that bringing candidates together to see how they interact better reveals strengths and weaknesses.

0390. **Bhakuni, Rosa I. "Community Connections."** *The High School Writing Center: Establishing and Maintaining One.* **Ed. Pamela B. Farrell. Urbana: NCTE, 1989. 143-45.** Suggests generating support for writing centers by interacting with the community through such activities as media coverage and writing competitions.

0391. **Bishop, Wendy. "Bringing Writers to the Center: Some Survey Results, Surmises, and Suggestions."** *The Writing Center Journal* **10.2 (1990): 31-44.** Claims writing center directors can most effectively increase student use rates by enlisting the help of instructors to promote the center.

0392. **Brannon, Lil. "Developing a Writing Center: What Can a Consultant Do?"** *The High School Writing Center: Establishing and Maintaining One.* **Ed. Pamela B. Farrell. Urbana: NCTE, 1989. 55-61.** Suggests value of bringing in an outside consultant to help establish a new writing center if the goal is to make writing a central activity in learning throughout the curriculum. As an outsider, this consultant can be an especially effective agent of change, particularly through in-service workshops.

0393. **Branscomb, H. Eric. "Persons, Places and Things in the Writing Center."** *Writing Lab Newsletter* **6.3 (1981): 1-5.** Discusses the conflicts between the expectations and demands placed upon the writing center and the realities of limited budgets and cutbacks. Considers how writing centers directors can best meet the center's responsibilities to students while still staying within restricted budgets.

0394. **Broder, Peggy. "Avoiding Friction Between the Writing Lab and the Composition Program."** *Writing Lab Newsletter* **5.4 (1980): 1-2.** Discusses how to avoid potential trouble spots in the relationship between the writing lab and the English department by establishing guidelines to clarify how the lab will assist students in working on papers and by securing copies of the instructors' assignments well in advance.

0395. **Brodersen, Karen, Diane Pregler, and Robert Marrs. "A Database Invades the Writing Center."** *Writing Lab Newsletter* **16.6 (1992): 11-14.** Discusses the difficulties of keeping accurate and meaningful records of tutorials and shows how a database partially solved one writing center's problems. Among other advantages, the database helped the director identify patterns of conference activities. Suggests such information can lead to improvements in training and assessment.

0396. **Brooks, Barbara, and Carol Lefelt. "Scheduling."** *The High School Writing Center: Establishing and Maintaining One.* **Ed. Pamela B. Farrell. Urbana: NCTE, 1989. 45-54.** Examines practical difficulties of scheduling students and professional staff in two suburban high schools of different sizes.

0397. **Brown, Alan. "What's an Assistant to Do?"** *Writing Lab Newsletter* **12.5 (1988): 8-9.** Describes how a new assistant writing center director's role evolved when he began to see it as an apprenticeship.

0398. **Brown, Alan. "Writing Labs: Why Do They Fail?"** *Writing Lab Newsletter* **7.4 (1982): 6.** Presents a series of questions for writing center staff to consider on why writing labs succeed or fail.

0399. **Brown, Lady Falls. "Stable Concept/Unstable Reality: Recreating the Writing Center."** *Writing Lab Newsletter* **14.8 (1990): 6-8.** Argues that writing centers must continually promote and recreate their services as they adjust to changes in faculty, students, and staff.

0400. **Bruffee, Kenneth A. "Two Related Issues in Peer Tutoring: Program Structure and Tutor Training."** *College Composition and Communication* **31.1 (1980): 76-80.** Discusses several issues related to writing centers: the advantages and disadvantages of setting up a tutoring program as a course requirement or as a drop-in service; whether to hire graduate student, professional, or peer tutors; and how to use peer criticism to train tutors effectively.

0401. **Carino, Peter, Lori Floyd, and Marcia Lightle. "Empowering a Writing Center: The Faculty Meets the Tutors."** *Writing Lab Newsletter* **16.2 (1991): 1-5.** Stresses the need for writing centers and the composition programs they serve to complement one another's work. Illustrates how presentations by one writing center's tutors during a composition workshop improved relations between the writing center and the faculty and enhanced the tutors' reputations on campus.

0402. **Carpenter, Carol. "The Learning Center as a Support System."** *Writing Lab Newsletter* **4.8 (1980): 6-7.** Contends that learning centers must reach out to students and faculty and offers methods to achieve this goal ranging from advertising the center's services to meeting with faculty in all disciplines.

0403. **Carter, Barbara B. "A Mini-Course Serves Many Purposes."** *Writing Lab Newsletter* **17.7 (1993): 14-16.** Describes a series of minicourses one writing center conducted to demonstrate its tutors' ability to assist students with a variety of writing tasks.

0404. **Chapman, David W. "The Rogue and the Tutor: A Tale."** *Writing Lab Newsletter* **11.7 (1987): 6.** Satirizes the writing center as Camelot in discussing the rather serious issue of a director dealing with a student who has falsely accused a tutor of failing to do her job.

0405. **Chiteman, Michael D. "From Writing Lab to Interdisciplinary Academic Support Center: Cost-Effective Guidelines."** *Writing Lab Newsletter* **8.7 (1984): 1-4. Rpt. in** *Writing Lab Newsletter* **9.3 (1984): 1-4.** Argues that the need for writing labs to offer additional tutorial services often falls victim to budget cuts. Suggests careful planning and connecting with other related services on campus can enable centers to expand services without extra funding.

0406. **Chiteman, Michael D. "The Writing Center and Institutional Politics: Making Connections with Administration and Faculty."** *Writing Lab Newsletter* **11.8 (1987): 1-4.** Advocates reaching out to faculty members and administrators to form alliances and increase the role of the writing center on campus. Urges directors to continue promoting the idea that the writing center is an essential ingredient in the educational mission of the university and the staff deserve professional status.

0407. **Clark, Irene Lurkis. "Integrating Lab and Classroom at a Large University."** *Writing Lab Newsletter* **5.7 (1981): 3-4.** Claims the writing lab should maintain active communication with the classroom instructors whose students attend the lab. Suggests lab tours, weekly reports to the instructor of his or her students' attendance in the lab, and publishing a writing lab newsletter as effective methods for maintaining contact.

0408. **Clark, Irene Lurkis. "Leading the Horse: The Writing Center and Required Visits."** *Writing Center Journal* **5.2/6.1 (1985): 31-34.** Argues against the idea that only students who are intrinsically motivated to come to the writing center will benefit from its services. Extrinsic motivations and required attendance can also help students improve their writing.

0409. **Cmielewski, Walter. "The High School Writing Center: Getting It Started and Keeping It Going."** *Writing Lab Newsletter* **18.5 (1994): 15-16.** Outlines the essential elements of establishing and maintaining a high school writing center: the necessary funding, possibly from Title monies; the support of the school's administration and faculty; and the determination to make the center a regular part of instruction. Briefly discusses presentations within the community to gain further support for the center.

0410. **Cobb, Loretta. "Overcoming a Financial Obstacle: Undergraduate Staffing in the Composition Lab."** *Writing Lab Newsletter* **7.4 (1982): 1-4.** Discusses the use of undergraduate peer tutors in a writing lab and discusses the advantages of using well-trained tutors who "can do a better job of teaching basic writing than another professional staff member."

0411. **Cobb, Loretta, and Elaine K. Elledge. "Peer Tutors as a Source of Power for Basic Writers."** *Teaching English in the Two-Year College* **9.2 (1983): 135-39.** Examines peer tutors as a particularly valuable resource for teaching basic writers. Provides criteria for selecting and evaluating applicants for tutoring positions.

0412. **Cobb, Loretta, and Elaine Kilgore Elledge. "Undergraduate Staffing in the Writing Center."** *Writing Centers: Theory and Administration.* **Ed. Gary A. Olson. Urbana: NCTE, 1984. 123-31.** Outlines program for staffing writing center with undergraduate peer tutors, touching on selecting, funding, training, and evaluating these tutors.

0413. **Collins, Norma Decker, and Brad Wilcox. "If Mohammed Won't Come to the Mountain: Encouraging Middle School Students to Use the Writing Center."** *Writing Lab Newsletter* **19.4 (1994): 10-11.** Outlines attempts to bring students into one middle school writing center. Suggests schools with similar goals begin by improving relations between the center and the faculty, bridging differences between theories of teaching (product vs. process), and overcoming negative student attitudes.

0414. **Corcoran, Amanda Inskip. "Accountability of Writing Center Consultants: How Far Can It Go?"** *Writing Lab Newsletter* **19.3 (1994): 11-14.** Examines problems that occur when students, professors, or administrators (and sometimes writing consultants themselves) assign responsibility for the quality of a given paper to the writing center, not the author. Suggests writing centers can avoid this situation through education of all parties as to the goal of tutoring and the ownership of student papers.

0415. Cosgrove, Cornelius. **"Explaining and Justifying Writing Centers: An Example."** *Writing Lab Newsletter* **17.8 (1993): 1-4.** Shares a letter circulated among an English department's faculty that clarifies the university writing center's mission and defends its policies and practices.

0416. Croft, Mary K. **"The Rites of Writing."** *Writing Lab Newsletter* **5.4 (1980): 7.** Discusses how bringing prominent writers to a campus conference on writing increased the campus's understanding of the value of writing. Describes setting up such a conference in terms of money, logistics, and reactions.

0417. Crump, Eric. **"Voices from the Net: Grappling with Institutional Contexts."** *Writing Lab Newsletter* **17.3 (1992): 10-12.** Discusses the difficulty writing centers often have of fitting into the institutional context of the university, including negotiating for money and status. WCenter correspondents recommend, among other advice, that writing center directors practice dogged persistence in pursuing their needs.

0418. Curtis, Deborah. **"A Reader Responds ... Writing Center Promotion—'The Hard Sell.'"** *Writing Lab Newsletter* **9.6 (1985): 6.** Recommends visiting with faculty members in their offices to discuss the writing center and making classroom presentations on the writing center's services as two methods of "hard sell" promotion.

0419. Davis, Kevin. **"Evaluating Writing Center Tutors."** *Writing Lab Newsletter* **16.7 (1992): 1-6.** Supports regular evaluations to help tutors improve, to formalize the workplace, to provide a basis for future letters of recommendation to employers or graduate schools, and to identify ineffective tutors. Offers evaluation forms other writing center directors can use.

0420. Davis, Kevin. **"Shopping: Peer Tutors as Cantaloupes."** *Writing Lab Newsletter* **10.2 (1985): 12-13.** Compares tutor selection and hiring to grocery shopping. Suggests directors look for several traits in tutors, including compassion, good reading and writing skills, and an openness to others' ideas.

0421. Delaney, Laurie, Helen Fuller, Jennifer Kay, and Gratia Murphy. **"Bridges Between Faculty and Tutors: An Honest Look at Teacher/Tutor Relationships."** *Writing Lab Newsletter* 18.3 (1993): 1-

3. Explores the problems tutors often face when they interpret professors' assignments, grades, and policies for students. Recommends directors clarify the academic chain of command and keep open lines of communication between the writing center and faculty members.

0422. **Deming, Mary, and Maria Valeri-Gold. "Letting Your Lab Earn Its Keep."** *Writing Lab Newsletter* **10.5 (1986): 13-14.** Urges writing center directors offer workshops for members of the community, enrichment programs for other local writing centers, special services for students with disabilities, and programs in research and teacher training. Argues that such offerings add to the center's usefulness and can bring in extra funds.

0423. **Devenish, Alan. "Decentering the Writing Center."** *Writing Lab Newsletter* **18.1 (1993): 4-7.** Argues that writing centers should find ways of projecting their services outside the walls of the center. Suggests directors send peer tutors to assist writers in classes across the curriculum, holding writing center hours in dormitories or other student-centered places, hosting creative writing readings and groups, and sponsoring workshops for the community and for other institutions.

0424. **Devet, Bonnie. "A Method for Observing and Evaluating Writing Lab Tutorials."** *The Writing Center Journal* **10.2 (1990): 75-83.** Offers advice and a form (a modified Flander's Interaction Analysis Categories form) for evaluating tutor performance. Emphasizes the importance of systematically evaluating writing center tutors.

0425. **Devet, Bonnie. "Workshops That 'Work.'"** *Writing Lab Newsletter* **11.5 (1987): 13-14.** Suggests a number of writing workshop topics that address particular concerns of student writers and help build a clientele for the center.

0426. **Dicks, R. Stanley. "Eight Suggestions to Attract More Students to Labs."** *Writing Lab Newsletter* **2.8 (1978): 1-2.** Suggests eight strategies to increase student use and prevent the lab from being regarded as a service for remedial students only.

0427. **Dickson, Gregory. "Starting a Writing Lab: An Argument for Haste."** *Writing Lab Newsletter* **10.9 (1986): 1-3.** Urges starting a writing lab without waiting to have all elements in place. Suggests eight steps new directors should follow.

0428. Dinitz, Susan. "Making the Medium the Message in Faculty Presentations, or, How to Get the Faculty to Value Peer Tutoring." *Writing Lab Newsletter* 12.1 (1987): 1-3. Describes a director's successful presentation to a university's faculty on how writing center tutors interact with student writers. Contends that having faculty members tutor each other can provide a graphic illustration of teacher-centered, authoritative, and ineffective tutoring practices.

0429. Donovan, Susan. "Writing Lab Make-Over." *Writing Lab Newsletter* 20.2 (1995): 8. Argues that a writing center's appearance affects the attitudes of writers, faculty, and administration. Suggests several ways to make the center look attractive and professional.

0430. Dossin, Mary. "Expectations." *Writing Lab Newsletter* 14.8 (1990): 12. Offers a list of policy statements outlining what a writing center will and will not do for students to help professors understand the collaborative philosophy and practices of the center.

0431. Eggers, Tilly. "Evaluation and Instruction." *Writing Lab Newsletter* 4.4 (1979): 4-5. Argues that numbers do not adequately reflect a writing center's accomplishments. Prefers that writing centers see student progress as the most important measure of a writing center's success.

0432. England, Donald. "Funding and Maintaining a Learning Lab." *Writing Lab Newsletter* 4.10 (1980): 1-3. Discusses means for inventing methods and strategies to generate the funds required to originate and maintain a learning lab. Focuses on funding through tuition and lab fees and describes the funding methods of the learning center at North Lake College (TX).

0433. Evans, Eileen B. "Crisis of Image: Promoting Your Center." *Writing Lab Newsletter* 10.8 (1986): 9-11. Argues that directors should actively promote the writing center. Offers approach that includes identifying an image consistent with the center's mission, doing an image assessment, devising a marketing strategy, using a variety of methods to reach the audience, and conducting surveys to evaluate progress.

0434. Farrell, Pamela. "Guest Artists Add Reverence for Writing." *Writing Lab Newsletter* 15.8 (1991): 7-8. Urges writing centers to sponsor readings and workshops with guest poets, playwrights, and fiction writers. Contends that professional writers can provide valuable feedback, help students to see themselves as working writers, and reinforce the need for revision.

0435. **Field-Pickering, Janet. "The Burden of Proof: Demonstrating the Effectiveness of a Computer Writing Center Program."** *Writing Lab Newsletter* **18.2 (1993): 1-3.** Discusses the issue of accountability to administrators by citing one high school writing center's budget-driven need to demonstrate its effectiveness in improving student writing. Offers advice on how to make a case for a center's effectiveness.

0436. **Fitzgerald, Sallyanne H. "Playing the Budget Game: The Story of Two Writing Centers."** *Writing Lab Newsletter* **18.5 (1994): 14-15.** Compares writing centers as two schools to demonstrate the greater financial security of a writing center that controls its own budget and serves the entire campus rather than a single department. Recommends that writing centers try to move as close as possible to that model and to cultivate support across the campus.

0437. **Fitzgerald, Sallyanne H. "Successes and Failures: Facilitating Cooperation Across the Curriculum."** *Writing Lab Newsletter* **13.1 (1988): 13-15.** Describes how a writing center gained campus support through a number of activities, including having tutors visit classes, providing information on student progress, and helping students and faculty with non-writing needs, such as academic advising.

0438. **Flynn, Tom. "Beginning a Skills-Development Center in a Small School."** *Tutoring Writing: A Sourcebook for Writing Labs.* **Ed. Muriel Harris. Glenview: Scott, Foresman, 1982. 170-78.** Uses a set of questions based on own experience in setting up a skills development center to aid others who may be asked to undertake a similar task.

0439. **Folks, Jeffrey J. "Using Regionally Oriented Materials in a Writing Center."** *Writing Lab Newsletter* **3.3 (1978): 1-2.** Discusses the development and use of regionally oriented materials as the basis for work with students in a writing/reading lab. Claims that students often respond with greater interest to "locally produced exercises than to the geographically neutral materials in many writing textbooks."

0440. **Forte, Imogene, Mary Ann Pangle, and Robbie Tupa.** *Cornering Creative Writing: Learning Centers, Games, Activities, and Ideas for the Elementary Classroom.* **Nashville: Incentive, 1974.** Suggests ways of establishing special classroom areas to encourage elementary students to write. Describes 52 varied "learning centers" that can be set up for student writing projects.

0441. Fowler, Carl. "The Writing Lab: Stepchild or Rightful Heir." *Writing Lab Newsletter* 6.10 (1982): 7-9. Discusses procedures a writing center should use in convincing administrators and faculty that it is "a legitimate child of education" in the value of its pedagogy and its services to students.

0442. Frankel, Penny, and Kay Severns. *Building a Writing Center: From Idea to Identity*. Lake Forest: Writing Center Consultants, n.d. A manual of guidelines for establishing writing centers at the middle and secondary school levels, based on the writing center established at Deerfield High School (Deerfield, IL). Covers the rationale for establishing a center, funding, staffing, training, and evaluation. A separate manual for training tutors is also available.

0443. Freisinger, Diana. "Beyond the Basics: Designing a Lab for All Students." *Writing Lab Newsletter* 7.2 (1982): 5-7. Discusses the "reigning stereotypes" of the writing lab as a fix-it shop for grammar deficiencies and suggests ways writing centers can be moved beyond remediation and offer services to all students.

0444. Freisinger, Diana. "Stretch the Lab." *Writing Lab Newsletter* 4.10 (1980): 6-7. Argues that faculty and students often define the writing lab too narrowly. Writing labs must find a broader identity than serving solely as an adjunct to freshman composition.

0445. Gajewski, Geoff. "The Tutor/Faculty Partnership: It's Required." *Writing Lab Newsletter* 15.10 (1991): 13-16. Discusses how assigning a tutor to each Freshman Studies section expanded the writing center's role and changed perceptions of peer tutoring.

0446. Gallo, Donald R. "Birthing a Writing Lab." *Writing Lab Newsletter* 3.7 (1979): 1-3. Offers advice to those who must plan and set up a writing lab, including such topics as seeking release time and gathering information and advice from others who have set up labs at other institutions.

0447. Gehrmann, S. Kay, and James Upton. "Beyond Tutoring: Expanding the Definition and Services of the High School Writing Center." *Writing Lab Newsletter* 14.8 (1990): 4-5. Describes how a high school writing center expanded its services beyond individual tutoring by visiting classes, sponsoring writing contests, publishing a student writing journal, and holding study skills nights.

**0448. George, Diana. "Talking to the Boss: A Preface."** *The Writing Center Journal* **9.1 (1988): 37-44.** Draws on information from writing center directors across the country to suggest ways to describe the multifaceted purpose of writing centers to administrators. Emphasizes the individual nature of writing center instruction, teaching goals writing centers and English departments share, and the nonremedial nature of tutoring.

**0449. Glassman, Susan. "Community and Communications in the Writing Center."** *Writing Lab Newsletter* **10.5 (1986): 1-3.** Advocates building a sense of community among writing center tutors through better communication. Also emphasizes the importance of communicating with the university community through newsletters and other publications.

**0450. Glassman, Susan. "Overcoming the 'No Show' Blues."** *Writing Lab Newsletter* **5.5 (1981): 7-8.** Discusses methods for dealing with students who do not keep appointments in the writing lab. Urges directors and tutors to realize that people's behavior patterns are established over time and often are not easily changed.

**0451. Glassman, Susan. "The Politics of the Drop-In Writing Center."** *Writing Lab Newsletter* **8.9 (1984): 1-3.** Claims that a drop-in writing center "functions as an extension of the faculty" and that this situation "necessarily complicates, to varying degrees, the student-instructor relationship." Discusses ways writing center directors can respond to the conflicts inherent in this structure.

**0452. Glassman, Susan. "Recruiting and Selecting Peer Tutors."** *Writing Lab Newsletter* **8.6 (1984): 1-4.** Discusses the difficulties in attracting good tutors when the writing center is unable to pay them. Argues that the recruiting and selecting process should reflect the atmosphere of the center as a workplace.

**0453. Graham, John Neil. "Community and the Writing Lab."** *The High School Writing Center: Establishing and Maintaining One.* **Ed. Pamela B. Farrell. Urbana: NCTE, 1989. 147-50.** Describes two assignments that take middle school students into the community, creating interest in the work of the writing center and support for it.

**0454. Guetschow, Paula. "Writing Labs That Hum."** *Writing Lab Newsletter* **5.9 (1981): 1-2.** Claims that good labs have directors who participate in tutor training, are located centrally, have sufficient space, and foster a relaxed atmosphere. Emphasizes the importance of "the highly developed handout file."

0455. **Harris, Jeanette. "Expanding the Writing Center Audience."** *WPA: Writing Program Administration* **6.3 (1983): 41-44.** Notes that writing centers have moved beyond remediation and beyond English departments and into the rest of the university community. Suggests ways of modifying public relations to change attitudes of faculty and students.

0456. **Harris, Jeanette. "Redefining the Role of the Writing Center."** *Writing Lab Newsletter* **7.3 (1982): 1-2.** Argues that writing centers directed exclusively toward remedial students or basic writers must redefine their role and finds ways to be integral components of a variety of programs or else face cutbacks or extinction as basic writing programs are reduced or eliminated.

0457. **Harris, Muriel. "Growing Pains: The Coming of Age of Writing Centers."** *The Writing Center Journal* **2.1 (1982): 1-8.** Points out recent growth of writing centers and suggests the continued misunderstanding of their activities may be attributed in part to poor public relations efforts. Suggests that writing centers emphasize their strength as an ideal teaching situation and develop more clearly focused research questions to demonstrate their effectiveness.

0458. **Harris, Muriel. "How Are Labs Evaluated?"** *Writing Lab Newsletter* **1.2 (1977): 3-6.** States that evaluation of writing centers is one of the central issues writing center personnel face. Provides two evaluation sheets used in the Purdue University Writing Lab as examples of one method of assessment.

0459. **Harris, Muriel. "Making the Writing Lab an Instructor's Resource Room."** *College Composition and Communication* **28 (1977): 376-78.** Discusses how faculty members can use resource files of handouts, articles, bibliographies, and books located in the writing lab.

0460. **Harris, Muriel. "Solutions and Trade-Offs in Writing Center Administration."** *The Writing Center Journal* **12.1 (1991): 63-79.** Cautions against a set approach to tutoring and administration because both are highly contextualized. Demonstrates the lack of absolutes by working through possible solutions to ten hypothetical dilemmas that might face writing center administrators.

0461. **Harris, Muriel, and Kathleen Blake Yancey. "Beyond Freshman Comp: Expanded Uses of the Writing Lab."** *The Writing Center Journal* **1.1 (1980): 41-49.** Points out that writing labs need to meet the needs of all courses involving writing and suggests ways of identifying and meeting those needs.

**0462. Harris, Muriel, and Tony Silva. "Tutoring ESL Students: Issues and Options."** *College Composition and Communication* **44 (1993): 525-37.** Writing center director and ESL coordinator discuss ways of implementing the following guidelines: focusing on global rather than local error; using studies in contrastive rhetoric to train tutors; resisting student pressure to correct all errors; setting realistic, long-term goals; providing ESL students linguistic information available to native speakers.

**0463. Hart, Dabney. "Peer Group Tutoring."** *Writing Lab Newsletter* **9.3 (1984): 11-12.** Discusses the advantages of having faculty teaching remedial English courses volunteer to work one hour a week in the writing lab as tutors.

**0464. Hartwell, Patrick. "The Writing Center and the Paradoxes of Written-Down Speech."** *Writing Centers: Theory and Administration.* **Ed. Gary A. Olson. Urbana: NCTE, 1984. 48-61.** Investigates writing of students who simply transcribe their spoken language without the refinements of discursive prose; suggests ways of identifying and working with such writers in the writing center.

**0465. Hashimoto, Irvin. "Writing Laboratory 'Image' or How Not to Write to Your Dean."** *The Writing Center Journal* **3.1 (1982): 1-10.** Criticizes "fuzzy" terminology and implicit anti-intellectualism in writing center scholarship. Also responds to Muriel Harris's "Growing Pains" (entry 0457), warning that defining writing centers in terms predicated on difference can be particularly dangerous in times of budget cuts.

**0466. Hashimoto, I.Y., and Roger Clark. "College Spelling Texts: The State of the Art."** *Writing Center Journal* **5.1 (1985): 1-13.** Claims textbooks are "inefficient" in teaching spelling because of their emphasis upon memorizing and recalling versus the more complex skill of applying knowledge. Urges researchers "to attack in a logical, theoretically sound fashion the problems of teaching spelling to college-age students."

**0467. Hatcher, Ruth. "The Fourth Hour."** *Writing Lab Newsletter* **7.4 (1982): 8-9.** Discusses how a community college added a fourth hour to the regular three-hour freshman English class and used this extra hour for tutorials and self-paced testing modules offered to students in the writing lab.

0468. Hayhoe, George. "Beyond the Basics: Expanded Uses of Writing Labs." *Tutoring Writing: A Sourcebook for Writing Labs.* Ed. Muriel Harris. Glenview: Scott, Foresman, 1982. 246-53. Discusses activities that can expand the scope of the writing lab beyond basic writing instruction, among them providing internships for graduate students, conducting workshops for faculty using writing in courses other than English, and becoming a site of the National Writing Project.

0469. Haynes-Burton, Cynthia. "'Thirty-something' Students: Concerning Transitions in the Writing Center." *Writing Lab Newsletter* 18.8 (1994): 3-4. Urges writing centers to hire tutors whose maturity and experience make them true peers of older students. Contends such tutors can help to ease students' transition from displaced worker to successful student.

0470. Healy, Dave. "From Place to Space: Perceptual and Administrative Issues in the Online Writing Center." *Computers and Composition* 12 (1995): 183-93. Focuses on administrative concerns of decentralizing the writing center, including effects of synchronous and asynchronous online tutoring on staffing, scheduling, and supervision. Examines some possible abuses of power connected with online tutorial records and monitoring of discussion lists.

0471. Held, Nadine. "Hire Junior College Students as Tutors? Why Not? (Ideas for Hiring and Funding Tutors at the Junior College)." *Writing Lab Newsletter* 10.1 (1985): 6-7. Discusses hiring policies of a junior college writing center. Recommends, in particular, hiring students from composition classes, likely to retain lessons learned about writing.

0472. Hemmeter, Thomas. "Spreading the Good Word: The Peer-Tutoring Report and the Public Image of the Writing Center." *WPA: Writing Program Administration* 9.1-2 (1985): 41-50. Claims that writing centers tend to neglect a valuable resource for improving the writing center's image—the well-written report of a peer tutor to the teacher of the student tutored.

0473. Hicks, Joyce. "A Reader Responds." *Writing Lab Newsletter* 9.7 (1985): 10-11. Discusses methods for promoting the writing center that range from writing thank you letters to faculty who refer students to seeking out nontraditional students to make them aware of the center's services.

0474. **Hilgers, Thomas L., and Joy Marsella.** *Making Your Writing Program Work.* **Newbury Park: Sage, 1992.** Single chapter ("Running a Writing Center") addresses writing center issues, describing and evaluating common models of organizing, staffing, and administering writing centers.

0475. **Hodgdon, David G. "Assessing a High School Writing Center: A Trek into the Frontiers of Program Evaluation."** *Writing Lab Newsletter* **14.8 (1990): 13-15.** Describes a four-part writing center evaluation system that examines the institutional contexts surrounding the center, any alternative strategies for accomplishing the center's goals, whether the center has met those goals, and statistical data on student use.

0476. **Hodges, Karen. "Writing Instruction in a (Non)Academic University Center."** *Writing Lab Newsletter* **8.2 (1983): 6-8.** Discusses the procedures used to set up a basic skills program for a student development center. Deals with the issue of setting up a program under student services as "extra-curricular" since only academic departments handle the "curricular."

0477. **Holbrook, Hilary Taylor. "Issues in the Writing Lab." ERIC/RCS Report.** *English Education* **20 (1988): 116-21. Rpt. in** *The Writing Center Journal* **9.2 (1989): 67-72.** Uses recent ERIC documents to summarize current discussion of three pressing writing center issues: staff training (particularly developing appropriate attitudes toward students), technology, and outreach.

0478. **Hollis, Karyn. "Hosting a Mini Peer Tutoring Conference: Easier Than You Might Think."** *Writing Lab Newsletter* **14.9 (1990): 14-15.** Offers advice on the logistics and expenses involved in planning a local peer tutoring conference.

0479. **Holmes, Leigh Howard. "Three Sources for Writing Lab Tutors."** *Writing Lab Newsletter* **3.4 (1978): 3.** Discusses securing tutors from classes in methods of teaching English and finding funding from work-study programs and the G.I. Bill.

0480. **Hylton, Jaime. "Evaluating the Writing Lab: How Do We Know that We Are Helping?"** *Writing Lab Newsletter* **15.3 (1990): 5-7.** Argues writing centers must go beyond mere head counting and anecdotal evidence to justify their existence to administrators. Includes specific questions aimed at determining how well the center satisfies particular objectives.

0481. Irace, Kathleen. "A Small College Writing Center: Writing Improvement on a No Frills Budget." *Writing Lab Newsletter* 4.9 (1980): 3-4. Describes the conflicts that arise when large numbers of students need remedial assistance and a department's budget is too small to set up a fully equipped skills center.

0482. Jacob, Greg. "Changing the Image of the Study Center." *Writing Lab Newsletter* 10.7 (1986): 9. Urges directors to promote their centers actively. Claims directors should not assume the university values or even knows about the center's services.

0483. Jolly, Peggy. "The Bottom Line: Financial Responsibility." *Writing Centers: Theory and Administration.* Ed. Gary A. Olson. Urbana: NCTE, 1984. 101-14. Discusses various possibilities of securing funding from within a university, local entrepreneurial sources, and local and federal grant programs.

0484. Jolly, Peggy B. "Funding a Writing Center." *Writing Lab Newsletter* 7.8 (1982): 1-4. Considers such sources of funding as the home department, university-wide initiatives, and external grants from state, regional, or national agencies.

0485. Jonz, Jon. "Overcoming 'Languageclassese.'" *Writing Lab Newsletter* 2.8 (1978): 4. Cautions that a "mastery approach" can leave learners with a sense of language as an object, not a process. Describes the creation of materials for a writing center course to teach rhetorical skills in a more integrated fashion.

0486. Jonz, Jon, and Jeanette Harris. "Decisions, Records, and the Writing Center." *Tutoring Writing: A Sourcebook for Writing Labs.* Ed. Muriel Harris. Glenview: Scott, Foresman, 1982. 216-26. Urges that records be kept and reported to different audiences for different purposes: to publicize successes, assess effectiveness, to provide meaningful data for decision makers.

0487. Kail, Harvey. "Evaluating Our Own Peer Tutoring Programs: A Few Leading Questions." *Writing Lab Newsletter* 7.10 (1983): 2-4. Suggests writing center directors evaluate peer tutoring programs by determining the historical, educational, and political reasons for establishing and maintaining the program.

0488. **Keene, Nadene A. "Portfolio Evaluation: Implications for Writing Centers."** *The Writing Center: New Directions.* **Ed. Ray Wallace and Jeanne Simpson. New York: Garland, 1991. 216-29.** Describes the portfolio evaluation system in place on one campus to demonstrate the impact of portfolios on the writing center and to suggest ways that writing centers might assist in making the system more effective.

0489. **Kilborn, Judith. "Cultural Diversity in the Writing Center: Defining Ourselves and Our Challenges."** *Writing Lab Newsletter* **19.1 (1994): 7-10.** Urges writing center directors to examine how they will help meet the growing needs of a culturally diverse student body. Gives tips on building a diverse clientele, recruiting minority staff, and fostering multicultural and linguistic sensitivity in tutors.

0490. **Killian, Dorothy J. "Establishing Attendance Policies in a Non-Required Learning Assistance Center."** *Writing Lab Newsletter* **6.9 (1982): 9-10.** Discusses a system of record keeping that allowed the staff to reward students who kept appointments with scheduled tutoring and to provide tutoring only as available to those who failed to keep appointments.

0491. **Kinkead, Joyce. "Outreach: The Writing Center, the Campus, and the Community."** *Writing Lab Newsletter* **10.3 (1985): 5-8.** Suggests various ways that writing centers wishing to thrive can serve increasingly wider circles of writers, including those in local secondary schools and in the community at large.

0492. **Kinkead, Joyce, and Jan Ugan. "Articulation Anyone?"** *Writing Lab Newsletter* **9.2 (1984): 8.** Discusses an outreach program of articulation between a university writing center and local high schools.

0493. **Kleimann, Susan, and G. Douglas Meyers. "Senior Citizens and Junior Writers: A Center for Exchange."** *The Writing Center Journal* **2.1 (1982): 57-60.** Describes successful program using retired professionals as tutors in a writing center dedicated to junior-level writing courses in specific disciplines.

0494. **Koring, Heidi. "The Lab Library: What Goes Where?"** *Writing Lab Newsletter* **8.3 (1983): 9-10.** Discusses ways to organize the library of print and audiovisual materials in a writing lab based upon "primary user categories."

0495. Koskinen, Patricia S., and Robert M. Wilson. *Developing a Successful Tutoring Program*. New York: Teachers College, 1982. Provides teachers and administrators wishing to establish a tutoring program with general guidelines applicable to all subjects and all grade levels. Contains many specific illustrations, limited primarily to language arts activities at the elementary school level.

0496. Kotker, Joan Garcia. "Expanding the Non-Credit Writing Lab." *Writing Lab Newsletter* 8.9 (1984): 10-11. Tells of how a writing lab, without an increase in staff, responded to the challenge of maintaining its drop-in base while also offering formal instruction on a semester-long basis to students in two sections of basic English.

0497. Lamb, Mary. "Evaluation Procedures for Writing Centers: Defining Ourselves Through Accountability." *Improving Writing Skills*. Ed. Thom Hawkins and Phyllis Brooks. New Directions for College Learning Assistance 3. San Francisco: Jossey-Bass, 1981. 69-82. Discusses statistics, questionnaires, pre- and posttests, follow-up on students' grades, external evaluation of writing centers by consultants, and the publication and professional activities of staff members as means for evaluating centers and addressing accountability issues.

0498. Larsen, Richard B. "A Note on Lab Layout." *Writing Lab Newsletter* 3.6 (1979): 3-4. Argues for the value of attention to decor, or layout, as one component of making a writing center aesthetically pleasing and psychologically reassuring to those who come to use the lab's services, particularly "the typical anxiety-ridden lab student."

0499. Lauby, Jacqueline. "A Reader Responds ... Understanding the Dyslexic Writer." *Writing Lab Newsletter* 9.5 (1985): 7-9. Discusses the services an academic support services center can offer dyslexic students under Section 504 of the Rehabilitation Act of 1973, including proofreaders to correct spelling errors, scribes to transcribe information from tapes, readers to tape printed material, and tutors trained to help dyslexics improve their writing.

0500. Lauby, Jacqueline. "Wanted: Someone Conversant with the Turabian Style Sheet to Help Edit My Thesis." *Writing Lab Newsletter* 8.9 (1984): 11-12. The author discusses her trials with MLA, APA, and Turabian documentation styles to argue that writing centers should provide "tutors-as-editors for graduate students and faculty in their disciplines." Claims there should be a "specialist" available who is conversant with each discipline's style sheet, jargon, journals, and method of argumentation.

0501. **Leahy, Richard. "Competency Testing and the Writing Center."** *WPA: Writing Program Administration* **15.3 (1992): 41-56.** Discusses the role one writing center plays preparing students to take the university's minimal competency writing exam. Argues that the exam, which some writing center personnel might see as burdensome, presents tutors with a chance to hone their skills and have a positive impact on the writers.

0502. **Leahy, Richard. "Competency Testing and the Writing Lab."** *Writing Lab Newsletter* **9.7 (1985): 12-14.** Discusses the impact upon a writing lab of a minimal competency exam required of all graduating students. Considers the greater need for facilities and staffing and how the lab can respond to students who do not pass.

0503. **Leibrock, Shannon M., and Lisa C. Bernbaum. "Awards for Writers Reward Writing Centers."** *Writing Lab Newsletter* **17.9 (1993): 12-14.** Suggests that sponsoring a writing contest can encourage student writers and focus positive attention on the writing center. Offers detailed anecdote about a particular contest that enhanced the writing center's image.

0504. **LeMoine, Jane P. "Overcoming Resistance to the Writing Center."** *Writing Lab Newsletter* **6.10 (1982): 2-4.** Describes a series of organizational steps a writing center used to increase student use and to avoid the stigma of remediation. Steps included moving the center under the administrative authority of the Humanities Department rather than the Learning Skills Center.

0505. **Liggett, Sarah. "Expanding the Writing Lab's Services: Meeting the Needs of Business Writers."** *Writing Lab Newsletter* **5.10 (1981): 1-3.** Discusses how the writing lab can select staff, prepare materials, and offer tutorials and minicourses for business writers.

0506. **Linden, Myra J. "Computer Academic Skills Center Management at Joliet Junior College."** *Writing Lab Newsletter* **3.10 (1979): 4.** Discusses the benefits of using keypunched time cards carrying student identification and course enrollment information as a method of record keeping.

0507. Lopez, Toni. "Co-Ordinating the Writing Lab with the Composition Program." *Writing Lab Newsletter* 4.1 (1979): 4-7. Discusses the benefits of coordinating lab services with the freshman composition program. Such an approach can keep the lab from being perceived as a "separate entity" from composition instruction or as "a last resort service to which only those students considered writing cripples are referred."

0508. Luce, Henry A. "High School-College Collaboration." *The High School Writing Center: Establishing and Maintaining One.* Ed. Pamela B. Farrell. Urbana: NCTE, 1989. 127-35. Lists benefits of collaborations between college and high school writing centers in dealing with the perceived writing crisis. Describes two such collaborations.

0509. Lunsford, Andrea. "Preparing for a Writing Workshop: Some Crucial Considerations." *Tutoring Writing: A Sourcebook for Writing Labs.* Ed. Muriel Harris. Glenview: Scott, Foresman, 1982. 164-69. Outlines the characteristics of successful writing centers and discusses ways of planning and developing a program that will have those characteristics. Stresses need for sustained, ongoing evaluation.

0510. Lupack, Barbara T. "Early Alert: Reaching Students in Time." *Writing Lab Newsletter* 8.9 (1984): 3-5. Discusses how an extensive nctwork of faculty referrals can help writing labs and learning centers reach remedial students early enough in their academic careers to be of greatest benefit.

0511. Lyons, Peter A. "Selecting Tutors: A Two-Step Process." *Writing Lab Newsletter* 7.8 (1983): 3-4. States that the recommendation of a colleague and an interview are the two most important aspects in tutor selection. Provides a series of interview questions.

0512. Maeck, Alexandra. "Report from a Correctional Institution: I Need Help." *Writing Lab Newsletter* 19.7 (1995): 13-14. Director laments the lack of funds that might help modernize her Los Angeles Community College (CA) writing center. Seeks advice on training and funding from writing center community.

0513. Marcus, Harriet. "The Writing Center: Peer Tutoring in a Supportive Setting." *English Journal* 73.5 (1984): 66-67. Describes the set-up and operation of a high school writing center at Oak Knoll School (NJ) that used honors English students as tutors and that helped to overcome students' negative attitudes toward writing.

0514. **Marcus, Harriet, and Pamela B. Farrell. "Staffing the Writing Center."** *The High School Writing Center: Establishing and Maintaining One.* **Ed. Pamela B. Farrell. Urbana: NCTE, 1989. 39-44.** Marcus provides philosophical reasons for staffing a high school writing center exclusively with students and describes its successful operation; Farrell examines operation of writing centers staffed with professionals.

0515. **Maring, Gerald H. "Computerizing Data in College Reading (and Writing) Centers for Accountability and Research."** *Reading World* **20.1 (1980): 16-28.** Outlines eight general steps for developing computerized data systems. Demonstrates ways Washington State University has been able to generate useful data for research and to document accountability.

0516. **Martin, Kathy. "The Writing Lab's Image."** *Writing Lab Newsletter* **8.7 (1984): 8.** Discusses strategies to overcome the image of the lab as a place for "dummies" by explaining the writing lab's purpose and improving classroom teachers' attitudes.

0517. **Masiello, Lea. "Qualitative and Quantitative Strategies for Assessing Writing Center Effectiveness."** *Writing Lab Newsletter* **16.6 (1992): 4-6.** Urges writing center directors to go beyond the collection of numerical data in evaluating the effectiveness of tutoring. Discusses one university's program that solicits a qualitative assessment of each tutorial from student writers.

0518. **McCracken, Nancy. "Evaluation/Accountability for the Writing Lab."** *Writing Lab Newsletter* **3.6 (1979): 1-2.** Argues that the most important measures writing lab directors can use to justify the lab's existence should focus on the individual student. Suggests error analysis of writing samples done at the start and the end of the term as one highly effective means of evaluation and accountability.

0519. **McCully, Michael. "The Writing Lab and Freshman Composition: A Mutual Re-Definition."** *Writing Lab Newsletter* **9.9 (1985): 1-5.** Discusses ways to involve composition instructors in the processes and philosophies of the writing lab. Suggestions range from making the writing lab a component of each composition course to reconstructing the composition courses so that lab activities will replace some regular class meetings.

0520. McFarland, Betty. "The Non-Credit Writing Laboratory." *Teaching English in the Two-Year College* 1.3 (1975): 153-54. Examines the use of non-credit writing laboratories to assist junior college students in meeting the demands of first-year English courses.

0521. McKenzie, Lee. "The Union of a Writing Center with a Computer Center: What to Put in the Marriage Contract." *Writing Lab Newsletter* 14.3 (1989): 1-2, 8. Looks at problems created by the merger of a writing center with a computer center managed by another department. Contends such a merger poses problems about who will supervise the center and how completely the two departments should mix.

0522. McMurrey, David A. "Writing Contests and Writing Labs." *Writing Lab Newsletter* 8.1 (1983): 11-12. Discusses the benefits of having writing labs sponsor writing contests. Advantages include promoting the writing lab to the academic community and focusing students' attention away from grades and toward the idea of writing as a craft.

0523. Melko, Jim. "A Materials Organization System for the Increased Effectiveness of Writing Skills Centers." *Writing Lab Newsletter* 6.10 (1982): 5-6. Describes a system of indexing books in writing lab libraries to aid tutor training.

0524. Meredith, Robert L. "The Departmental Handbook." *Writing Lab Newsletter* 3.10 (1979): 1-2. Discusses the benefits of having English department faculty write a handbook of rhetoric and usage for the writing lab. Such a project helps to coordinate the activities of the lab with regular English classes.

0525. Miller, Gaylier. "A Functioning Writing Laboratory: Seven Operational Truisms." *Writing Lab Newsletter* 7.1 (1982): 7-9. Discusses the illusions and the realities that accompany such truisms as "Everyone can learn to write" and "Self-concept is directly related to learning." Reflects upon how these truths and illusions can influence writing center operations.

0526. Mills, Eva B., and Stella Nesanovich. "Helping the Reluctant Student." *Writing Lab Newsletter* 7.8 (1983): 7-9. Discusses the reasons students are reluctant to use a writing lab and suggests how lab administrators can overcome these obstacles and boost attendance.

0527. Mohr, Ellen. "Credit in the Writing Center." *Writing Lab Newsletter* 13.10 (1989): 13-16, 10. Reports on a series of one-credit courses offered by a writing center with an emphasis on sentence pattern, proofreading, composing, practical writing, and research skills. Contends that such classes not only produce revenue, but offer needed, individualized instruction that traditional classroom teaching cannot provide.

0528. Morrissey, Thomas J. "Increasing Student Use of the Drop-In Writing Center." *Writing Lab Newsletter* 5.1 (1980): 8. Discusses a program of placing peer tutors in composition classes as preceptors and participants in group discussions as one method of increasing student use of the writing center.

0529. Moss, Frederick K. "Writing Labs Within Skills Programs." *Writing Lab Newsletter* 7.5 (1983): 5-6. Discusses the advantages of combining a writing lab's tutoring services with those of a learning assistance program that emphasized reading and math skills. Argues that writing labs have a better chance at survival if they combine with other programs and work from a position of "strength in numbers."

0530. Murphy, Marguerite P. "Publicity and Success." *The Writing Lab Newsletter* 4.3 (1979): 1-2. Discusses methods of promoting the writing lab from encouraging academic advisors to refer students to presenting information at orientation sessions for new faculty and students.

0531. Nash, Thomas. "Hamlet, Polonius, and the Writing Center." *The Writing Center Journal* 1.1 (1980): 34-40. Compares Hamlet (the detached evaluator) to teachers and Polonius (the problematic speaker) to students; represents tutor as caught between them. Urges that writing center directors intervene early in the writing process by seeking more teacher involvement (e.g., obtaining assignments), training tutors in prewriting heuristics, and tailoring heuristics to fit particular assignments.

0532. Neuleib, Janice. "Evaluating a Writing Lab." *Tutoring Writing: A Sourcebook for Writing Labs*. Ed. Muriel Harris. Glenview: Scott, Foresman, 1982. 227-32. A general discussion of kinds of records that may be useful for evaluating the work of a writing lab and of kinds of resources available.

0533. Neuleib, Janice. "Proving We Did It." *Writing Lab Newsletter* 4.7 (1980): 2-4. Argues that proving a writing facility has been effective requires a clear plan of action, covering goals, staffing, record keeping, "good press and visibility," and regular reports to administrators and faculty.

0534. Neuleib, Janice. **"Questions Which Need Answers."** *Writing Lab Newsletter* 1.2 **(1977): 3.** Offers sets of questions on such issues as scope of writing labs, staffing, materials, financing, operation, evaluation, and problem areas.

0535. Neuleib, Janice, and Maurice Scharton. **"Grammar Hotline."** *College English* **44 (1982): 413-16.** Describes and categorizes calls to grammar hotline operated in the writing center.

0536. Neumann, Betty B. **"A Reader Asks ... Peer Tutors in the Two-Year Colleges?"** *Writing Lab Newsletter* **9.10 (1985): 10.** Points out that, while four-year colleges can draw upon juniors, seniors, and graduate students for peer tutors, two-year colleges have only freshmen and sophomores available. Considers the advantages, disadvantages, and difficulties involved in this situation.

0537. Nieves, Julie. **"Non-Credit Students in the Writing Lab."** *Writing Lab Newsletter* **7.5 (1983): 8-9.** Discusses students' use of a writing lab in one of two ways—taking individualized audio-tutorial courses for credit or choosing to work in the lab on a non-credit basis. Considers the advantages and disadvantages of each approach for students and for lab administration.

0538. Nigliazzo, Marc. **"Some Writing Labs Are Failing: Reasons Why."** *Writing Lab Newsletter* **4.9 (1980): 5-6.** Discusses some reasons writing labs fail, ranging from the "I want one like yours" syndrome, to excessive reliance on machinery, to inadequate planning and direction, to failing to attract and serve students.

0539. North, Steve. **"Writing Lab Staffs."** *Writing Lab Newsletter* **2.10 (1978): 2-5.** States that those involved in staffing a writing lab should consider cost, continuity, expertise, training, and the four main "labor pools"—undergraduates, graduate students, professionals, and nonprofessionals such as "faculty wives or husbands" and "qualified and interested community people."

0540. O'Hear, Michael F. **"Building Administrator and Faculty Awareness."** *Writing Lab Newsletter* 2.8 **(1978): 3.** Discusses the value of sharing monthly progress reports with administrators and academic

departments as a way of keeping administrators and faculty aware of a
writing skills center's programs and effectiveness.

0541. **Olson, Gary A. "Establishing a Writing Center in the Junior or
Community College."** *Community College Review* **9.2 (1981): 19-26.**
Discusses issues related to establishing a writing center in a two-year
college, ranging from selling the idea to the English department and
administration to staffing and tutor training.

0542. **Olson, Gary A. "Establishing and Maintaining a Writing Center in
a Two-Year College."** *Writing Centers: Theory and Administration.*
**Ed. Gary A. Olson. Urbana: NCTE, 1984. 87-100.** Outlines step-by-
step procedure for setting up a writing center, including such
considerations as funding, location, staffing, and training.

0543. **Olson, Gary A. "Writing Center Atmosphere: An Experiment."**
*Writing Lab Newsletter* **5.1 (1980): 6.** Describes the use of tapes of
Mozart as background music to overcome the "sterile silence" of the
writing center. Reports that students and tutors felt more relaxed and
anxiety free.

0544. **Palumbo, Donald. "Efficient Use of Writing Lab Staff."** *Writing Lab
Newsletter* **5.7 (1981): 4-5.** Argues that a quantitative analysis of lab use
patterns can aid the writing lab director in organizing available staff time
more effectively.

0545. **Perdue, Virginia, and Deborah James. "Teaching in the Center."**
*Writing Lab Newsletter* **14.10 (1990): 7-8.** Argues the need for
exploring the differences between teaching in the writing center and in
the classroom. Contends that knowledge of these differences would add
to the writing center's effectiveness and allow directors to demonstrate
its contribution to student learning.

0546. **Perkins, Lorraine. "Encouraging Student Attendance."** *Writing Lab
Newsletter* **5.10 (1981): 7-8.** Discusses the use of referral forms from
instructors as one means of encouraging student use of the writing lab.

0547. **Perkins, Lorraine. "'N.S.'"** *Writing Lab Newsletter* **4.9 (1980): 5.**
Discusses ways to reduce the number of "no shows"—students who make
appointments in the writing lab and then fail to keep them.

0548. **Popken, Randall L. "The Context-Sensitivity Problem in Models and
Exercises for the Writing Lab."** *Writing Lab Newsletter* **13.6 (1989):**

**11-12.** Argues that writing lab directors, instead of eliminating computerized lab exercises, should design exercises that carefully match form and context. Suggests that exercises too often pair informal writing samples with formal writing exercises and vice versa.

0549. **Ports, Michele J. "The Tutor's Corner: Iacocca's Magic and Writing Center 'Sales.'"** *Writing Lab Newsletter* **10.9 (1986): 7.** Emphasizes the need to market the writing center's services by making it more attractive and accessible to student writers.

0550. **Richardson, Linda. "What Can You Do Except Tutor?"** *Writing Lab Newsletter* **3.1 (1978): 6.** Discusses the value of minicourses or writing workshops as one response to two problems writing centers face: (1) the logistics of conducting one-to-one tutorials with large numbers of students and (2) the difficulties tutors face in saying "the same thing" over and over to students.

0551. **Rochelle, Larry. "The ABCs of Writing Centers."** *Writing Lab Newsletter* **6.1 (1981): 7-9.** Discusses Alienation, Budget, Conflict, Determination, Emptiness, Furniture, Grades, the Hot-line, Individualized Instruction, Judges and Jury, and the King as central issues in writing center administration.

0552. **Rochelle, Larry. "The ABCs of Writing Centers (Part II)."** *Writing Lab Newsletter* **6.2 (1981): 8-10.** Discusses the relationship of the Learning Center; Materials; the Neighborhood; Operations; Peer Tutors; the Queen; Referrals; the Secretary/Receptionist; Tea, Coffee, Soft Drinks, Food, Smoking, etc.; the Unusual; Visitors; and When Exasperated Yell "Zounds!" to administering the writing center.

0553. **Rodis, Karen. "Mending the Damaged Path: How to Avoid Conflict of Expectation When Setting up a Writing Center."** *The Writing Center Journal* **10.2 (1990): 45-57.** Examines conflicting expectations of composition teachers and tutors about the writing center's mission. While tutors teach all aspects of writing, instructors often see writing centers as remedial skills centers and communicate this viewpoint to their students. Suggests directors promote the center as nonremedial, encourage voluntary attendance, and hire professional staff.

0554. **Runciman, Lex. "Should Writing Lab Conferences Be Required for Composition Students?"** *Writing Lab Newsletter* **11.9 (1987): 12-14.** Describes a program to increase writing center use by requiring first-year composition students to participate in tutorials. Student survey indicates most had not heard of the center before being required to go, the tutorials were a positive experience, and they would recommend that others use the center.

0555. Ryan, Maureen. "An Inter-Office Memo." *Writing Lab Newsletter* 9.6 (1985): 7-8. Text of a memo from a writing center director to faculty, explaining the center's role in student-centered instruction.

0556. Saling, Joseph, and Kelly Cook-McEachern. "Building a Community of Writers in a Required Lab: A Paradox and a Dilemma." *Writing Lab Newsletter* 17.3 (1992): 13-15. Relates the experience of building a collaborative, student-centered environment despite rules requiring students to visit the lab. Recommends viewing students who come to the writing center as colleagues.

0557. Saloman, Patricia. "Starting from Scratch: Developing a Tutor-Training Program." *Writing Lab Newsletter* 19.1 (1994): 15. Describes the implementation of a tutor training course that clarified the distinction between tutoring and proofreading, emphasized interpersonal skills, and provided information on tutoring ESL students.

0558. Sbaratta, Philip. "Teaching Composition in the Portable Writing Laboratory." *College Composition and Communication* 27 (1976): 202-04. Describes the application of writing center principles to a developmental English class. Classroom activities were limited to writing, the teacher serving as "editor." Includes writing assignments.

0559. Scharton, Maurice, and Janice Neuleib. "Establishing a Unified Record-Keeping System in a Writing Laboratory." *Writing Lab Newsletter* 6.9 (1982): 7-9. Discusses a computerized record keeping system as an ideal means for information management. Describes how the system was created and considers the types and categories of information that should be tracked in a writing lab.

0560. Schwalm, David E. "E Pluribus Unum: An Administrator Rounds Up Mavericks and Money." *Writing Center Perspectives.* Ed. Byron L. Stay, Christina Murphy, and Eric H. Hobson. Emmitsburg: NWCA Press, 1995. 53-62. Recounts the development of the writing center at Arizona State University West from the point of view of the central administrator of the university to demonstrate the complex factors affecting administrative decisions.

0561. Seigle, Natalie R. "Designing a Writing Lab for MBA Students." *Writing Lab Newsletter* 7.4 (1982): 5. Discusses the issues that surround offering tutorial services to MBA students, including how many minicourses the lab should offer and whether group or one-to-one tutorials are better for this population.

0562. Severns, Kay. "A Secondary School Success Story for Writing Enthusiasts." *Writing Lab Newsletter* 13.4 (1988): 12, 16. Offers advice, based on lessons learned from a successful program, on how to set up and staff a high school writing center.

0563. Sherwood, Steve. "How to Survive the Hard Times." *Writing Lab Newsletter* 17.10 (1993): 4-8. Argues that writing centers facing budget cuts can increase their chances of survival by justifying their cost effectiveness, practicing judicious self-promotion, avoiding marginalization, allying themselves with other learning centers, and moving the center out of the English department.

0564. Simmons, Nancy, and Jane Brill. "Resources for Writing Centers." *English Journal* 74.6 (1985): 78-79. Lists and evaluates books useful for operating a high school writing center and advises that writing centers invest more heavily in professional staff than in computers.

0565. Simpson, Jeanne. "Perceptions, Realities, and Possibilities: Central Administration and Writing Centers." *Writing Center Perspectives.* Ed. Byron L. Stay, Christina Murphy, and Eric H. Hobson. Emmitsburg: NWCA Press, 1995. 48-52. Examines common misperceptions about the way central administration operates and suggests productive ways for writing center directors to deal with administrators.

0566. Simpson, Jeanne. "Planning for Computers in the Writing Center: First Drafts." *Writing Lab Newsletter* 17.7 (1993): 13-14. Examines ways to design a state-of-the-art computer room for a writing center. Recommends anticipating problems with noise, heat, and breakdowns. Suggests setting up computers in clusters or islands to facilitate tutoring.

0567. Simpson, Jeanne. "The Role of Writing Centers in Student Retention Programs." *The Writing Center: New Directions.* Ed. Ray Wallace and Jeanne Simpson. New York: Garland, 1991. 102-09. Points out value of writing centers in the crucial area of student retention through academic assistance, mentoring, and developing peer relationships. Suggests ways that writing centers can be involved in residence halls, academic assistance programs, advising, and orientation programs, the four areas of campus life that most affect student success.

0568. **Simpson, Jeanne. "To Arms! To Arms! Defending the Writing Center."** *Writing Lab Newsletter* 7.2 (1982): 2-3. Responds to Phyllis A. Sherwood's "The Rise and Fall of Basic English and the Writing Lab" (entry 0194) by explaining rhetorical strategies and organizational moves directors can use in defending their writing centers from cutbacks and elimination.

0569. **Skelton, James. "Starting a Writing Center: The Agony and the Ecstacy."** *Writing Lab Newsletter* 11.1 (1986): 1-4. A humorous look at the pains and pleasures of starting a university writing center on a tight budget. Urges new directors who are upset by the chaos to realize that the confusion and unpredictability of start-up are half the fun.

0570. **Skulicz, Matthew. "The Director of Developmental English as Meatball."** *Writing Lab Newsletter* 8.7 (1984): 5. Discusses one director's response to a composition instructor's view that a student should be moved from a regular composition class to a developmental one simply because the student exhibited spelling errors in an otherwise well-written paper.

0571. **Smith, C. Michael. "Efficiency and Insecurity: A Case Study in Form Design and Records Management."** *Writing Centers: Theory and Administration.* Ed. Gary A. Olson. Urbana: NCTE, 1984. 115-22. Uses a case study to demonstrate how to simplify writing center forms and improve record keeping efficiency.

0572. **Smoot, Joyce. "Public Relations and the Writing Center Director: Making the Center Visible On and Off Campus."** *Writing Lab Newsletter* 11.1 (1986): 6-8. Recommends promoting the writing center's services by offering workshops and making presentations to a variety of audiences. Specifically suggests offering workshops through the university's extended education program.

0573. **Solinger, Rickie. "Starting Small and Thinking Big: An Administrator's Viewpoint."** *Improving Writing Skills.* Ed. Thom Hawkins and Phyllis Brooks. New Directions for College Learning Assistance 3. San Francisco: Jossey-Bass, 1981. 61-68. Claims that writing centers face "diminished financial support and institutional ambivalence about support services on the campus." However, contends that literacy crises and the instructional requirements of non-traditional students make writing centers "extremely useful and even indispensable facilities."

0574. Sorenson, Sharon. **"The High School Writing Lab: A Management Plan (Part II)."** *Writing Lab Newsletter* **6.2 (1981): 2-4.** Describes a plan under Title IV-c Innovative Education to provide individualized tutoring for 350 high school students.

0575. Sorenson, Sharon. **"The High School Writing Lab: Its Establishment (Part I)."** *Writing Lab Newsletter* **6.1 (1981): 1-3.** Discusses procedures for setting up writing labs at the high school level and argues that solving the problems of funding and scheduling are the central concerns.

0576. Sorenson, Sharon. **"The High School Writing Lab: Its Evaluation (Part III)."** *Writing Lab Newsletter* **6.3 (1981): 6-7.** Describes a formal evaluation plan for the high school writing center based upon pre- and posttesting of students and the use of student attitudinal surveys.

0577. Sorenson, Sharon. **"The High-School Writing Lab: Its Feasibility and Function."** *Tutoring Writing: A Sourcebook for Writing Labs.* **Ed. Muriel Harris. Glenview: Scott, Foresman, 1982. 186-95.** Argues that a writing center is not only feasible but highly desirable in high schools, providing the individualized attention needed by students at all levels. Briefly suggests solutions for problems of funding and scheduling as well.

0578. Sorenson, Sharon. **"Working with Students."** *The High School Writing Center: Establishing and Maintaining One.* **Ed. Pamela B. Farrell. Urbana: NCTE, 1989. 85-87.** Addresses difficulty in providing appropriate individualized instruction for the wide range of clients using the writing center in a high school of 1,500 students. Describes structural and organizational limits imposed to make lab function smoothly with commercially prepared materials that allowed students to move at their own pace.

0579. Speiser, William A., and Pamela B. Farrell. **"The High School Writing Lab/Center: A Dialogue."** *The High School Writing Center: Establishing and Maintaining One.* **Ed. Pamela B. Farrell. Urbana: NCTE, 1989. 9-22.** Uses dialogue between two directors of high school writing centers to introduce issues covered in this collection, emphasizing philosophical distinction between terms *lab* and *center*.

0580. Steward, Joyce S., and Mary K. Croft. *The Writing Laboratory: Organization, Management, and Methods.* Glenview: Scott, 1982. Presents a brief overview of "the lab phenomenon" (history, underlying philosophy of individualized instruction, populations served, and financing), then examines day-to-day operations in more detail. Topics covered include selecting and training staff (including peer tutors), setting up conference teaching and small group instruction sessions, and managing the writing center (scheduling, record keeping, evaluation, and publicity). Contains sample forms and extensive bibliography.

0581. Stratton, Russ. "A Note on the Collapse: Let Them Eat Cake." *Writing Lab Newsletter* 7.2 (1982): 1-2. Responds to Phyllis A. Sherwood's "The Rise and Fall of Basic English and the Writing Lab" (entry 0194) by speculating on the reasons an English department may have voted to discontinue the services of a writing lab.

0582. Stroud, Cynthia K. "Writing Center Workshops: A Way to Reach Out." *Writing Lab Newsletter* 5.2 (1980): 1-3. Discusses the use of workshops on writing skills as a means of establishing rapport with students, the English department, and faculty in all disciplines. Suggests ways such workshops benefit the writing center and increase its profile on campus.

0583. Sullivan, Patrick. "Do You Object to Tutors Assisting Your Students with Their Writing?" *Writing Lab Newsletter* 10.4 (1985): 6-8. Discusses faculty objections to writing center tutoring, based on suspicion that tutors help students too much. Suggests directors inform instructors about what the center will and will not do for students, promote the center, and keep instructors informed about specific students' use of the center.

0584. Taufen, Phyllis M. "What Do You Do When the Budget is Zero?" *Writing Lab Newsletter* 11.9 (1987): 1-3. Illustrates how a writing center with a dedicated staff of volunteers from a number of disciplines can operate effectively without a budget. Contends that a concern for student writers and a commitment to improving the quality of writing across the university are key ingredients of a writing center's success.

0585. Tiedt, Iris M. *Individualizing Writing in the Elementary Classroom.* Urbana: NCTE and ERIC, 1975. Justifies individualized instruction and discusses the best procedures to attain this end, especially the design and operation of a writing center.

0586. Tovey, Duane R. *Writing Centers in the Elementary School.*
Bloomington: Phi Delta Kappa Educational Foundation, 1979. Offers
a rationale for establishing a writing center in the elementary school and
provides detailed lists of activities, materials, and equipment to improve
children's thinking skills through writing.

0587. Towns, Cheryl Hofstetter. "Serving the Disabled in the Writing
Center." *Writing Lab Newsletter* 14.3 (1989): 14-16. Suggests writing
centers can assist students with disabilities by offering a reader/taping
service, giving easy access to computers, providing duplication paper for
carbon copies of class notes, and making other accommodations. Stresses
the importance of tutor training, particularly in maintaining an
empowering yet professional attitude toward students with disabilities.

0588. Truscott, Robert Blake. "Tutoring the Advanced Writer in a Writing
Center." *Writing Lab Newsletter* 9.10 (1985): 14-15. Discusses the
development of minicourses in creative writing, career writing, and
stylistics as ways of attracting advanced writers to the writing center.

0589. Upton, James. "Expanding Services of the High School Writing
Center." *Writing Lab Newsletter* 15.1 (1990): 6-7. Recommends high
school writing centers expand their services by having tutors make
presentations to classes, conduct short writing seminars, sponsor writing
contests, and work with instructors in developing writing assignments
and improving their own writing projects.

0590. Upton, James. "Filling the Room: Public Relations." *The High
School Writing Center: Establishing and Maintaining One.* Ed.
Pamela B. Farrell. Urbana: NCTE, 1989. 77-80. Describes the
publicity campaign used to promote a newly opened high school writing
center, including such strategies as publications, contests, and classroom
visits.

0591. Upton, James. "From the Center Out." *Writing Lab Newsletter* 14.1
(1989): 15-16. Explores the logistics of expanding the writing center's
services into the community. Contends the benefits in student
improvement and community goodwill outweigh the extra work
involved.

0592. Upton, James. "The High School Writing Center: The Once and
Future Services." *The Writing Center Journal* 11.1 (1990): 67-71.
Claims high school centers can play a significant role in addressing
literacy problems and enhancing academic skills of secondary students.

0593. Upton, Jim. "What's in a Name?" *Writing Lab Newsletter* 13.2 (1988): 4, 8. Contends that the word *writing* in *writing center* may cause some high school science and social science teachers to avoid referring their students for tutoring. Suggests schools should name centers carefully.

0594. Waldrep, Thomas D. "Redefining the Writing Center: Helping Clients Alter Their Composing Processes." *CEA Forum* 12.3 (1982): 1-2. Argues writing centers should focus on helping students deal with the composing process rather than on correcting errors.

0595. Waldrep, Tom. "A New Model for Writing Centers." *Teaching English in the Two-Year College* 8.3 (1982): 201-05. Urges that writing centers extend their services, not only intensifying their work with basic writers but moving out into the university and community at large to deal with writing and literacy issues in a number of venues.

0596. Walker, Carolyn. "Communications with the Faculty: Vital Links for the Success of Writing Centers." *Writing Lab Newsletter* 16.3 (1991): 11-16. Contends that a writing center must have faculty endorsement to be effective. Describes one center's bid to gain support by reporting on students' progress, assigning tutor liaisons to classes, and participating in new faculty orientation.

0597. Walker, Jim. "Record Keeping and Specific Feedback: Prerequisites to Realized Potential in Writing-Lab Function." *Writing Lab Newsletter* 5.2 (1980): 5-7. A narrative of three writing labs that established inadequate systems of record keeping and feedback and the implications of this failure to the writing labs' operations and eventual success or failure.

0598. Wallace, Ray. "Sharing the Benefits and the Expense of Expansion: Developing a Cross-Curricular Cash Flow for a Cross-Curricular Writing Center." *The Writing Center: New Directions*. Ed. Ray Wallace and Jeanne Simpson. New York: Garland, 1991. 82-101. In order to focus on the recurring problem of funding, traces a brief history of the transformation of the remedial "writing lab" into a broader "writing center" that addresses needs of many disciplines. Argues that the wider range of professional services of the "writing center" entitle it to funding from all areas it serves.

0599. Warde, William B., Jr. "Ensuring the Success of a New Writing Center Program." *Writing Lab Newsletter* 7.9 (1983): 8-10. Argues that a writing center's success largely depends upon keeping the university community informed of the center's services and successes. Encourages writing center directors to blow their own horns in announcing use rates, student successes, and future plans.

0600. **Ware, Elaine. "Crisis Intervention in the Writing Center."** *Writing Lab Newsletter* **10.10 (1986): 5-8.** Explores problems posed by emotionally troubled students who disrupt activities in the writing center. Suggests discussing crisis intervention during tutor training.

0601. **Westcott, Holly. "A Different Kind of Writing Center."** *Writing Lab Newsletter* **10.5 (1986): 8-11.** Describes a writing center that offers self-paced writing courses rather than drop-in tutorial services. Contends such classes allow students to follow an established schedule and receive immediate feedback from instructors.

0602. **Whitt, Margaret. "Writing Center Travels to Residence Halls."** *Writing Lab Newsletter* **15.3 (1990): 15-16.** Describes the logistical difficulties (eventually overcome) of opening a branch writing center in residence halls three nights a week. Suggests this approach as a viable way of expanding services.

0603. **Wolcott, Willa. "Establishing Writing Center Workshops."** *The Writing Center Journal* **7.2 (1987): 45-49.** Claims that workshops meet the specific needs of students and also help writing centers to expand their roles on campus. Offers a six-step process for organizing workshops.

0604. **Wolcott, Willa. "A Writing Center Reaches Out."** *Writing Lab Newsletter* **5.9 (1981): 7-9.** Discusses five methods by which a writing center can broaden the scope of its programs on a campus: laboratory classes, independent skills programs for referrals and volunteers, minicourses, diagnostic testing of writing skills, and incorporation into courses in the curriculum.

0605. **Wolterbeek, Marc. "Resisting and Accepting Writing Centers: A Personal View."** *Writing Lab Newsletter* **11.5 (1987): 10-11.** Discusses the role of faculty resistance or acceptance in the success or failure of a writing center. Argues that fear of the unknown causes most of the resistance while teachers who welcome challenge and change generally accept and assist the development of a new writing center.

0606. **Woodward, Pauline. "The Writing Center's Fate."** *Writing Lab Newsletter* **5.10 (1981): 8-9.** Argues that writing centers will not be funded unless they earn strong support from three constituencies: students who need help with their writing, able students interested in writing as a craft, and faculty members interested in incorporating writing into their pedagogy.

0607. **Wright, Anne. "Establishing a High School Writing Lab."** *Writing Lab Newsletter* **17.5 (1993): 4-6.** Offers step-by-step advice on setting up a high school writing center. Suggests schools first formulate the center's philosophy, then find a location, choose equipment (including computers and software), and hire staff.

0608. **Wright, Anne. "Keeping Records in the Writing Lab."** *The High School Writing Center: Establishing and Maintaining One.* **Ed. Pamela B. Farrell. Urbana: NCTE, 1989. 93-97.** Describes a model record keeping form and periodic reports generated from it.

0609. **Wright, Sharon. "Getting the Biggest Bang for the Buck in the Writing Center."** *Writing Lab Newsletter* **18.8 (1994): 14-16.** Offers writing center directors a five-step process for spending their limited funds most efficiently: determine needs, plan conference area, plan computer area, choose equipment, and establish a budget.

0610. **Yahner, William. "Explaining and Justifying Writing Centers: One MORE Example."** *Writing Lab Newsletter* **18.2 (1993): 5-6.** Offers writing center directors who seek to avoid the budget axe a format for demonstrating their centers' usefulness. Focuses primarily on the writing center's role in retention, facilitating faculty development, and supporting writing across the curriculum programs.

0611. **Yee, Nancy. "Writing Proficiency Examinations: A New Perspective on Writing Labs."** *Writing Lab Newsletter* **10.1 (1985): 3-6.** Sees the writing center as an essential element in addressing student writing problems, particularly at universities requiring writing proficiency examinations. Includes poll indicating how many universities requiring such examinations have writing centers.

# Writing Across the Curriculum

0612. **Aarons, Victoria, and Willis A. Salomon. "The Writing Center and Writing Across the Curriculum: Some Observations on Theory and Practice."** *Focuses* **2.2 (1989): 91-102.** Claims that the "cross-curricular implications" of writing centers have been neglected because of the false assumption that writing can be taught apart from the methods and subject matters of the academic disciplines. Argues for a clearer understanding of the writing center's role in relation to writing in all disciplines.

0613. **Adams, Katherine H. "Satellite Writing Centers: A Successful Model for Writing Across the Curriculum."** *The Writing Center: New Directions.* **Ed. Ray Wallace and Jeanne Simpson. New York: Garland, 1991. 73-81.** Describes three writing centers serving different discourse communities (arts and sciences, journalism, law) and suggests the benefits of these satellites of the drop-in center that serves the entire campus.

0614. **Asselin, Bonnie, and Nancy Schultz. "Optimizing the Writing Center for an Interdisciplinary Course."** *Writing Lab Newsletter* **12.9 (1988): 5-6.** Describes how a writing center prepared its tutors to assist students in an interdisciplinary composition and psychology course.

0615. **Besser, Pam. "Bridging the Gap: The Theoretically and Pedagogically Efficient Writing Center."** *Writing Lab Newsletter* **16.3 (1991): 6-8.** Points to the growing need, particularly in community colleges, for interdisciplinary writing centers equipped and staffed to assist students from all disciplines and educational backgrounds.

0616. Bizzaro, Patrick. "Writing Center Assistance to Writing Across the Curriculum." *Writing Lab Newsletter* 10.8 (1986): 3-5. Outlines a three-stage program to improve writing among college students by instituting a writing across the curriculum program supported by a campus-wide writing center. The program involves the creation of the center, the establishment of a university writing center steering committee, and the development of a writing across the curriculum program.

0617. Brooks, Barbara. "Writing Across the Curriculum." *The High School Writing Center: Establishing and Maintaining One.* Ed. Pamela B. Farrell. Urbana: NCTE, 1989. 137-41. Describes a number of successful writing center sponsored projects for working with disciplines other than English, not only working with students but also helping teachers develop assignments and computing skills.

0618. Chase, Geoffrey W. "Integrating the Writing Center into the Curriculum." *Writing Lab Newsletter* 9.6 (1985): 1-4. Argues that writing as a way of learning provides opportunities and a theoretical framework for integrating the writing center into writing instruction across the disciplines.

0619. Cozzens, Christine S. "The Writing Center and the Senior Thesis: A Context for Writing as Teaching." *Writing Lab Newsletter* 13.9 (1989): 11-14. Examines a tutoring program in which classroom writing instructors act as mentors for students from a variety of disciplines working on senior thesis projects.

0620. Devet, Bonnie, Peter Cramer, Alice France, Forest Mahon, Mary-Jane Ogawa, Tammy Raabe, and Brandon Rogers. "Writing Lab Consultants Talk About Helping Students Writing Across the Disciplines." *Writing Lab Newsletter* 19.9 (1995): 8-10. Commentary from peer tutors in a writing across the curriculum program, touching on ways tutors responded to different students across the disciplines, rhetorical strategies used by such students, and benefits to the tutors from the experience. Concludes that tutors often do their best work when they respond to discipline-specific writing as nonexperts in that discipline.

0621. Dinitz, Susan, and Diane Howe. "Writing Centers and Writing-Across-the-Curriculum: An Evolving Partnership." *The Writing Center Journal* 10.1 (1989): 45-51. Chronicles the process of setting up a writing center writing across the curriculum program partnership.

Presents three models of such a partnership, one requiring students to visit the writing center, another assigning tutors to particular classes, and a third using tutors to facilitate in-class peer critique groups. Explores drawbacks and advantages of each model.

0622. **Dixon, Mimi Still, and Maureen S. Fry. "Raising Consciousness Across the Curriculum: How Faculty Can Own Responsibility for Student Writing."** *Writing Lab Newsletter* **16.2 (1991): 12-15.** Examines the role of faculty attitudes in the successful integration of a university writing center and writing across the curriculum program. Illustrates how the writing center helped raise the faculty's consciousness of the importance of writing in the learning process and got the faculty to accept responsibility for helping students improve their writing.

0623. **Fearing, Bertie E., and W. Keats Sparrow. "Tutoring Business and Technical Writing Students in the Writing Center."** *Writing Centers: Theory and Administration.* **Ed. Gary A. Olson. Urbana: NCTE, 1984. 215-26.** Provides ways to help tutors deal with business and technical writing students in the writing center by outlining six basic principles of technical writing.

0624. **Feirn, Mary. "Writing in Health Science: A Short Course for Graduate Nursing Students."** *Writing Lab Newsletter* **13.5 (1989): 5-8.** Describes a short, noncredit course one writing center offered graduate nursing students in order to address discipline-specific writing problems and supplement individual writing conferences.

0625. **Freisinger, Diana, and Jill Burkland. "Talking About Writing: The Role of the Writing Lab."** *Language Connections: Writing and Reading Across the Curriculum.* **Ed. Toby Fulwiler and Art Young. Urbana: NCTE, 1982. 167-79.** Uses sample paper to illustrate both the tutoring process and the role the writing center can play in a writing across the curriculum program. Outlines a five-step general plan of action for the tutor: talk, read, praise, question, decide on course of action.

0626. **Fulwiler, Toby. "The Case for Faculty Workshops."** *Writing Lab Newsletter* **4.2 (1979): 4-5.** Argues that neither the composition teacher nor the writing lab tutor is likely to bring about a permanent change in student writing behavior unless that change is reinforced in the student's courses in all disciplines. Writing labs can be instrumental in training faculty to see the benefits of writing instruction by offering workshops on issues and techniques.

0627. **Gaskins, Jake. "How We've Grown as a Writing (Across the Curriculum) Center." *Writing Lab Newsletter* 16.8 (1992): 6-8.** Describes how a writing center's successful incorporation into a writing across the curriculum program led to improved facilities, a higher level of expertise for the staff, more faculty commitment, and better teamwork among directors of the writing program.

0628. **Grattan, Mary. "The Writing Center as a Consulting Service for Content Area Faculty." *Writing Lab Newsletter* 9.7 (1985): 1-3.** Discusses four practices that help make the writing center the focal point of a writing across the curriculum program: content area writing labs, assignment guides, worksheets, and writing booklets.

0629. **Grattan, Mary C., and Susan P. Robins. "Content Area Models: A Key to Student Writing Improvement in Writing Center Programs." *Teaching English in the Two-Year College* 9.2 (1983): 117-21.** Suggests that faculty members from various content areas work together with the English department to teach composition and provide the writing center with models of writing used in those content areas.

0630. **Harris, Muriel. "The View from the Writing Lab: Another Way to Evaluate a Writing Program." *WPA: Writing Program Administration* 5.2 (1981): 13-19.** Claims writing labs offer another means to evaluate the efficacy of writing programs. Offers guidelines for evaluating writing labs in relation to writing programs, ranging from what kinds of help writing labs provide students to whether the lab is a resource place for teachers as well as students.

0631. **Harris, Muriel. "The Writing Center and Tutoring in WAC Programs." *Writing Across the Curriculum: A Guide to Developing Programs.* Ed. Susan H. McLeod and Margot Soven. Newbury Park: Sage, 1992. 155-74.** Points out writing centers can offer writing across the curriculum programs "a pedagogically and theoretically sound" approach to teaching students to write in the disciplines. Claims tutoring should take place in a writing center because its supportive atmosphere aids peer tutors as true collaborators with students.

0632. **Haviland, Carol Peterson. "Writing Centers and Writing-Across-the-Curriculum: An Important Connection." *Writing Center Journal* 5.2/6.1 (1985): 25-30.** Argues that writing centers' connections to writing across the curriculum programs can help writing centers escape the "fix-it shop" roles they must so frequently assume and thus neglect a larger focus on the thinking/writing skills that build confident, competent writers.

0633. **Hocks, Elaine. "A Method of Interpreting and Writing About Literature."** *Writing Lab Newsletter* **8.9 (1984): 6-9.** Discusses the ways in which writing center tutors can be of help to students who are writing papers for literature courses. Emphasizes identifying the theme and the plot of the literary work and then applying an "algebraic" system of plot plus three elements in order to analyze the work's meaning.

0634. **Holderer, Robert W. "Holistic Scoring: A Valuable Tool for Improving Writing Across the Curriculum."** *Writing Center Perspectives.* **Ed. Byron L. Stay, Christina Murphy, and Eric H. Hobson. Emmitsburg: NWCA Press, 1995. 132-45.** To help improve writing in all disciplines, recommends that writing center help instructors develop a scoring guide (drawing on principles of analytic, primary trait, and holistic scoring) that can be used during drafting.

0635. **Hollis, Karyn. "More Science in the Writing Center: Training Tutors to Lead Group Tutorials on Biology Lab Reports."** *The Writing Center: New Directions.* **Ed. Ray Wallace and Jeanne Simpson. New York: Garland, 1991. 247-62.** Recounts successful attempt to prepare student tutors from the humanities to work with students from the hard sciences, illustrating the formats and other conventions with which they need to become familiar.

0636. **Hughes, Bradley T. "Writing Center Outreach: Sharing Knowledge and Influencing Attitudes About Writing."** *The Writing Center: New Directions.* **Ed. Ray Wallace and Jeanne Simpson. New York: Garland, 1991. 39-55.** Describes an outreach program for teachers of all disciplines, consisting of both brief classroom visits and longer instructional units presented to classes. Discusses advantages of such a program and provides detailed advice for planning and implementing it.

0637. **Hymes, Kate. "Interdisciplinary Programs and the Writing Lab: The Evolution of a College Writing Lab."** *Writing Lab Newsletter* **5.5 (1981): 5-7.** Argues that the writing lab has a necessary and important role to play in an interdisciplinary writing program because the lab is usually the only instructional facility on campus not constrained by traditional educational and evaluative structures.

0638. **Impson, Beth, Burl Self, Susan Dorsey, Lucinda Hudson, and Laura Johnson. "Integrating WAC and Tutoring Services: Advantages to**

Faculty, Students, and Writing Center Staff." *Writing Lab Newsletter* 16.2 (1991): 5-8, 11. Discusses the value of forming a close partnership between a university's writing center and writing across the curriculum program. The partnership benefits all parties through a clarification of writing assignments, a wider distribution of tutoring services, and a sharper focus on the special problems students in writing-intensive courses are likely to face.

0639. Kiedaisch, Jean, and Sue Dinitz. "'Look Back and Say "So What"': The Limitations of the Generalist Tutor." *The Writing Center Journal* 14.1 (1993): 63-74. Questions the value of generalist tutors' work with students from various academic disciplines. Correlates a tutor's discipline-specific knowledge and high quality tutoring of students from that discipline. Concludes that training tutors in all disciplines would be impractical. Suggests alternative solutions, including campuswide discussions on how each discipline can teach writing more effectively.

0640. Kiedaisch, Jean, and Sue Dinitz. "Using Collaborative Groups to Teach Critical Thinking." *Writing Center Perspectives*. Ed. Byron L. Stay, Christina Murphy, and Eric H. Hobson. Emmitsburg: NWCA Press, 1995. 179-86. Describes a set of tutoring sessions in which small groups of students from an art history class meet with a tutor for discussions before they begin drafting papers; examines the role of the tutor in developing critical thinking skills in these group sessions.

0641. Kinkead, Joyce, Nanette Alderman, Brett Baker, Alan Freer, Jon Hertzke, Sonya Mildon Hill, Jennifer Obry, Tiffany Parker, and Maryann Peterson. "Situations and Solutions for Tutoring Across the Curriculum." *Writing Lab Newsletter* 19.8 (1995): 1-5. In connection with the writing across the curriculum program at Utah State, discusses nine problematic situations that may arise between tutor and student and suggests possible solutions and tradeoffs tutors can draw upon. Also discusses solutions to problems tutors might face in their relationships with professors.

0642. Leahy, Richard. "A Lot of Pleasure, a Bit of Agony: Producing a Newsletter for the Faculty." *The Writing Center: New Directions*. Ed. Ray Wallace and Jeanne Simpson. New York: Garland, 1991. 145-56. Discusses the advantages of a newsletter in publicizing the writing center and especially in enhancing the writing across the curriculum program.

0643. Leahy, Richard. "What the College Writing Center Is—And Isn't." *College Teaching* 38.2 (1990): 43-48. Explains why confusion often surrounds perceptions of writing centers. Defines writing center services available to students in all disciplines and ways their instructors can make writing center services more effective.

0644. Leahy, Richard. "Writing Assistants in Writing-Emphasis Courses: Toward Some Working Guidelines." *Writing Lab Newsletter* 16.9-10 (1992): 11. Discusses some of the problems that occurred when professors misused the writing assistants assigned to their writing-intensive, discipline-specific courses. Provides handout used to clarify the writing assistants' duties.

0645. Leahy, Richard. "Writing Centers and Writing-for-Learning." *The Writing Center Journal* 10.1 (1989): 31-37. Rpt. in 0007. Urges instructors teaching writing across the curriculum courses to make use of expressive ("writing for learning") as well as transactional (writing for a finished product) assignments. Contends that expressive writing can help students better understand the writing process and the concepts being taught in the class. Also suggests writing centers help students with journal writing and freewriting and sponsor ongoing workshops on writing for learning to faculty.

0646. Maimon, Elaine P. "Tourists, Travelers, and Citizens: Teaching Writing in the Twenty-First Century." *Focuses* 4.2 (1991): 109-15. Discusses the writing center as a focal point for writing across the curriculum, which is described as the "leading wedge toward a reform pedagogy that enfranchises students as world citizens."

0647. Mills, Moylan C., and Patricia Rizzolo. "New Directions for the Writing Center: Reaching Beyond the Traditional Center to Provide Additional Student Services and Support for Faculty—A Case Study." *Writing Lab Newsletter* 7.6 (1983): 4-5. Discusses outreach programs used to interact with faculty in all disciplines and inform them of the writing center's offerings as well as to assess what services the writing center could provide to faculty.

0648. Moore, Shelee. "The Tutor's Corner: Robotics and English." *Writing Lab Newsletter* 11.6 (1987): 7. Using an anecdote, illustrates how a peer tutor with no knowledge of engineering helped a student work through a paper on robotics by asking questions that led the student to reassess his writing.

0649. Moreland, Kim. "The Writing Center: A Center for Writing-Across-the-Curriculum Activities." *Writing Lab Newsletter* 10.3 (1985): 1-4. Describes a program in which writing center staff work closely with instructors from all disciplines to improve their students' writing skills. Program involves visiting classrooms, meeting with groups of students in the writing center, and helping the professors to improve their writing assignments.

0650. Murphy, James. "Tutors and Fruitflies." *Writing Lab Newsletter* 15.9 (1991): 5-6. Describes how a writing center director and a genetics professor collaborated in training tutors to assist students with scientific papers.

0651. Papay, Twila Yates. "Compounding Interest: A Writing Center for Teachers." *Teaching English in the Two-Year College* 9.2 (1983): 157-60. Describes writing center involvement in in-service training for teachers, stressing its benefits in helping teachers in all disciplines see themselves as writers and as teachers of writing.

0652. Pemberton, Michael A. "Rethinking the WAC/Writing Center Connection." *The Writing Center Journal* 15.2 (1995): 116-33. Critiques the relationship between writing centers and university writing across the curriculum programs. Contends their missions are often oppositional since the writing center emphasizes a *"pedagogy of the generic"* and writing across the curriculum emphasizes writing for particular academic disciplines. Suggests ways to reconcile the writing center/writing across the curriculum relationship by clarifying the mission of each.

0653. Powers, Judith K., and Jane V. Nelson. "Rethinking Writing Center Conferencing Strategies for Writers in the Disciplines." *Writing Lab Newsletter* 20.1 (1995): 12-15. Contends the typical "model" of tutoring encourages "physical and psychological isolation from the rest of the campus writing community." Explores a new approach to assisting students across the disciplines that involves forming a three-way collaborative partnership among student, tutor, and instructor.

0654. Robbins, Susan P., and Mary C. Grattan. "The Role of Writing Centers in Writing Across the Curriculum." *Writing Lab Newsletter* 7.1 (1982): 4-5. Discusses the writing center's role in tutoring, classroom presentations, and faculty consultations as steps in establishing a writing across the curriculum program at a community college.

0655. **Rothman, Donald L. "Tutoring in Writing: Our Literacy Problem."** *College English* **39 (1977-78): 484-90.** Describes setting up writing center at the University of California—Santa Cruz, with eight tutors from various disciplines to deal with writing problems on campus. Suggests that writing centers become forums for analyzing the basic campus-wide assumptions about education and pedagogy.

0656. **Rowan, Katherine. "Equipping Your Writing Center to Assist Journalistic Writers."** *Writing Lab Newsletter* **15.2 (1990): 1-7.** Distinguishes between journalistic articles and the academic essays students commonly bring to the writing center. Offers short lessons on specific principles of journalism, and suggests tutors prepare handouts on such topics as interviewing, notetaking, leads, and feature writing.

0657. **Samson, Donald. "Tutoring Technical Students in the Writing Center."** *The Writing Center: New Directions.* **Ed. Ray Wallace and Jeanne Simpson. New York: Garland, 1991. 230-46.** Points out the increasing number of technical students needing to be tutored in writing centers, often by other students in communications fields; suggests ways to prepare writing center staff for this challenge, noting the advantages accrued to the student.

0658. **Scanlon, Leone. "Where Does the Writing Center Fit In?"** *Writing Lab Newsletter* **3.8 (1979): 4.** Contends that the writing center can play an important role in promoting the goal of writing throughout the curriculum. Claims the writing center, by nature and definition, lends itself well in practice to the support of interdisciplinary programs.

0659. **Scanlon, Leone C. "Recruiting and Training Tutors for Cross-Disciplinary Writing Programs."** *Writing Center Journal* **6.2 (1986): 37-41.** Emphasizes drawing tutors from a range of disciplines so that they can work more effectively with students' assignments in all disciplines. Also argues that tutor training should include theories about what is unique to different types of discourse in disciplines.

0660. **Smith, Louise Z. "Independence and Collaboration: Why We Should Decentralize Writing Centers."** *Writing Center Journal* **7.1 (1986): 3-10.** Discusses the value of decentralizing the writing center as "a site of specialized knowledge" so that writing centers can work in conjunction with writing across the curriculum programs in extending knowledge across a campus.

**0661. Thaiss, Chris. "Of Havens, Nodes, and No-Center Centers."** *Focuses* **5.1 (1992): 16-26.** Explores the role of the writing center in meeting the evolving needs of the university. Examines the writing center's ties to writing across the curriculum and the consequent "decentering" of its mission. Suggests that the writing center become a clearing house that matches student writers with experts writing in a particular discipline.

**0662. Upton, James. "A Midwife's Guide to Writing for Learning Assignments."** *Writing Lab Newsletter* **15.7 (1991): 12-13.** Describes the "writing to learn" assignments that one high school writing center developed and distributed to teachers. Suggests that teachers can use the assignments to encourage students to explore their ideas through writing. Also lists several "assignments from hell" by way of negative example.

**0663. Waldo, Mark. "The Last Best Place for WAC: The Writing Center."** *WPA: Writing Program Administration* **16.3 (1993): 15-26.** Argues that writing centers provide a "definable space for expertise, with identifiable goals and services that a campus will need to initiate and sustain WAC."

**0664. Waldo, Mark L. "What Should the Relationship Between the Writing Center and Writing Program Be?"** *The Writing Center Journal* **11.1 (1990): 73-80.** Argues that writing centers and university writing programs should be equal partners in teaching writing, forming a symbiotic relationship that uses the strengths of each to provide maximum benefit to the university and its students. Suggests this "powerful union" is too often prevented because English departments view writing centers as inferior.

**0665. Wallace, Ray. "Writing Across the Curriculum: A Faculty Survey."** *Writing Lab Newsletter* **11.5 (1987): 8-10.** Citing the results of a survey of 153 faculty members, identifies the types of writing tasks assigned by various disciplines. Also indicates that most professors listed "overall paper organization, content quality, and development of ideas" as the most useful aspects of writing to master for future success.

**0666. Wallace, Ray. "The Writing Center's Role in the Writing Across the Curriculum Program: Theory and Practice."** *The Writing Center Journal* **8.2 (1988): 43-48. Rpt. in 0007.** Discusses goals and guidelines of the writing center and writing across the curriculum partnership. Details positive actions the writing center took in coordinating the program, including hosting a workshop on designing appropriate writing assignments, recruiting qualified tutors from other disciplines, and creating a weekly tutor training workshop.

0667. **Wilson, Lucy, and Olivia LaBouff. "Going Beyond Remedial: The Writing Center and the Literature Class."** *Writing Center Journal* **6.2 (1986): 19-27.** Discusses writing center workshops on specific reading and writing assignments for literature courses. Describes how writing center personnel worked with English faculty as a way of escaping the "fix-it shop" image of the writing center.

0668. **Wolff, William C. "Writing Services: A New Role for the Writing Center and Faculty."** *The Writing Center: New Directions.* **Ed. Ray Wallace and Jeanne Simpson. New York: Garland, 1991. 110-32.** Describes a workshop organized by a writing center director for faculty and staff, focusing on a particular writing project to encourage forming peer writing groups in various academic areas. Examines the responses of faculty members from five disciplines.

0669. **Yarmove, Jay. "Interlock: A Proposal for a 'Cosmopolitan' Writing Lab."** *Writing Lab Newsletter* **11.10 (1987): 8-9.** Contends that writing centers should hire tutors from a variety of disciplines, able to help student writers in technical, business, and scientific fields. Contends that too many writing centers are suited primarily to help students from English classes.

# Educational Technology

0670. Adams, Ronald. "*PREWRITE*: A Software Review." *Writing Lab Newsletter* 9.10 (1985): 11-12. Discusses the benefits of *PREWRITE*, a companion software program to Mimi Schwartz's textbook, *Writing for Many Roles*.

0671. Baker, Jeffrey S. "An Ethical Question About On-Line Tutoring in the Writing Lab." *Writing Lab Newsletter* 18.5 (1994): 6-7. Questions ethics of on-line tutoring because of the loss of interpersonal contact that can result in students' understanding of complex concepts and the possibility that a student may actually incorporate the tutor's on-line response into his or her own text. Claims on-line dialogue does not permit the "conceptual indeterminacy" and potential creativity, of verbal conversation.

0672. Balester, Valerie. "Electronic Discourse for Writing Consultants." *Writing Lab Newsletter* 18.9 (1994): 10-12. Examines the benefits of using an electronic mail bulletin board for discussions among writing consultants. Benefits include allowing consultants who could not meet face to face to keep in touch, air differences, share insights, make suggestions for improvements of writing center services, bond as a group.

0673. Batson, Trent. "The Alliance for Computers and Writing." *Writing Lab Newsletter* 18.2 (1993): 7. Announces the creation and goals of the Alliance for Computers and Writing.

0674. Berta, Renee. "Micro Style: Computer Modifications for Disabled Students." *Writing Lab Newsletter* 14.9 (1990): 6-7. Urges writing centers to make computers more accessible to students with disabilities.

Suggests centers consider accommodating three primary groups (those with visual, orthopedic, and learning disabilities) by installing speech synthesizers or photosensitive keyboards activated by light wands.

0675. **Brown, Alan. "Coping with Computers in the Writing Center."** *Writing Lab Newsletter* **15.4 (1990): 13-14.** Discusses the effects computers had on a small university's writing center and reviews the strengths and weaknesses of several software programs aimed at helping students improve their writing.

0676. **Brown, Jane Lightcap. "Teaching Word Processing: A Cooperative Effort."** *Writing Center Journal* **6.2 (1986): 11-17.** Discusses how word processing can be taught collaboratively in the writing center by using peer tutors trained as computer assistants.

0677. **Campbell, John, and Greg Larkin. "NAUWriter: A Total, Automated Writing Environment."** *EDU Magazine* **48 (1988): 11- 13.** Describes the development and implementation of NAUWriter, a system of computer instruction in writing, at Northern Arizona University, that combines lesson materials about writing and tools with which writers can actually write. Describes its use in an English department writing lab and other facilities across campus.

0678. **Chappell, Virginia A. "Theorizing in Practice: Tutor Training 'Live, from the VAX Lab.'"** *Computers and Composition* **12 (1995): 227-36.** Describes one portion of tutor training program in which students participate in a weekly E-mail discussion of the connections between their experience as tutors and assigned readings in composition theory and research. Finds these discussions more satisfactory than journals in fostering collaborative pedagogy.

0679. **Child, Robert D. "***PROTEUS***: A Software Review."** *Writing Lab Newsletter* **9.10 (1985): 12-13.** Discusses the operation and pros and cons of *PROTEUS: The Idea Processor,* a prewriting software program that offers students five options for getting started—freewriting, looping, listing, the 5 W's, and cubing.

0680. **Clark, Irene Lurkis. "The Writing Center and the Research Paper: Computers and Collaboration."** *The Writing Center: New Directions.* **Ed. Ray Wallace and Jeanne Simpson. New York: Garland, 1991. 205-15.** Describes *Project Jefferson,* a hypertext instructional program designed to teach students a systematic process for conducting research, and demonstrates how employment of that computer program in the writing center allows students to collaborate on learning those skills.

0681. Crisp, Sally. "You *Can* Teach an Old Dog New Tricks: Observations on Entering the Computer Age." *Writing Lab Newsletter* 11.3 (1986): 12-14. Discusses the various ways a writing center put its new computer cluster to work for student writers, using computers to teach principles of revision, the writing process, word processing, and problem solving.

0682. Crump, Eric. "A Dialogue on OWLing in the Writing Lab: Some Thoughts on Michael Spooner's Thoughts." *Writing Lab Newsletter* 18.6 (1994): 6-8. Responding to Michael Spooner (entry 0752), claims the changing nature of writing (from print to electronic media) will eventually change the nature of tutoring as well. Argues that writing centers need to continue providing face-to-face tutoring while they embrace the new computer technologies and the possibilities they offer for online tutoring.

0683. Crump, Eric. "Online Community: Writing Centers Join the Network World." *Writing Lab Newsletter* 17.2 (1992): 1-5. Explains the purpose and benefits of WCenter, an electronic forum for writing center specialists. Argues that the E-mail distribution list supplements other communication outlets, such as *Writing Lab Newsletter* and *Writing Center Journal*. Also claims that WCenter offers writing center personnel moral support, a sense of community, and a chance to participate in ongoing, informal discussions about issues that concern them.

0684. Crump, Eric. "Voices from the Net: E-mail: Rebirth of Letter Writing?" *Writing Lab Newsletter* 18.5 (1994): 10-11. Presents on-going conversation from WCenter on the advantages of E-mail as a mode of communication. Among other comments, suggests E-mail may revive letter writing, but in a form that reflects the language and speed of the new medium.

0685. Crump, Eric. "Voices from the Net: Putting Out the Welcome Mat for Tutors." *Writing Lab Newsletter* 17.8 (1993): 10-12. Assures peer tutors that they are welcome to join the discussion on WCenter and discusses ways to make E-mail more accessible to undergraduates.

0686. Crump, Eric. "Voices from the Net: Shaping Writing Center Computer Labs." *Writing Lab Newsletter* 17.6 (1993): 4-6. Offers discussion from WCenter correspondents about the ideal computer lab for writing centers. Suggestions include planning for plenty of space, purchasing laptops for flexible and unobtrusive computing power, and installing laser printers.

0687. Cullen, Roxanne, and Sandra Balkema. "Generating a Professional Portfolio in the Writing Center: A Hypertext Tutor." *Computers and Composition* 12 (1995): 195-201. Describes role of one writing center in school-wide, discipline-specific portfolio assignments. Describes advantages of constructing a hypercard program on portfolio development, with input from instructors in various disciplines, rather than training tutors as specialized readers.

0688. Davis, Kevin. "Data Bases in the Writing Center: The PC as Administrative Record Keeper." *Writing Lab Newsletter* 11.10 (1987): 5-6. Lauds the personal computer's potential for keeping and accessing information about student visits to the writing center. Recommends, in particular, the *Appleworks Data Base*.

0689. Donnelly, Anne. "Educational Technology Serves Diverse Student Needs." *EDU Magazine* 48 (1988): 17-18. Discusses the use of educational technology in the Learning Center at the State University of New York—College of Agriculture and Technology to address the writing, reading, and computational needs of an increasingly diverse student population.

0690. Douglas, Michael A. "A Successful Individualized Writing Lab Module." *Journal of Developmental Education* 16.3 (1993): 24-26. Reports success of using teacher-prepared, computer-assisted module for underprepared students faced with a state-mandated writing exam. Students using this method succeeded at a higher rate than those using more traditional methods.

0691. Emmett, Bill. "Another View of *WANDAH: HBJ Writer*." *The Writing Center Journal* 8.1 (1987): 55-58. Acknowledges weaknesses of the program but recommends it as successful in its limited mission. Contends it offers some students valuable help.

0692. Farrell, Pamela B. "Computers Interact with Writers and Tutors." *The High School Writing Center: Establishing and Maintaining One.* Ed. Pamela B. Farrell. Urbana: NCTE, 1989. 107-10. Maintains that computers facilitate collaboration among students, providing a neutral ground for discussion and offering immediate feedback and ease in revision.

0693. **Farrell, Pamela B. "Writer, Peer Tutor, and the Computer: A Unique Relationship."** *The Writing Center Journal* **8.1 (1987): 29-33.** Presents the computer as neutral meeting ground for tutor and student and as writing partner. Suggests that tutoring at the computer enhances collaboration.

0694. **Fort, Jerry Sue. "Testing Retrieval Skills in the Middle School Writing Lab."** *English in Texas* **24.3 (1993): 10-12.** Describes a series of exercises in which students use computers to decipher a numerical/linguistic code to retrieve information and learn grammar skills and deductive reasoning. Concludes that writing labs offer teachers and students opportunities for creative word processing classes that test and enhance thinking skills.

0695. **Gaskins, Jake, and Mason Emerson. "More Apples in Another Center."** *Writing Lab Newsletter* **10.6 (1986): 1-2.** Contends that adding computers to the writing center helps tutors tailor their instruction to meet the needs of individual writers.

0696. **Greene, Wendy Tibbetts. "What Should a Computer-Assisted Composition Lab Be?"** *Writing Lab Newsletter* **10.7 (1986): 10-12.** Discusses one writing center's struggle to convert the faculty and students into computer users. Concludes that the computer lab needs to be convenient and must reserve time for faculty-only use in order to win converts.

0697. **Grubbs, Katherine. "Some Questions About the Politics of On-Line Tutoring in Electronic Writing Centers."** *Writing Lab Newsletter* **19.2 (1994): 7, 12.** Expresses concerns about tutoring on line, including interpersonal power issues and the loss of face-to-face contact with students.

0698. **Harris, Muriel, and Michael Pemberton. "Online Writing Labs (OWLs): A Taxonomy of Options and Issues."** *Computers and Composition* **12 (1995): 145-59.** Outlines widely available technologies (E-mail, Gopher, Worldwide Web, newsgroups, synchronous chat systems, automated file retrieval systems) and factors to consider in choosing among them. Among those factors are network security, computer illiteracy, institutional missions, writing center missions, computing center priorities, and programmers' attitudes.

0699. **Hobson, Eric. "Coming in Out of the Silence."** *Writing Lab Newsletter* **17.6 (1993): 7-8.** Applauds the sense of community and the quality of advice, experience, and information writing center personnel derive from WCenter, the E-mail discussion group.

0700. **Holdstein, Deborah. "Computerized Instruction in Writing at the Illinois Institute of Technology: Practice, Editing, and Motivation for the Engineering Student." *Writing Lab Newsletter* 8.7 (1984): 6-8.** Argues that computerized instruction allows students to practice basic skills and develop the confidence to overcome writing anxiety. Describes the program of computerized instruction and its benefits for engineering students, many of whom are "reluctant" writers needing "fine tuning."

0701. **Hollis, Karyn. "Scheduler, Record Keeper, Teacher: The Computer in the Writing Program at Dickinson College." *Writing Lab Newsletter* 15.1 (1990): 11-13.** Discusses the various ways in which the writing center at Dickinson College (PA) uses computers, focusing primarily on programs such as *Idealog* and *Access* that facilitate writing.

0702. **Holmes, Leigh Howard. "Expanding Turf: Rationales for Computers in Writing Labs." *Writing Lab Newsletter* 9.10 (1985): 13-14.** Argues that including computers in writing labs helps counter the perception of the lab as a place only for remedial writers. Since all students can come to the lab to use computers to word process and text analyze their papers, the function and atmosphere of the lab change.

0703. **Holmes, Leigh Howard. "Word Processing Theme Comments in the Writing Lab." *Writing Lab Newsletter* 8.6 (1984): 6-7.** Discusses the value of developing software that would enable tutors and teachers to annotate student papers rather than use the customary grammar checklist.

0704. **Jacobsen, Beatrice. "The Apple in the Center." *Writing Lab Newsletter* 9.3 (1984): 9-10.** Tells of the introduction of an Apple II computer into a writing center's offerings and its benefits for freewriting and final editing.

0705. **Johanek, Cindy, and Rebecca Rickly. "Online Tutor Training: Synchronous Conferencing in a Professional Community." *Computers and Composition* 12 (1995): 237-46.** Describes the synchronous conferencing system (*Daedalus INTERCHANGE*) used in tutor training program and examines transcripts excerpted from four sessions to show how the system supports the goals of the training program.

0706. **Jordan-Henley, Jennifer, and Barry Maid. "MOOving Along the Information Superhighway: Writing Centers in Cyberspace."** *Writing Lab Newsletter* **19.5 (1995): 1-6.** Describes a Cyberspace project to create an Internet writing center to join tutors at the University of Arkansas—Little Rock with students at Roane State Community College (TN). Argues that the resulting MOO (a multi-user, real-time, synchronous computer link) disrupts the traditional classroom hierarchy, gives students more responsibility for their own learning, and enhances narrative and computer programming skills.

0707. **Jordan-Henley, Jennifer, and Barry M. Maid. "Tutoring in Cyberspace: Student Impact and College/University Collaboration."** *Computers and Composition* **12 (1995): 211-18.** Describes and evaluates impact of collaboration in which students at Roane State Community College (TN) used E-mail to send papers to graduate student tutors at the University of Arkansas—Little Rock, for comments and subsequently had a synchronous conference at a cyberspace writing center. Writers devoted increased time to revision, while tutors reflected on differences in tutoring styles under differing conditions.

0708. **Kemp, Fred. "Getting Smart with Computers: Computer-Aided Heuristics for Student Writers."** *The Writing Center Journal* **8.1 (1987): 3-10.** Challenges the "replacement fallacy," the belief that computers can or should replace the human tutor. Proposes using heuristic computer-assisted learning programs with composition students. Describes several heuristic programs (*Topoi, SEEN, Writer's Helper, Idealog, LOGO*) that writing center directors might use to augment tutorials.

0709. **Kinkead, Joyce. "Computer Conversations: E-Mail and Writing Instruction."** *College Composition and Communication* **38.3 (1987): 337-41.** Discusses various ways to use E-mail to teach writing. Includes description of a tutor, based in the writing center, who replies to questions about writing within 24 hours of receiving a transmission.

0710. **Kinkead, Joyce. "The Electronic Writing Tutor."** *Writing Lab Newsletter* **13.4 (1988): 4-5.** Examines advantages and disadvantages of tutoring via E-mail. Suggests writing centers should prepare to offer this service to give nontraditional students access to writing assistance.

0711. **Kleen, Janice. "The Teaching of Spelling: A Success Story."** *Writing Lab Newsletter* **6.4 (1981): 1-2.** Discusses the success of using a filmstrip, *Spelling Techniques: Tactile Kinesthetic Method*, to teach spelling to students in the writing center.

0712. **Kotler, Lorne. "Teacher and Computer Joining Forces in a Writing Lab."** *Writing Lab Newsletter* **7.7 (1983): 1-3.** Discusses a computer-based instructional management system called RSVP (Response System with Variable Prescriptions) that was developed by faculty at a community college "to manage with prescriptive feedback the learning of a heterogeneous group of students." Discusses the benefits of this system to writing lab and classroom instruction.

0713. **Kriewald, Gary L. "Computer-Programmed Instruction in Elements of Grammar for Students with Remedial Problems in Writing."** *Writing Lab Newsletter* **4.6 (1980): 4-5.** Discusses a program of computerized instruction known as *WRITE 101-105*, designed as an adjunct to a writing center's tutorial program in composition. Considers the special benefits of this program for students who display " chronic deficiencies in elementary composition."

0714. **Leder, Priscilla. "Software for the Writing Lab: A Series of Reviews."** *Writing Lab Newsletter* **13.6 (1989): 13-16.** Reviews computer software programs of interest to writing centers, including *PROTEUS, MARK-UP, DOUBLE-UP, RHUBARB, RAPID RECALL II*, and *Norton Textra Writer*.

0715. **Levin, Robert L. "Microcomputers in the Writing Center."** *Writing Lab Newsletter* **10.6 (1986): 8-11.** Notes the fear with which many students and faculty members approach computers. Numbers among the advantages computers their ability to change the instructional context of writing, to improve the ease of composition and revision, and to level the playing field for students with disabilities.

0716. **Loxterman, Alan S. "A Multi-Media Writing Text."** *Writing Lab Newsletter* **5.1 (1980): 5-6.** Reports on the successful use of *Process One: A College Writing Program* in individualized tutorials with two students. *Process One* combines a college level rhetoric and grammar with film strips and cassettes that correspond to each chapter.

0717. **Luchte, Jeanne. "Computer Programs in the Writing Center: A Bibliographical Essay."** *The Writing Center Journal* **8.1 (1987): 11-19.** Focuses on how writing center tutors can use the computer in helping student writers compose. Examines how computers benefit student writers in the prewriting, organizing, drafting, revising, and proofreading stages of the composing process. Surveys various software programs aimed at facilitating composition.

0718. Marek, Margaret-Rose. "The Life and Times of a Writing Center Technical Coordinator." *Writing Lab Newsletter* 14.5 (1990): 15-16. A humorous look at the problems associated with installing and debugging a writing center's computer cluster.

0719. Marshall, Rick. "Word Processing and More: The Joys and Chores of a Writing Lab Computer." *Writing Lab Newsletter* 11.10 (1987): 1-4. Examines the many benefits of bringing computers into a writing center but cautions that tutors and staff will require extensive training before they can help students take full advantage of hardware and software.

0720. Mason, Richard. "Unnecessary Hangups." *Writing Lab Newsletter* 3.4 (1978): 1-2. Argues that, while a healthy skepticism is needed, "unrealistic negativism" toward the use of machines and commercial program materials "can stymy progress in writing lab development."

0721. Mason, Richard G. "Computer Assistance in the Writing Lab." *Writing Lab Newsletter* 6.9 (1982): 1-5. Explains how computer-assisted instruction (CAI) works in the writing lab and discusses it pros and cons. Focuses on text-processing and text-analysis software and also discusses the challenges CAI will pose for writing labs in the future.

0722. Maxwell, Mark. "Writing Centers Offer Personal Touch in the World of Computer Composition." *Communication: Journalism Education Today* 24.2 (1991): 2-5. Describes a high school writing center in a computerized tutoring room, where students can get individual assistance with their writing and become familiar with computer technology at the same time. Outlines common activities and problems of one such center.

0723. Nelson, Jane, and Cynthia A. Wambeam. "Moving Computers into the Writing Center: The Path to Least Resistance." *Computers and Composition* 12 (1995): 135-43. Urges that writing centers take a leading role in implementing technology on campuses by forming alliances with information technologists. Such collaborative efforts as online writing labs (OWLs) and computer classrooms can help shape future directions of writing instruction.

0724. Neuleib, Janice, and Maurice Scharton. "Tutors and Computers, an Easy Alliance." *The Writing Center Journal* 11.1 (1990): 49-58. Chronicles the entry of the writing center at Illinois State University into the computer age. Discusses drawbacks (including administrators' assumptions that computers can eventually replace human tutors) and advantages of using computers in writing and tutoring. Lists results of a survey of second-generation computer users, concluding that, despite drawbacks, computers help students of all levels master writing.

0725. Nigliazzo, Marc. "Audiovisual Instruction in a Writing Laboratory." *Tutoring Writing: A Sourcebook for Writing Labs*. Ed. Muriel Harris. Glenview: Scott, Foresman, 1982. 147-52. Discusses advantages and disadvantages of various audiovisual instructional media and computer-assisted learning programs, recommending that these technologies supplement rather than replace tutorials.

0726. Norton, Don, and Kristine Hansen. "The Potential of Computer-Assisted Instruction in Writing Labs." *Tutoring Writing: A Sourcebook for Writing Labs*. Ed. Muriel Harris. Glenview: Scott, Foresman, 1982. 153-62. An introduction to computer-assisted instruction that outlines its potential advantages and disadvantages and discusses areas in which it is most effective.

0727. O'Donoghue, Rosemary. "Entering Electronic Reality." *Writing Lab Newsletter* 17.2 (1992): 6. Relates difficulties writing center director experienced in logging on to BITNET and WCenter.

0728. O'Hear, Michael F. "Homemade Instructional Videotapes: Easy, Fun and Effective." *Writing Lab Newsletter* 7.6 (1983): 1-4. Describes how a writing lab staff wrote scripts and selected music for instructional videotapes that were filmed by the media department. Claims using inexpensive, homemade videotapes reduces the jargon in writing instruction and gets students more interested in learning.

0729. Partenheimer, David. "One View of *WANDAH: HBJ Writer*." *The Writing Center Journal* 8.1 (1987): 49-54. Praises computer-assisted learning but criticizes this particular program as ineffective and even "pedagogically dangerous."

0730. Pitel, Vonna J. "Making the Writing Center Feel at Home in the Library." *Book Report* 10.2 (1991): 38-39. Describes how a computerized writing center was implemented in a high school library, discusses the cooperation of the teacher and librarian in designing and implementing writing assignments, and outlines the way the library supports the writing center.

0731. **Pitel, Vonna J. "Reading, Writing, and Research: A Writing Center in the IMC."** *Writing Notebook: Creative Word Processing in the Classroom* **8.4 (1991): 36-37.** Describes advantages of setting up the writing center as part of an instructional media center, provides preliminary guidelines for establishing such a center, and gives examples of popular writing assignments.

0732. **Posey, Evelyn. "Micro Style."** *Writing Lab Newsletter* **13.3 (1988): 8-9.** Discusses the ambivalence some writing center directors feel toward computers. Attempts to persuade technophobic directors that computers belong in writing centers because they heighten student motivation to write and facilitate the writing and revision processes.

0733. **Posey, Evelyn. "Micro Style: Prewriting Options: Moving Beyond the Word Processor."** *Writing Lab Newsletter* **15.2 (1990): 12-13.** Discusses such computer programs as *Mindwriter, SEEN,* and *Writer's Helper, Stage II* that are designed to help students in their prewriting stages and encourage a recursive approach to writing.

0734. **Posey, Evelyn. "Micro Style: Purchasing Software for the Writing Center."** *Writing Lab Newsletter* **13.9 (1989): 6-8.** Briefly reviews a number of software packages (*Bank Street Writer III, WordPerfect, Microsoft Word, Writer's Workshop, Mindwriter, Descant, Norton Textra Writer, Writer's Helper,* and *HBJ Writer*) writing center directors might consider purchasing.

0735. **Posey, Evelyn. "Micro Style: Using a Word Processor to Enhance Prewriting."** *Writing Lab Newsletter* **14.4 (1989): 12-13.** Examines two ways of enhancing students' prewriting abilities via computer: "invisible writing" (writing with the monitor off) and "cooperating audience" (stationing two readers beside the computer to ask for clarification or elaboration of ideas).

0736. **Posey, Evelyn. "Micro Style: Which One Should I Buy?"** *Writing Lab Newsletter* **13.6 (1989): 7-8.** Offers advice to writing center directors trying to decide which personal computers to purchase for their writing centers. Examines advantages and disadvantages of the two major types of computers—IBM compatibles and Macintoshes. Also recommends specific monitors and printers.

0737. **Reimer, Daniel. "Teaching Theresa."** *Writing Lab Newsletter* **9.1 (1984): 1-2.** Discusses the use of a TRS-80 computer (nicknamed "Theresa") to teach editing skills to students in the writing lab.

0738. **Rhyan, Donald. "Autotutor: A Branching Self-Instruction Program."** *Writing Lab Newsletter* **2.6 (1978): 2.** Discusses the Autotutor System, an individual viewing console into which 35 mm filmstrip cassettes are loaded. The system offers individualized, programmed learning to writers.

0739. **Rosaschi, Gaylene. "Computer-Assisted Instruction."** *Writing Lab Newsletter* **2.7 (1978): 4.** Reports on the use of the Time-Shared, Interactive, Computer-Controlled Information Television (TICCIT) computer system in the writing center at Brigham Young University (UT). The system allows students the option of choosing their own learning strategy as they move through units on Rules, Examples, Practice Problems, and Helps.

0740. **Roth, Emery, II. "Computer Miracles and Tutor Restraint."** *Writing Lab Newsletter* **13.5 (1989): 10-12.** Discusses the benefits computers reap for middle school writing students. Contends that students who ordinarily put little effort into writing sit and write for hours at the computer. Also argues that when students are intensely engaged in work on computers, tutors do more harm than good by volunteering their help.

0741. **Scharton, Maurice. "The Third Person: The Role of the Computer in Writing Centers."** *Computers and Composition* **7.1 (1989): 37-48.** Employs case studies to examine the effectiveness of computer in four areas: tutor-student interaction, editing, large scale structural revision, and printing.

0742. **Schmidt, Deborah A. "The Tutors' Corner."** *Writing Lab Newsletter* **11.7 (1987): 7.** Discusses the role of word processors in helping motivate and teach students to rethink and revise their texts. Suggests that computers allow students to temporarily forget the need to make corrections and focus on expressing their ideas.

0743. **Selfe, Cynthia.** *Creating a Computer-Supported Writing Facility: A Blueprint for Action.* **Advances in Computers and Composition Studies. Houghton: Michigan Technological University, 1989.** A practical guide for establishing and maintaining a computer-supported facility for writing instruction. Divided into three major sections: "Planning for a Computer-Supported Writing Facility," "Operating a

Computer-Supported Writing Facility," and "Improving a Computer-Supported Writing Facility."

0744. **Selfe, Cynthia. "Creating a Computer-Supported Writing Lab: Sharing Stories and Creating Vision."** *Computers and Composition* **4 (1987): 44-65.** Discusses the design of a computer-based writing lab, focusing on planning, funding, staffing, and issues of physical space. Suggests that computer-assisted writing instruction complements many dimensions of the writing tutorial.

0745. **Serico, Joseph G. "Making the Computer Writing Center a Reality."** *Writing Lab Newsletter* **10.9 (1986): 5-6.** Discusses the virtues of making computers available to students in a high school writing center. Contends that computers attract nonremedial students to the center and allow tutors to address process-oriented issues with these writers.

0746. **Shurbutt, S. Bailey. "Integration of Classroom Computer Use and the Peer Evaluation Process: Increasing the Level of Composition Proficiency Through Student Revision."** *The Writing Center Journal* **8.1 (1987): 35-42.** Contends computers help students become less reluctant to make major structural revisions of their essays, enhancing student creativity and fluency. Cites case studies to demonstrate advantages of combining computer use with peer evaluation.

0747. **Sills, Caryl. "Text and Texture: The Advantages of Computer Networks for Writing Instruction."** *Composition Chronicle* **3.7 (1990): 4-6.** Discusses advantages of teaching writing in a writing lab computer center, including allowing students to share texts through an interactive network, carry on electronic dialogues, and respond quickly to collaboratively written projects. Another advantage is immediate and reliable dissemination of teaching materials.

0748. **Simons, Susan. "CAI: Instruction and Change in the Writing Center."** *Writing Lab Newsletter* **20.1 (1995): 11, 16.** Cites the changes in writing and writing instruction brought about by increased use of computers in composition. Contends that by working at computers, student writers discover, on their own, that text is fluid and writing is a recursive process. Urges tutors to consider these changes in determining how best to assist writers.

0749. **Simons, Susan, Jim Bryant, and Jeanne Stroh. "Recreating the Writing Center: A Chance Collaboration."** *Computers and Composition* **12 (1995): 161-70.** Writing center director, instructional designer, and computer coordinator describe their collaboration in introducing computers into a community college writing center. Focuses on their search for a satisfactory teaching/learning theory and their search for effective ways of forecasting change and providing support for computer users.

0750. **Sipe, Betty Barbara. "Why Computer Assisted Instruction?"** *The High School Writing Center: Establishing and Maintaining One.* **Ed. Pamela B. Farrell. Urbana: NCTE, 1989. 119-24.** Outlines benefits of computer-assisted instruction and briefly describes a number of available software programs.

0751. **Slattery, Pat. "Technology in the Writing Center: Do We Need It?"** *Writing Lab Newsletter* **11.9 (1987): 6-7.** Examines how 12 writing centers use audio, video, and computer technologies. Finds that none of the centers uses audio equipment as an effective teaching tool, that several use video equipment in tutor training, and that nearly all provide students with access to or instruction on computers.

0752. **Spooner, Michael. "A Dialogue on OWLing in the Writing Lab: Some Thoughts About Online Writing Labs."** *Writing Lab Newsletter* **18.6 (1994): 6-8.** Argues against taking the tutoring function online because of the value of face-to-face contact—complete with facial expression, tone of voice, gestures, and pauses for thought—between tutor and student. Also poses ethical questions about an online tutor's editing text rather than teaching writing.

0753. **Stoddart, Pat. "Revising Aids: A Step Beyond Word Processing."** *The High School Writing Center: Establishing and Maintaining One.* **Ed. Pamela B. Farrell. Urbana: NCTE, 1989. 111-18.** A detailed examination of a software program called *Writer's Aid and Author's Helper* (*WANDAH*), which bundles prewriting and revising activities with an integrated word-processing program.

0754. **Strenski, Ellen, and TA-TALKers. "Virtual Staff Meetings: Electronic Tutor Training with a Local E-Mail Listserv Discussion Group."** *Computers and Composition* **12 (1995): 247-55.** Describes an online discussion group that supplements weekly meetings for 50-member staff of students. Presents the advantages of this system over other electronic delivery systems and suggests potential difficulties.

0755. **Sunstein, Bonnie. "Using Computer Software in the Writing Center."** *Writing Lab Newsletter* **11.5 (1987): 1-2.** Advises choosing by asking several questions about its use, including "What will it do to meet our objectives for better writing and thinking?"

0756. Sunstein, Bonnie, and Joan Dunfey. "A Sampling of Software for the Writing Center." *Writing Lab Newsletter* 11.5 (1987): 2-5. Provides a detailed list of computer programs that writing center directors might find useful. Acknowledges that, since software is constantly changing, the list had already become obsolete upon publication.

0757. Sweeney, Sharon. "Networking Computers at the Learning Center." *Writing Lab Newsletter* 11.9 (1987): 8-9. Shares experience in setting up and running a computer network at a learning center. Suggests directors choose software carefully and consult with network specialists before buying equipment. Warns that the network will likely suffer a number of glitches during its first semester of operation.

0758. Vasile, Kathy, and Nick Ghizzone. "Computer-Integrated Tutoring." *Writing Lab Newsletter* 16.9-10 (1992): 17-19. Describes various strategies tutors can employ in helping students revise on the computer. The strategies include isolating each sentence on the screen to highlight repetition and other problems, underlining key ideas, and cutting and pasting.

0759. Veit, Richard C. "Are Machines the Answer?" *Writing Lab Newsletter* 4.4 (1979): 1-2. Discusses the pros and cons of human contact in writing labs versus machine-assisted instruction and concludes that "humanistic labs" have more to offer students than do programs and machines.

0760. Wood, Gail F. "Making the Transition from ASL to English: Deaf Students, Computers, and the Writing Center." *Computers and Composition* 12 (1995): 219-26. Details series of five two-hour tutoring sessions with a deaf student (whose first language is American Sign Language), carried out entirely in written English via computer. Reports significant increase in fluency and critical awareness of text over the course of the sessions.

0761. Wright, Anne. "Equipment for the Writing Lab/Center." *The High School Writing Center: Establishing and Maintaining One*. Ed. Pamela B. Farrell. Urbana: NCTE, 1989. 103-06. Encourages use of computers, and recommends general types of software. Points out that, in her own writing center, programs on usage, grammar, and punctuation go unused.

# Tutoring Theory

0762. Ady, Paul. "Fear and Trembling at the Center: Student Perceptions about the Tutorial." *Writing Lab Newsletter* 12.8 (1988): 11-12. Finds students were frightened to go to the writing center for help, primarily because they feared criticism. Contends that for a majority of students the writing center is a place "that inspires fear and trembling." Discusses how students' perceptions changed after visiting the center, how centers can diminish student fears, and implications for tutor training.

0763. Allen, Nancy J. "Who Owns the Truth in the Writing Lab?" *Writing Center Journal* 6.2 (1986): 3-9. Argues that decisions on the roles tutors will play in the writing center "reflect fundamental theoretical differences in our goals for a tutorial and in our viewpoint toward writing itself."

0764. Almasy, Rudolph. "The Nature of Writing-Laboratory Instruction for the Developing Student." *Tutoring Writing: A Sourcebook for Writing Labs.* Ed. Muriel Harris. Glenview: Scott, Foresman, 1982. 13-20. Distinguishes between classroom and supplemental writing center instruction, pointing out advantages of the latter.

0765. Almasy, Rudolph, and David England. "Future Teachers as Real Teachers: English Education Students in the Writing Laboratory." *English Education* 10.3 (1979): 155-62. Discusses how the writing center at West Virginia University used English Education majors as peer tutors. Describes how this blend of the theoretical with the practical would help makes these education majors better teachers due to their understanding of individualized instruction.

0766. Anderson, James E., Ellen M. Bommarito, and Laura Seijas. "Writing-Center Tutors Speak Out: An Argument for Peer Tutoring as Teacher Training." *Improving Writing Skills*. Ed. Thom Hawkins and Phyllis Brooks. New Directions for College Learning Assistance 3. San Francisco: Jossey-Bass, 1981. 35-37. Three former tutors discuss how they changed their career goals and entered graduate programs in composition to become writing teachers. Reflect upon how their tutoring experiences enrich their teaching and also their understanding of students.

0767. Arkin, Marian. "Training Writing-Center Tutors: Issues and Approaches." *Improving Writing Skills*. Ed. Thom Hawkins and Phyllis Brooks. New Directions for College Learning Assistance 3. San Francisco: Jossey-Bass, 1981. 25-33. Discusses tutoring as "a distinct and permanent alternative to teaching" and claims tutors should recognize that their contributions to instruction complement classroom teaching and are not inferior to it. Argues tutors must be given a professional identity by developing programs and materials, writing articles, and conducting workshops.

0768. Ashton-Jones, Evelyn. "Asking the Right Questions: A Heuristic for Tutors." *The Writing Center Journal* 9.1 (1988): 29-36. Argues that tutors function simultaneously in three different roles (teacher, intervener, and text expert), each role having duties and purposes that conflict with the others. Offers four categories of heuristic questions to help tutors formulate their own approach to tutoring: establishing rapport, exploring potential, discovering strategies, and ongoing self-review.

0769. Baker, Tracey. "Critical Thinking and the Writing Center: Possibilities." *The Writing Center Journal* 8.2 (1988): 37-41. Argues tutoring that employs inferential reasoning, controlled composition, and sentence combining exercises strengthens students' ability to think critically. Also recommends using Socratic questioning to help students rethink their ideas, thereby making use of their critical thinking abilities.

0770. Barnett, Robert W. "The Invisible Couch in the Tutoring of Writing." *Writing Lab Newsletter* 20.4 (1995): 10-12. Claims that tutors must acknowledge that "on-the-spot counseling is sometimes inevitable" because tutors don't just work with papers but with the real students whose lives affect their writing. Offers narrative examples and general guidelines to suggest that an understanding of the tutor's role as counselor should be an integral part of tutor training.

0771. **Bell, Elizabeth. "The Peer Tutor: The Writing Center's Most Valuable Resource." *Teaching English in the Two-Year College* 9.2 (1983): 141-44.** Describes role of peer tutor in dealing with students, arguing that well-trained peer tutors are particularly adept in guiding other students through the complexities of the writing process.

0772. **Bell, James Harrington. "Tutoring in a Writing Center." Diss. U of Texas at Austin, 1989. *DAI* 50-09A (1989): 2763.** Examines the power relationships in writing center conferences using Thomas J. Reigstad's typology of teacher-centered, structured participation, collaborative, or student-centered conferences. Finds tutors act more often as evaluators than as peers and that most of the conference talk studied focused on finding a thesis and/or how to develop support for a thesis.

0773. **Bishop, Wendy. "Writing from the Tips of Our Tongues: Writers, Tutors, and Talk." *The Writing Center Journal* 14.1 (1993): 30-43.** Explores the role of talk in writing and tutoring, affirming the value of the verbal interchanges between tutor and student. Discusses ownership of text, debunking the "myth of solitary genius" and supporting social constructionist notions of making meaning through collaboration.

0774. **Bizzaro, Patrick, and Hope Toler. "The Effects of Writing Apprehension on the Teaching Behaviors of Writing Center Tutors." *The Writing Center Journal* 7.1 (1986): 37-43.** A survey of 20 writing center tutors identifies types of writing apprehension focused on evaluation, stress, and product; finds that tutors sometimes transmit their writing apprehension by mentioning negative rather than positive aspects of students' writing, acting in an adversarial manner, focusing on errors, and running tutor-oriented conferences.

0775. **Blau, Susan. "Issues in Tutoring Writing: Stories from Our Center." *Writing Lab Newsletter* 19.2 (1994): 1-4.** Points out differences between what writing center consultants claim to do in tutorials and what they really do. Uses five scenarios about dependency, passivity, inappropriate topics, racism, and proofreading to challenge writing center orthodoxy.

0776. **Bloom, Sophie. *Peer and Cross-Age Tutoring in The Schools: An Individualized Supplement to Group Instruction.* United States. Dept. of Health, Education, and Welfare. National Institute of Education. Washington: GPO, 1976.** Provides a brief history of peer tutoring and an overview of the educational theory underlying it. Describes the role of peer tutoring as a supplement to classroom instruction, focusing primarily on reading and other language arts activities in the elementary grades. Includes extensive annotated bibliography on tutoring.

0777. Boswell, James, Jr. "Should Community College Students be Peer Tutors?" *Writing Lab Newsletter* 11.8 (1987): 5-6. Discusses the pros and cons of using freshman and sophomore students as peer tutors in community college writing centers. Justifies the use of peer tutors, claiming they offer a level of encouragement and empathy instructors cannot always provide.

0778. Bowen, Betsy Anne. "Talking About Writing: Collaborative Revision in the Peer Writing Conference." Diss. Carnegie-Mellon U, 1988. *DAI* 49-10A (1988): 2953. Examines the cognitive strategies of participants in tutoring conferences and the relationship between those strategies and the composing process. Claims that the cognitive process model of revision can help explain positive results between tutor and student.

0779. Bramley, Wyn. *Group Tutoring.* New York: Nichols, 1979. Focuses on theories of small group teaching, with particular emphasis upon the interpersonal skills needed by tutors. Draws contrasts between the American system and theories of tutoring and the British. Also contrasts theories of group tutoring with those of one-to-one conferencing.

0780. Broglie, Mary. "From Teacher to Tutor: Making the Change." *Writing Lab Newsletter* 15.4 (1990): 1-3. Argues English teachers who tutor in the writing center must undergo a transformation in philosophy. Claims that tutors and teachers differ in their response to student writing, in how they present themselves, and in their views on whether authority resides in themselves or the student writer.

0781. Brooks, Jeff. "Minimalist Tutoring: Making the Student Do All the Work." *Writing Lab Newsletter* 15.6 (1991): 1-4. Rpt. in 0008. Argues tutors must guard against doing too much work for students. Sets out a minimalist philosophy of tutoring through a series of practical tips on how to focus collaborative efforts on improving student writers (rather than merely perfecting their papers).

0782. Bruffee, Kenneth A. "Peer Tutoring and the 'Conversation of Mankind.'" *Writing Centers: Theory and Administration.* Ed. Gary A. Olson. Urbana: NCTE, 1984. 3-15. Rpt. in 0007. Arguing that thought and writing are both based in conversation, Bruffee offers peer tutoring as a model for instruction in writing centers and throughout the humanities.

0783. **Bruffee, Kenneth A. "Staffing and Operating Peer-Tutoring Writing Centers."** *Basic Writing: Essays for Teachers, Researchers, and Administrators.* **Ed. Lawrence Kasden and Daniel R. Hoeber. Urbana: NCTE, 1980. 141-49.** Argues for the educational effectiveness of using peer tutors in basic writing centers. Claims that peer tutoring "supplements formal classroom instruction in writing by offering an alternative, long-range context for learning."

0784. **Budhecha, Parag K. "The Role of Audience Awareness in Making the Writing Center an Integral Part of the Composition Curriculum."** *Arizona English Bulletin* **35.2 (1993): 29-34.** Argues that, because a writer's awareness of audience is so integral to his or her success, the tutor's role as a representative of that audience is valuable to both tutor and writer. Affirms Linda Flower's distinction between "writer-based" and "reader-based" prose and claims that audience awareness theory links the writing center and the composition curriculum because both graders (classroom instructors) and tutors serve as audiences for student writing.

0785. **Butterworth, Nancy K. "Responding Responsibly to Subjective Viewpoints in Student Writing."** *Focuses* **7.2 (1994): 89-100.** Examines the dilemma of dealing with papers expressing views a tutor finds objectionable and applies Thomas Gordon's concept of "active listening" to suggest a nondirective approach.

0786. **Callaway, Susan J. "Collaboration, Resistance, and the Authority of the Student Writer: A Case Study of Peer Tutoring." Diss. U of Wisconsin—Milwaukee, 1993.** *DAI* **54-07A (1993): 2555.** Argues that a student's "developing authority as a writer is a complex response to her varying relationships to others in the environment of writing." Her negotiation of authority through peer tutoring does not necessarily involve a "happy collaboration" but can occur through resistance and contention. Thus, "theoreticians should begin to address the needs of students who think of themselves as writers independent of the academy's sanction."

0787. **Chapman, David. "Evaluating the Writing Conference."** *Writing Lab Newsletter* **14.5 (1990): 4-8.** Focuses on evaluating writing conferences and concludes that tutors are harsher critics of tutorials than students.

Also finds a troublesome correlation between less successful conferences and students rated as having poor writing ability.

0788. **Chapman, David. "Requiem for a Writing Center."** *Writing Lab Newsletter* 14.4 (1989): 7-8. Offers a satirical look at what could happen to a writing center that embraces a directive, tutor-centered philosophy known as "power tutoring."

0789. **Chase, Geoffrey W. "Problem-Solving in the Writing Center: From Theory to Practice."** *The Writing Center Journal* 7.2 (1987): 29-35. Applies the problem-solving approach of Don Koberg and Jim Bagnall to tutor training. Suggests this seven-stage approach (acceptance, analysis, definition, ideation, selection, implementation, evaluation) provides tutors with a framework for understanding and teaching the writing process.

0790. **Coogan, David. "E-Mail Tutoring, a New Way to Do New Work."** *Computers and Composition* 12 (1995): 171-81. Describes an experiment in tutoring by E-mail and examines the impact of changed conditions on tutoring. Points out that previous computer use in writing centers (autotutorial and word processing) reflected dominant composition models of the time (current-traditional and process, respectively), whereas E-mail seems more nearly aligned with current concern for the social dimensions of writing and learning.

0791. **Coogan, David. "Towards a Rhetoric of On-Line Tutoring."** *Writing Lab Newsletter* 19.1 (1994): 3-5. Explores a number of practical, philosophical, and ethical issues posed by E-mail tutoring. Contends that on-line tutoring returns the attention of tutor and student to where it belongs—on the act of writing.

0792. **Cosgrove, Cornelius. "Conferencing for the 'Learning-Disabled': How We Might Really Help."** *Dynamics of the Writing Conference: Social and Cognitive Interaction.* Ed. Thomas Flynn and Mary King. Urbana: NCTE, 1993. 95-102. Critiques term *learning-disabled*, cautioning against an unquestioning acceptance of this "disease model." Suggests that conferences and process-oriented approaches are the best strategies for dealing with students diagnosed as learning disabled.

0793. **Crisp, Sally, Ruby Bayani, Earnest Cox, Donna Crossland, Chad Fitz, Darryl Haley, Paige James, Briget Laskowski, Ferrol Lattin, Kerri Lowry, Leroy Mayfield, Lisa Mongnobove, Cheryl Patterson, and Charlesena Walker. "Assertive Collaboration in the Writing**

**Center: Discovering Autonomy Through Community."** *Writing Lab Newsletter* **16.7 (1992): 11-16.** Sees *assertive collaboration* as a more accurate description of what goes on in the writing center than *peer tutoring.* Defines *assertive collaboration* as a relationship in which equals work together toward a common goal. Argues that assertive collaboration promotes discovery and clarification of meaning, proactive learning, communication, a sense of community, and creativity.

**0794. Davis, Kevin. "Notes from the Inside."** *Teaching English in the Two-Year College* **18.1 (1991): 18-21.** Argues that peer tutors are particularly suited to their work because their status as students enables them to interpret assignments and professorial expectations.

**0795. DeCiccio, Albert. "Is Gentran Taking the Peer Out of Peer Tutor?"** *Writing Lab Newsletter* **11.6 (1987): 1-5.** Examines the dangers of increased credibility for peer tutors and writing centers. Contends that, as peer tutors assume formalized, "mini-teacher" roles through which they transmit previously generated knowledge, they distance themselves from student writers and undercut their usefulness as peer respondents.

**0796. DeCiccio, Albert. "The Writing Center and Peer Tutoring: Some Observations."** *Writing Lab Newsletter* **12.5 (1988): 3-5.** Discusses whether the peer tutor should scrve as the student writer's equal or as a mini-teacher. Makes strong case for the value of dialogue-based collaboration between student and tutor.

**0797. DeCiccio, Albert C. "Literacy and Authority as Threats to Peer Tutoring: A Commentary Inspired by the Fifth Annual Conference for Peer Tutors in Writing."** *Writing Lab Newsletter* **13.10 (1989): 11-12.** Discusses dangers posed to peer tutoring, collaborative learning, and student empowerment by fears of a literacy crisis and retrenching of teaching authority.

**0798. Edmunds, Jane, Lorraine Lordi, Violet Dagdigian, and Leslie VanWagner. "Authority: Issues and Insights."** *Writing Lab Newsletter* **15.3 (1990): 11-14.** Distinguishes among the guide role (for first-time clients), the counselor role (for clients returning for more help), and the mentor role (for clients who view themselves more as writers than students). Discusses the levels of authority tutors assume in each relationship.

**0799. Farrell, John Thomas. "Some of the Challenges to Writing Centers Posed by Graduate Students."** *Writing Lab Newsletter* **18.6 (1994): 3-**

5. Argues graduate students have little patience with tutors who patronize them, often have an exaggerated sense of anxiety about returning to school, and may rely on outmoded concepts about writing.

0800. **Fishman, Judith. "On Tutors, the Writing Lab, and Writing."** *Tutoring Writing: A Sourcebook for Writing Labs.* **Ed. Muriel Harris. Glenview: Scott, Foresman, 1982. 86-93.** Discusses seeing peer tutors evolve as writers and as teachers of writing, moving away from hunting errors and learning to respond to writers and their writing. Discussion of the general implications of this process to the goals and philosophies of tutoring.

0801. **Fitzgerald, Sallyanne H. "Collaborative Learning and Whole Language Theory."** *Intersections: Theory-Practice in the Writing Center.* **Ed. Joan A. Mullin and Ray Wallace. Urbana: NCTE, 1994. 11-18.** Argues that whole language theory underlies successful collaboration and helps to explain its success. Illustrates by describing how successful tutoring sessions incorporate a full range of language activities (speaking, writing, listening, reading).

0802. **Fletcher, David C. "On the Issue of Authority."** *Dynamics of the Writing Conference: Social and Cognitive Interaction.* **Ed. Thomas Flynn and Mary King. Urbana: NCTE, 1993. 41-50.** Analyzes a student-tutor conference, demonstrating that it is to a large extent a struggle for authority; suggests ways tutors can grant authority to the student writer.

0803. **Flynn, Thomas. "Promoting Higher-Order Thinking Skills in Writing Conferences."** *Dynamics of the Writing Conference: Social and Cognitive Interaction.* **Ed. Thomas Flynn and Mary King. Urbana: NCTE, 1993. 3-14.** Surveys the research on individualized instruction, higher-order thinking, interaction between novices and experts, and productive interactions in writing conferences. Points out that more research is needed on the cognitive dimension of writing conferences to complement the more customary attention to the social level.

0804. **Formo, Dawn M., and Jennifer Welsh. "Tickling the Student's Ear: Collaboration and the Teacher/Student Relationship."** *Writing Center Perspectives.* **Ed. Byron L. Stay, Christina Murphy, and Eric H. Hobson. Emmitsburg: NWCA Press, 1995. 104-11.** Examines some shortcomings of collaborative pedagogy, particularly its tendency to reinforce the hierarchy it attempts to displace; explores the ambiguity of metaphors applied to teacher/student relationship, particularly those related to family. Questions link between these issues and current debates about intellectual property and sexual harassment.

0805. **Freedman, Aviva. "A Theoretic Context for the Writing Lab."** *Tutoring Writing: A Sourcebook for Writing Labs.* **Ed. Muriel Harris. Glenview: Scott, Foresman, 1982. 2-12.** Outlines five-stage, recursive model of writing process as theoretic context for tutoring writing.

0806. **Gillam, Alice M. "Collaborative Learning Theory and Peer Tutoring Practice."** *Intersections: Theory-Practice in the Writing Center.* **Ed. Joan A. Mullin and Ray Wallace. Urbana: NCTE, 1994. 39-53.** Reviews recent critiques of collaborative learning and outlines three models of peer tutoring and their basis in collaborative learning theory. Uses an individual peer tutoring session to demonstrate both the power and limitations of theory to illuminate the session.

0807. **Graves, Richard L. "Breakthroughs: The Satori Experience."** *Focuses* **1.1 (1988): 20-28.** Applies the Zen principle of satori (intuitive breakthrough) to tutoring practice—in particular, to helping students overcome their mental blocks toward writing. Stresses the motivational value of such breakthrough experiences and urges tutors and teachers to understand and avoid stifling them.

0808. **Haas, Teri Sinclair. "A Case Study of Peer Tutors' Writing Conferences with Students: Tutors' Roles and Conversations About Composing." Diss. New York U, 1986.** *DAI* **47-12A (1987): 4309.** Examining the interactions of college peer tutors with students during weekly conferences in a writing center, finds that tutors and students acted as collaborators and talked of the ideas in the students' texts during prewriting or early draft conferences. However, when students brought in teacher-marked drafts, the teacher's purpose controlled the conference; the tutoring pair was constrained by comments that often concerned features of surface correctness. When following teachers' comments, the tutors often became mini-teachers rather than peer collaborators, and students lost control of the conferences and their texts.

0809. **Ham, Elisa. "'T.E.A.C.H.': Five Steps to Applying the Humanistic Approach to Tutoring."** *Writing Lab Newsletter* **20.4 (1995): 15-16.** Draws upon the learning theories of humanistic psychologists such as Carl Rogers, Arthur Combs, and William Glasser and relates these ideas to writing center theory in claiming that Trust, Equality, Acceptance, Care, and Honesty are core values in student-centered tutoring.

0810. **Harada, Janet Louise. "Peer Tutoring as a Social Process." Diss. U of California—Santa Barbara, 1979.** *DAI* **44-09A (1984): 2897.** Contends that successful peer tutoring is a developmental process with four identifiable phases: (1) a social bond between the participants is established, (2) the ways of doing tutoring tasks are explored and tutor and tutee develop a common orientation to the task, (3) the selection and standardization of procedures occurs, and (4) specialization augments individual skills learned in tutoring. Contends that the phases take time to develop and that, if they do not develop in sequence, difficulties arise that hamper successful completion of the tutoring tasks.

0811. **Harred, Larry D., and Thomas J. Russo. "Using Small Groups Effectively in the Lab: Strategies for Improving Student Self-Confidence."** *Writing Lab Newsletter* **12.1 (1987): 7-10.** Describes a pilot program involving discussion groups of freshman writing students led by peer tutors. Contends the groups, meeting without the teacher, fostered a positive, supportive atmosphere for collaboration among the writers. Concludes a majority of students gained a sense of self-efficacy during the course of the program.

0812. **Harris, Muriel. "Collaboration Is Not Collaboration Is Not Collaboration: Writing Center Tutorials vs. Peer-Response Groups."** *College Composition and Communication* **43.3 (1992): 369-383.** Examines differences in perspectives, assumptions, goals, agenda-setting, methods, and outcomes of classroom peer-response groups and writing center tutorials. Argues that although proponents of both activities emphasize the value of "collaboration," they do not use the term in the same way. Suggests peer-response groups primarily help students satisfy requirements of a particular course, whereas tutoring helps students address a wider spectrum of writing skills and problems.

0813. **Harris, Muriel. "Diagnosing Writing-Process Problems: A Pedagogical Application of Speaking-Aloud Protocol Analysis."** *When a Writing Can't Write: Studies in Writer's Block and Other Composing-Process Problems.* **New York: Guilford, 1985. 166-81.** Emphasizes the usefulness of "speaking-aloud protocols" in diagnosing and solving students' writing process problems in the writing lab. Argues such protocols "are extremely helpful in getting at individual composing problems," such as writer's block, by revealing whether a student's composing strategies lack variety, flexibility, and complexity and are productive or inhibitive.

0814. **Harris, Muriel. "A Grab-Bag of Diagnostic Techniques."** *Teaching English in the Two-Year College* **9.2 (1983): 111-15.** Outlines several techniques for assessing writing difficulties of students referred to the writing center, including using structured interviews, asking students to use compose-aloud protocols, and questioning students about their knowledge of a given topic.

0815. **Harris, Muriel. "Individualized Diagnosis: Searching for Causes, Not Symptoms of Writing Deficiencies."** *College English* **40 (1978-79): 318-23.** Warns against premature diagnosis and offers a list of questions used to gain insight into students' attitudes in their first visit to the writing center.

0816. **Harris, Muriel. "Individualized Diagnosis: Searching for Causes, Not Symptoms of Writing Deficiencies."** *Tutoring Writing: A Sourcebook for Writing Labs.* **Ed. Muriel Harris. Glenview: Scott, Foresman, 1982. 53-65.** Reprint of entry 0815. Includes commentary by Vincent D. Puma and response by Harris. Puma objects that Harris offers no real methods for determining causes of error but still deals with symptoms and that her questionnaire investigates student attitudes that are already evident. Harris explains what had been cut from the article due to editorial demands, including her discussion of ways to work backward from particular errors to their sources.

0817. **Harris, Muriel. "Individualized Instruction in Writing Centers: Attending to Cross-Cultural Differences."** *Intersections: Theory-Practice in the Writing Center.* **Ed. Joan A. Mullin and Ray Wallace. Urbana: NCTE, 1994. 96-110.** Draws on work in contrastive rhetoric to illustrate differences in ways cultural differences are reflected in language and then suggests ways for tutors to recognize and deal with these differences in writing center clientele.

0818. **Harris, Muriel. "The Ins and Outs of Conferencing."** *The Writing Instructor* **6 (1987): 87-96.** Applies lessons learned from writing lab tutorials to the teacher-student conference. Contends that the one-to-one conference reinforces the perspective of writing as a process, encourages questioning of concepts, permits teacher and student to engage in a more in-depth exchange of ideas, and provides an opportunity for the teacher to tailor comments to fit a student's particular needs.

0819. **Harris, Muriel.** *Teaching One-to-One: The Writing Conference.* **Urbana: NCTE, 1986.** Examines rationale for teaching through individual conferences and discusses benefits of this method. Analyzes elements of successful conferences. Suggests appropriate diagnostic activities and strategies for conferences. Draws on a wide variety of disciplines, including counseling, cognitive psychology, cultural anthropology, and ESL.

0820. **Hartman, Hope J. "Factors Affecting the Tutoring Process."** *Journal of Developmental Education* **14.2 (1990): 2-6.** Analyzes factors affecting the tutoring process, such as cognition, affect, variables in the academic context, and features of the nonacademic environment. Discusses the Integrated Learning Model as a theoretical framework for thinking about tutoring programs and their effectiveness.

0821. **Hawkins, Nathaniel. "An Introduction to the History and Theory of Peer Tutoring in Writing."** *A Guide to Writing Programs: Writing Centers, Peer Tutoring Programs, and Writing Across the Curriculum.* **Ed. Tori Haring-Smith, Nathaniel Hawkins, Elizabeth Morrison, Lise Stern, and Robin Tatu. Glenview: Scott, Foresman, 1985. 7-18.** Examines recent history of peer tutoring, particularly the political and social context in which it emerged. Briefly indicates the variety of training programs available across the country and explores the challenges the practice faces.

0822. **Hawkins, Thom. "Dealing with Criticism."** *Writing Lab Newsletter* **4.2 (1979): 2-4.** Claims that students who come to the writing center often misconstrue criticism as condemnation or censure. Argues that students can better understand criticism if they learn what it is like to give it, and develops a reader-response model based upon Kenneth Bruffee's "The Brooklyn Plan" (entry 0095). Contends this model of how to evaluate content and interact with the author and other critics can be of benefit in tutor training.

0823. **Hawkins, Thom. "Intimacy and Audience: The Relation between Revision and the Social Dimension of Peer Tutoring."** *College English* **42 (1980): 64-69. Rpt. in** *Tutoring Writing: A Sourcebook for Writing Labs.* **Ed. Muriel Harris. Glenview: Scott, Foresman, 1982. 27-31.** Uses journals from peer tutors in writing center at the University of California—Berkeley, to investigate the effectiveness of peer tutoring, concluding that the social dimension (particularly empathy) makes the practice successful.

0824. **Healy, Dave. "Countering the Myth of (In)dependence: Developing Life-Long Clients."** *Writing Lab Newsletter* **18.9 (1993): 1-3.** Counters the notion that student dependency is detrimental and that the need for tutoring ends when students become competent writers. Contends repeat customers, rather than implying that the writing center has failed in its mission, point to the center's effectiveness in teaching writers to collaborate.

0825. **Hemmeter, Thomas. "Live and On Stage: Writing Center Stories and Tutorial Authority."** *The Writing Center Journal* **15.1 (1994): 35-50.** Advises tutors to view tutoring as a narrative performance in order to react flexibly to student needs, share power with students, and explore various roles a tutor must adopt. Looks skeptically at formulaic, rule-bound tutoring relationships and advocates a tutoring style that accommodates the writing center's "troubled, divided, unstable, and contentious" reality.

0826. **Hettich, Rebecca Livengood. "Writing Apprehension: A Critique."** **Diss. Purdue U, 1994.** *DAI* **56-02A (1995): 494.** Claims writing apprehension is a problem for students and for teachers and writing center specialists who recognize apprehension in the behaviors of students but have no practical and reliable means of intervention. Examines the research on this subject to conclude that three interrelated concepts have bearing on the understanding and treatment of writing apprehension: agency, individuality, and attitude.

0827. **Hey, Phil, and Cindy Nahrwold. "Tutors Aren't Trained—They're Educated: The Need for Composition Theory."** *Writing Lab Newsletter* **18.7 (1994): 4-5.** Presents 10 reasons why a knowledge of composition theory is valuable to tutors and essential to tutor training. Concludes that a basic understanding of theoretical principles can generate a wide range of practical responses.

0828. **Hobson, Eric. "Tutors' Column: Warning: Tutoring May Make You a Researcher."** *Writing Lab Newsletter* **16.9-10 (1992): 9.** Discusses the tendency of tutors to question what they do and how they can improve. Suggests such questions lead tutors to become researchers, to seek answers by observing tutoring practices and turning to theory.

0829. **Hubbuch, Susan. "Some Thoughts on Collaboration from a Veteran Tutor."** *Writing Lab Newsletter* **16.1 (1991): 1-3, 8.** Expresses doubts about accepting collaborative learning as the dominant theory underlying writing centers. Argues that viewing collaboration in the writing center idealistically, as a meeting of minds between two equals, fails to convey the reality that students who come to the writing center view tutors as experts. Emphasizes the empowering force of allowing students to make their own choices about topics, ideas, and word usage.

0830. **Hubbuch, Susan M. "A Tutor Needs to Know the Subject Matter to Help a Student With a Paper: ___Agree ___Disagree ___Not Sure."** *The Writing Center Journal* **8.2 (1988): 23-30.** Contrasts tutors' roles in assisting students with English composition assignments and discipline-specific assignments. Acknowledges tutors with extensive knowledge of a discipline can ask appropriate questions and understand technical terms, but argues generalist tutors force students to take more responsibility for their work and help students clarify their ideas.

0831. **Hunter, Kathleen R. "Tutor Talk: A Study of Selected Linguistic Factors Affecting Tutor-Writer Interaction in a University Writing Center." Diss. Indiana University of Pennsylvania, 1993.** *DAI* **54-10A (1994): 3727.** Examines the conversations that comprised writing tutorial sessions in a university writing center by studying various kinds of linguistic utterances and focusing on the parts played by questioning in the writing conference. Suggests five directions for writing tutors, ranging from paying attention to their clients' agendas to trusting their instincts about the flow of a conference.

0832. **Hynds, Susan. "Perspectives on Perspectives in the Writing Center Conference."** *Focuses* **2.2 (1989): 77-90.** Argues that, even though writing centers have popularized the writing conference model, little is known about what actually goes on in conferences beyond "anecdotal reflections." Attempts to provide a "systematic inquiry" into this "rapidly growing phenomenon."

0833. **Jacoby, Jay. "Shall We Talk to Them in 'English': The Contributions of Sociolinguistics to Training Writing Center Personnel."** *Writing Center Journal* **4.1 (1983): 1-14.** Argues that peer tutors often model their approach to tutoring on teachers without realizing that "teacher behaviors" frustrate and alienate many learners. One way to create the awareness that "talking like teachers" can be frustrating is to introduce into tutor training more work in interpersonal communication and in sociolinguistics—"in how language functions beyond the communication of information to establish and maintain social relationships."

0834. **Jacoby, Jay. "What a Peer Tutor Is Not."** *Writing Lab Newsletter* **7.9 (1983): 5-7.** Argues against writing labs that combine faculty tutors with peer tutors by claiming that the peer tutors' advice and comments are better received by student writers. Claims that "peer tutors have an advantage over faculty tutors in gaining student confidence and establishing rapport." Peer tutors are also perceived as "less intimidating" and as "genuine collaborators in a learning effort."

0835. Jackson, Alan. "Writing Centers: A Panorama to Teaching and the Profession." *Writing Lab Newsletter* 18.6 (1994): 1-2, 12. Claims working in a writing center can help composition specialists develop the skills, experiences, and insights into students and student writing they will need to become excellent classroom teachers.

0836. Janangelo, Joseph. "The Polarities of Context in the Writing Center Conference." *The Writing Center Journal* 8.2 (1988): 31-36. Illustrates the pitfalls and possibilities in tutorial dialogues caused by differences in the personal contexts of tutor and student. Shows, in one case, how a tutor's assumption of shared common knowledge backfired while, in another case, the tutor's admission of ignorance led the student to clarify an essay's meaning.

0837. Johanek, Cindy. "Learning Styles: Issues, Questions, and the Roles of the Writing Center Tutor." *Writing Lab Newsletter* 16.4-5 (1992): 10-14. Shows how Kolb's Learning Style Type Indicator can inform the tutor-writer relationship. Indicates a familiarity with different ways writers perceive and process information can lead to more effective, student-centered tutoring.

0838. Johnson, JoAnn B. "Reevaluation of the Question as a Teaching Tool." *Dynamics of the Writing Conference: Social and Cognitive Interaction*. Ed. Thomas Flynn and Mary King. Urbana: NCTE, 1993. 34-40. Draws on psychological research to demonstrate the limited utility of questioning in writing conferences, suggesting a judicious mixture of paraphrasing and imperative statements to engage students more thoroughly in critical thinking.

0839. Johnson, JoAnn B. "Re-Evaluation of the Question as a Teaching Tool." *Writing Lab Newsletter* 10.4 (1985): 1-4. Draws on the theories of Jean Piaget, L.S. Vygotsky, Carl Rogers, and Jerome Bruner to examine the effectiveness of asking questions in tutorials. Suggests that some questions, rather than encouraging learning, have a chilling effect on student responses. Contends that a tutor's well-chosen statements, if they require a response from the student, "created longer, more reflective responses."

0840. Johnson-Shull, Lisa. "Tutors' Column: Teaching Assistants Learn Teaching Tips by Tutoring." *Writing Lab Newsletter* 18.9 (1993): 13. Recounts how one graduate student learned to be a better teacher by tutoring in the writing center. Contends other prospective teachers could benefit from such experience.

0841. Johnstone, Anne. "The Writing Tutorial as Ecology: A Case Study." *The Writing Center Journal* 9.2 (1989): 51-56. Uses a case study to illustrate Marilyn Cooper's concept of the writing center tutorial as ecology. Shows how tutors' expectations affect what students write and how students' "individual acts of writing" in turn affect what tutors expect.

0842. Jolly, Peggy. "Three Approaches to Teaching: The Laboratory Alternative." *Writing Lab Newsletter* 5.2 (1980): 3-4. Describes one-to-one tutoring, self-paced instruction, and computer-assisted instruction in the writing lab as positive alternatives to traditional classroom instruction.

0843. Joyner, Michael A. "The Writing Center Conference and the Textuality of Power." *The Writing Center Journal* 12.1 (1991): 80-89. Explores the interplay of the objective and subjective in writing center conferences. Takes issue with policies that forbid, as unethical, tutors' ventures into subjective aspects of students' ideas. Supports poststructuralist ideas in rejecting notions of individual genius and individuality (and therefore of subjectivity). Urges tutors to bring an awareness of "the political nature of writing" to tutoring.

0844. Kail, Harvey. "Collaborative Learning in Context: The Problem with Peer Tutoring." *College English* 45 (1983): 594-99. Discusses collaborative learning in the context of the large-scale institutionalization of this model into the pedagogical structure of higher education. Contrasts the service model of peer tutoring—in which peer tutors satisfy the learning demands of the teacher—with the collaborative model in which peer tutoring programs change the writing environment.

0845. Kail, Harvey, and John Trimbur. "The Politics of Peer Tutoring." *WPA: Writing Program Administration* 11.1-2 (1987): 5-12. Rpt. in 0007. Contrasts two forms of peer tutoring programs—the writing center model and the curriculum-based model in which peer tutors are assigned to help students in a particular course. Examines the political underpinnings, advantages, disadvantages, and effects on student writers of both models: curriculum-based tutors, as extensions of the university's writing program, transmit knowledge; writing center tutors collaborate in the creation of knowledge—a change not only in the learning patterns but in the power structure of the academy.

0846. **Kellett, David A.J. "The Cognitive Benefits of Peer Tutoring and Peer Collaboration." Diss. U of Nottingham, 1989. *DAI* 50-12A (1989): 3897.** Examines whether tutors derive cognitive benefits from tutoring or collaborating with tutees who have less information or poorer cognitive strategies. Claims that tutors do receive cognitive benefits and that "neo-Piagetian socio-cognitive conflict theory can be successfully applied to the problem of designing styles of effective peer collaboration."

0847. **Kilmer, Mary. "Tutor—Know Yourself." *Writing Lab Newsletter* 11.10 (1987): 13-14.** Discusses assumptions tutors make, based on their own preferences, about students' personalities and needs. Suggests tutors avail themselves of the Myers-Briggs Type Indicator to understand how aspects of their own personalities might impede effective tutoring.

0848. **King, Mary. "Teaching for Cognitive Growth." *Writing Lab Newsletter* 7.7 (1983): 7-9.** Discusses issues involved in theories of developmental education—whether development itself is a natural course of growth that can be assisted, or whether developmental education should address students who exhibit deficiencies compared to what their capacities "should be" for success in college. Reflects upon the significance of these theories to writing instruction.

0849. **King, Mary. "What Can Students Say about Poems? Reader Response in a Conference Setting." *Dynamics of the Writing Conference: Social and Cognitive Interaction*. Ed. Thomas Flynn and Mary King. Urbana: NCTE, 1993. 69-79.** Uses a writing center conference about a paper on literature to demonstrate the value of reader-response criticism in helping students find a sense of ownership in responding to and understanding literature.

0850. **Kirkpatrick, Carolyn. "The Case for Autotutorial Materials." *Improving Writing Skills*. Ed. Thom Hawkins and Phyllis Brooks. New Directions for College Learning Assistance 3. San Francisco: Jossey-Bass, 1981. 15-23.** Makes a case for writing labs and centers to consider the value of the autotutorial (self-instructional) method, even though the tutoring method is usually held in higher regard. Autotutorial methods allow students to work independently.

**0851. Lassner, Phyllis. "Conferencing: The Psychodynamics of Teaching Contraries."** *Writing Center Journal* **4.2 (1984): 22-30.** Discusses how the teaching environment of conferencing enables tutors to encourage "both the nurturing and critical processes leading students to a greater control over their ability to generate and revise writing."

**0852. Lassner, Phyllis. "The Politics of Otherness: Negotiating Distance and Difference."** *Intersections: Theory-Practice in the Writing Center.* **Ed. Joan A. Mullin and Ray Wallace. Urbana: NCTE, 1994. 148-60.** Uses feminist theories of difference to examine peer tutoring and the notion of "peerness," looking at collaborations between tutor and writer in which both parties clearly differ and in which they seem alike and finding coercion possible in both.

**0853. Lassner, Phyllis. "The Politics of Peer Tutoring."** *Writing Lab Newsletter* **12.1 (1987): 4-6.** Cautions against letting peer tutoring harden into a specific pattern because the social and political undercurrents of regions and particular universities differ (as do their students' needs). To prevent peers from becoming authority figures instead of collaborators and co-learners, suggests their training should include ongoing reflection about their impact on the learning processes of student writers.

**0854. Leahy, Richard. "Rhetorical Analysis in Writing Assistant Training."** *Writing Lab Newsletter* **20.4 (1995): 1-4.** Discusses the value of formal training in rhetorical analysis of student texts to writing assistant training programs. Bases this conclusion on the fact that many writing assistants, though skilled writers, "do not necessarily know how to think or talk in a systematic way about the structure, development, or writer-reader relationship of longer, more complex student drafts."

**0855. Leahy, Richard. "When the Going is Good: Implications of 'Flow' and 'Liking' for Writers and Tutors."** *The Writing Center Journal* **15.2 (1995): 152-62.** Attributes much of the enjoyment writers feel to flow, "a heightened sense of awareness and enjoyment in an activity we do well." Reflects on the importance of liking a piece well enough to look past its flaws to see its potential. Contends that understanding these emotions could make writing assistants more effective.

**0856. Lotto, Edward. "The Texts and Contexts of Writing."** *The Writing Center Journal* **9.1 (1988): 13-20.** Portrays the writing center as a setting in which numerous contexts for writing (and evaluation of writing) converge. Examines the assumptions of other disciplines that impact on the tutor-student relationship. Demonstrates how each discipline's views about writing depend on its views about the nature of knowledge (e.g., scientists hold that knowledge lies outside language and humanists hold that knowledge is a function of language). Recommends tutors keep such differences in mind.

0857. **Lotto, Edward. "The Writer's Subject is Sometimes a Fiction."** *Writing Center Journal* **5.2/6.1 (1985): 15-20.** Argues writers engage in a complex process of fictionalizing a "subject" by putting previous experience into words. A tutor's role is to be sensitive to this process since "the meaning and the subject exist in a web of shared language and shared experience."

0858. **Lyons, Greg. "Validating Cultural Difference in the Writing Center."** *The Writing Center Journal* **12.2 (1992): 145-58.** Urges that directors train tutors to practice John Trimbur's "utopian" view of consensus to affirm the differences in culture, gender, class, and learning styles that nontraditional students bring to the writing center.

0859. **Macdonald, Andrew F. "Peer Tutoring and the Problem of Rhetorical Superiority."** *Freshman English News* **7.3 (1979): 13-15.** Contends that peer tutoring works against the concept of "rhetorical superiority" in which all writers in academic and non-academic settings seek to win favor from individuals in the position to accept or reject their work. Concludes peer tutoring gives writers a false sense of how their work will be judged in future professional settings.

0860. **MacDonald, Ross B. "An Analysis of Verbal Interaction in College Tutorials."** *Journal of Developmental Education* **15.1 (1991): 2-12.** Uses a coding system, the MacDonald Tutoring Interaction Codes, to extend sociolinguistic research in education into peer tutoring through a micro-level analysis of talk. Finds results contradict tutor trainers' commonly held belief that tutors lead tutees to answers by asking skillful questions. Much of the time, tutor and tutee are explaining information to each other. Discusses implications of this finding to research, practice, and tutor training.

0861. **MacDonald, Ross B. "Group Tutoring Techniques: From Research to Practice."** *Journal of Developmental Education* **17.2 (1993): 12-18.** Argues that tutor training programs should include training in small group dynamics and group tutoring techniques and not focus exclusively on training for one-to-one conferencing. Group tutoring will become the reality as schools' financial resources shrink, students' needs for tutoring increase, and exemplary tutors are in short supply.

0862. **MacDonald, Ross Barclay. "Tutoring: A Descriptive Investigation of Four One-to-One Community College Tutorials." Diss. U of California—Davis, 1988.** *DAI* **49-07A (1988): 1686.** Uses sociolinguistic methods and the IREAM coding system of initiation, reply, evaluation, addition, and marker moves to examine verbal interactions in tutorials. Socio-cognitive theory confirms that tutors and tutees construct and rehearse shared understandings about tasks in a sequence.

0863. **Maid, Barry, Sally Crisp, and Suzanne Norton. "On Gaining Insight into Ourselves as Writers and as Tutors: Our Use of the Myers-Briggs Type Indicator."** *Writing Lab Newsletter* **13.10 (1989): 1-5.** Explains the Myers-Briggs Type Indicator and suggests this tool offers a window into how personality affects writing and tutoring.

0864. **Major, James S., and Jean S. Filetti. "'Type'-Writing: Helping Students Write With the Myers-Briggs Type Indicator."** *Writing Lab Newsletter* **15.4 (1990): 4-6.** Discusses how a college requires all new students to take the Myers-Briggs Type Indicator test and uses this information in tutoring at its Research and Writing Center. Contends that a knowledge of each writer's personality preferences helps tutors effectively meet each student's needs.

0865. **Mann, Ann Ferguson. "A Quantitative and Qualitative Evaluation of a Peer Tutor-training Course: A Cognitive-developmental Model." Diss. North Carolina State U, 1992.** *DAI* **53-07A (1993): 2226.** Evaluates the effectiveness of a peer tutor-training course for college tutors and contends that peer tutoring represents a role-taking activity that, when properly monitored and supervised, can foster the cognitive and social development of tutors while providing academic assistance and support for other college students.

0866. **Martin, Frances. "Close Encounters of an Ancient Kind: Readings on the Tutorial Classroom and the Writing Conference."** *The Writing Center Journal* **2.2 (1982): 7-17.** Annotated bibliography of 30 books and articles on the tutorial approach to teaching writing, both in classroom settings and individually.

0867. **Marx, Michael Steven. "Bringing Tutorials to a Close: Counseling's Termination Process and the Writing Tutorial."** *The Writing Center*

*Journal* **11.2 (1991): 51-60.** Draws on psychological counseling techniques to suggest how to end long-term tutor-student relationships humanely and productively. While acknowledging termination is a recursive process, recommends a three-step approach: (1) assessing the student's progress as a writer, (2) gracefully bringing the relationship to a close, (3) leaving the student with a sense of self-reliance.

0868. **Masiello, Lea. "Collaborative Pedagogy and Perry's Stages of Cognitive Growth: Some Thoughts on Conferences as Learning Environments."** *Writing Lab Newsletter* **12.8 (1988): 1-2.** Contends that the collaborative pedagogy of writing centers kindles tutors' cognitive growth from dualistic to multiplistic to relativistic stages of thinking.

0869. **Masiello, Lea. "Tutor-Instructor Collaboration in the Writing Center and the Classroom."** *Writing Lab Newsletter* **13.4 (1988): 13-15.** Argues that collaboration between writing center tutors and classroom instructors benefits students, instructors, and tutors. Cautions that collaboration succeeds most often when the tutor and instructor are flexible and agree on a pedagogical approach to writing.

0870. **Matsuhashi, Ann, Alice Gillam, Rance Conley, and Beverly Moss. "A Theoretical Framework for Studying Peer Tutoring as Response."** *Writing and Response.* **Ed. Chris M. Anson. Urbana: NCTE, 1989. 293-316.** Defines peer tutoring as a "response event," focusing on the feedback processes at work during language transactions. Tutoring is viewed as a "to and fro" feedback strategy that emphasizes the intermediate stages between current text and ideal text.

0871. **Maxwell, Martha. "The Effects of Expectations, Sex, and Ethnicity on Peer Tutoring."** *Journal of Developmental Education* **15.1 (1991): 14-18.** Surveys studies of peer tutoring in many disciplines, revealing a significant correlation between the success of tutorial sessions and a variety of factors: tutee expectations, the proximity of college class of tutor and tutee, and the ethnicity and gender of both parties. Examines the potential impact of these findings on tutor training.

0872. **McCall, William. "Writing Centers and the Idea of Consultancy."** *The Writing Center Journal* **14.2 (1994): 163-71.** Joins the ongoing discussion of whether writing center personnel should call themselves *tutors* or *consultants*. Concludes that *tutor* carries meanings that undermine the mission of writing centers and advocates making the change to *consultant*.

0873. McClure, Susan Harpham. "An Observational Study of the Behavior of First Semester College Students as Tutors in a Writing Center." Diss. Indiana U of Pennsylvania, 1990. *DAI* 51-03A (1990): 0193. This study of first-semester tutors with no formal training finds the tutors stayed on task, addressed students' drafts, and dealt with "both higher and lower compositional concerns." Students were satisfied with the tutors, viewing them as listeners, evaluators, and partners in writing. Suggests that student writers influence the conference and the tutors' style.

0874. Medway, Frederic J. "A Social Psychological Analysis of Peer Tutoring." *Journal of Developmental Education* 15.1 (1991): 20-26, 32. Reviews research in peer tutoring in many areas, focusing on the contextual and situational factors that result in successful tutoring. Calls for tutor training programs to draw more thoroughly on this existing body of research.

0875. Melnick, Jane F. "The Politics of Writing Conferences: Describing Authority Through Speech Act Theory." *Writing Center Journal* 4.2 (1984): 9-21. Views writing center conferences as "intellectual dialogue" and uses the sociolinguistic concept of "membershipping"—the process by which speakers share varying degrees of intellectual belonging in a conversation—to argue for the validity of sociolinguistics and speech act theory for enhancing conference effectiveness and for tutor training.

0876. Mohr, Ellen. "Model of Collaboration: The Peer Tutor." *Writing Lab Newsletter* 16.1 (1991): 14-16. Extols peer tutoring as a collaborative model for the writing center and for the composition classroom. Details the techniques one writing center uses in tutoring and tutor training to encourage successful peer collaboration.

0877. Montgomery, Nancy. "Facilitating Talk about Student Texts in Small Writing Groups." *Focuses* 7.2 (1994): 79-88. Observed the tutor as a facilitator in small group discussions held in a writing center. Concludes that a successful "workshop" of this type must give priority to "the essential acts of collaboration" (sharing, mirroring, assessing, and suggesting), for which students need to be trained carefully.

0878. Morrison, Margaret. "Peer Tutors as Postmodern Readers in a Writing Center." *Freshman English News* 18.2 (1990): 12-15. Claims a knowledge of postmodern theories of interpretation can alert peer tutors to the dangers of imposing their own ideology upon the writer's text. Peer tutors need to know that there are no determinate meanings in understanding texts.

0879. **Mullin, Anne E. "*Differance*: Aiding the Writer to Reader Shift."** *Writing Lab Newsletter* **19.6 (1995): 4-5.** Discusses the difficult movement student writers must make from writer to reader in order to become critics of their own work. Suggests that the writing center provides a place where such a shift in roles can take place. Argues that tutoring, especially sessions that involve reading papers aloud, can help students make the necessary change in point of view.

0880. **Murphy, Christina. "Freud in the Writing Center: The Psychoanalytics of Tutoring Well."** *The Writing Center Journal* **10.1 (1989): 13-18. Rpt. in 0008.** Argues the tutor-student relationship differs from the teacher-student relationship because it is voluntary, more personal, and aimed at solving the particular student's problems. Suggests that psychoanalytic principles of personal empowerment through interaction offer a theoretical bridge between expressionist and social constructionist theories.

0881. **Nardini, Gloria. "Peer Tutors and the Making of Meaning."** *Writing Lab Newsletter* **14.10 (1990): 14-15.** Endorses peer tutoring as perhaps more effective than teaching in helping students express and clarify meaning. Supports contentions with an interactive dialogue between a student and a peer tutor.

0882. **Nash, Thomas. "Derrida's 'Play' and Prewriting for the Laboratory."** *Writing Centers: Theory and Administration.* **Ed. Gary A. Olson. Urbana: NCTE, 1984. 182-96.** Discusses invention and prewriting in tutorials, offering a variety of models of invention ranging from Aristotle's *topoi* to Derrida's concept of *differance*.

0883. **Neil, Lynn Riley. "Individual Student-Teacher Conferences: Guiding Content Revision with Sixth Graders."** *The Writing Center Journal* **7.2 (1987): 37-44.** Chronicles study of writing conferences in Utah elementary school. Draws upon the theories of Donald Graves and Donald Murray to argue that individual student-teacher conferences do encourage young children to revise.

0884. **Neuleib, Janice. "The Friendly Stranger: Twenty-Five Years as 'Other.'"** *College Composition and Communication* **43.2 (1992): 231-43.** Discusses the difficulties academics have in relating closely enough to their disadvantaged students' perspectives to help them improve as writers. Contends teachers must "decenter" in order to understand the alienated nonreader, nonwriter values of their students. Suggests this decentering often involves learning with and from, as opposed to teaching, these students.

0885. Nixon-John, Gloria D. "The High School Writing Center—A Room for One-on-One Student Tutoring." *Teaching and Change* 1.4 (1994): 369-79. Describes a high school writing center for private student peer tutorials without the teacher present and how the students themselves modified some of the tutoring protocols to create a more interactive and social constructionist tutoring environment.

0886. North, Stephen. "Writing Center Diagnosis: The Composing Profile." *Tutoring Writing: A Sourcebook for Writing Labs.* Ed. Muriel Harris. Glenview: Scott, Foresman, 1982. 42-52. Provides a diagnostic instrument (the composing profile), an open-ended set of strategies for teaching writing, and principles for bringing students together with those strategies. The composing profile becomes the basis for writing center consultation.

0887. Novak, Cynthia Cornell. "College-Bound Writers: An Attributional Study of the Effects of Writing-Specific Self-Concept, Success and Failure, and Normative Versus Mastery Feedback on the Motivated Behavior of Help Seeking." Diss. U of California, Los Angeles, 1992. *DAI* 53-12A (1993): 4258. Examines the influence of writing-specific self-concept and the types of feedback students receive from teachers and writing center tutors upon the psychological processes involved in the motivated behavior of help seeking. Finds that students' confidence about their writing abilities, successful performance, and the cognitive intent to seek help were reliable predictors of actual help seeking. Feedback from teachers and tutors had little motivational effect.

0888. Onore, Cynthia. "In Their Own 'Write': A Portrait of the Peer Tutor as a Young Professional." *The Writing Center Journal* 3.1 (1982): 20-31. Includes essays by three peer tutors (entries 1064, 1173, 1257) summarizing their experiences in the writing center. Introductory commentary points out that these narratives demonstrate these tutors' abilities to connect their own experience as writers with other writers' situations, as well as their flexibility and insight.

0889. Pemberton, Michael A. "Dependency in the Writing Center: Psychological Profiles and Tutorial Strategies." *Research and Teaching in Developmental Education* 10.2 (1994): 63-70. Reviews literature on dependency in psychological research and suggests possible methods writing tutors can use in reducing dependency of writing center clients.

0890. **Powers, Judith K. "Assisting the Graduate Thesis Writer Through Faculty and Writing Center Collaboration."** *Writing Lab Newsletter* **20.2 (1995): 13-16.** Claims the "model" conferencing strategies that work for undergraduate writers do not work for graduate thesis or dissertation writers. Explores the unique problems facing graduate students and suggests a new model for working with them, involving consultation and collaboration with the students' dissertation advisors.

0891. **Powers, Judith. "Bending the 'Rules': Diversifying the Model Conference for the ESL Writer."** *Writing Lab Newsletter* **17.6 (1993): 1-3, 8.** Argues tutoring ESL writers often requires tutors to use a more directive approach than they would use with a native-English writers. Views standard tutoring techniques, such as having students read aloud and attempt to "edit by ear," as of little use to ESL students. Suggests tutors often teach ESL students more effectively by violating "rules" against editing or proofreading a paper.

0892. **Powers, Judith K. "Rethinking Writing Center Conferencing Strategies for the ESL Writer." Rpt. in 0008.** *The Writing Center Journal* **13.2 (1993): 39-47.** Contends few writing center tutors are adequately trained in the intricacies of assisting ESL writers. Demonstrates how the collaborative approach tutors use to good effect with native writers often fails when applied to ESL writers, who have different cultural values, needs, rhetorical strategies, and attitudes toward the tutor-student relationship. Suggests tutors may have to intervene more directly in the ELS writers' texts, acting less as collaborators than as "informants."

0893. **Raign, Kathryn Rosser. "Stasis Theory Revisited: An Inventional Technique for Empowering Students."** *Focuses* **2.1 (1989): 19-26.** Claims the inventional strategies of stasis theory, drawn from classical rhetoric, can aid tutors in helping students understand the requirements and implications of writing assignments.

0894. **Raines, Helon Howell. "Tutoring and Teaching: Continuum, Dichotomy, or Dialectic?"** *The Writing Center Journal* **14.2 (1994): 150-62.** Proposes a dialectical model of tutoring that puts tutoring and teaching in opposition and in concert. Rather than attempting to unify the roles, seeks to bring the best aspects of each to the other. Incl<sub></sub>des narrative examples of tutors practicing this model.

**0895. Redfern, Jenny R. "Peer Tutoring as a Subversive Activity."** *Writing Lab Newsletter* **10.7 (1986): 1-2.** Views peer tutoring as a chance for tutor and student to "overturn their perceptions of how both composing and teaching are achieved" by helping them see writing as a process, engaging in shared learning, and restoring authority to the student writer.

**0896. Rehberger, Dean. "Negotiating Authority Among Writing Centers, Writing Programs, Peer Tutors and Students."** *English in Texas* **25.4 (1994): 50-54.** Contends that having peer tutors work with teachers in writing classrooms offers a new way of understanding the complexities of authority by shifting the teacher/student dynamic from familiar roles and forcing teachers, tutors, and students to reevaluate their subject positions.

**0897. Reigstad, Tom. "The Writing Conference: An Ethnographic Model for Discovering Patterns of Teacher-Student Interaction."** *The Writing Center Journal* **2.1 (1982): 9-20.** Recounts systematic ethnographic investigation of 40 conferences conducted by 10 teachers. Derives and describes three conference models (teacher-centered, collaborative, student-centered) and calls for further research.

**0898. Roberts, Ian F. "Writing Centers as Centers of Controlled Learning, Too."** *Writing Lab Newsletter* **17.4 (1992): 12-13.** Critiques aspects of the "midwife" metaphor for tutoring as naive yet seeks to expand upon the principles underlying this metaphor. Sees the midwife approach as more controlling than its advocates appear willing to admit and urges tutors to acknowledge the positive side of such control.

**0899. Roswell, Barbara Sherr. "The Tutor's Audience Is Always a Fiction: The Construction of Authority in Writing Center Conferences." Diss. U of Pennsylvania, 1992.** *DAI* **53-11A (1993): 3830.** This ethnographic study of a peer tutor staffed writing center investigates how undergraduate tutors and writers construct authority in their talk about text. Concludes "(1) that writing center conferences cannot be understood apart from the layers of institutional context in which they are embedded and (2) that the poststructural notion of subject positions can productively inform the sociolinguistic methods often used to study conference talk."

0900. Rottenberg, Annette T. "Learning to Teach by Tutoring." *Writing Lab Newsletter* 12.10 (1988): 11-12. Contends that tutoring in a writing center provides solid preparation for college composition teachers by introducing tutors to aspects of the writing process, revealing weaknesses in teachers' assignments, and giving tutors insight into students' attitudes, strengths, and weaknesses.

0901. Runciman, Lex. "Defining Ourselves: Do We Really Want to Use the Word *Tutor*?" *The Writing Center Journal* 11.1 (1990): 27-34. Discusses connotations of the word *tutor*. Contends that, despite the positive images of the British tutoring system that *tutor* might create, the term too often carries remedial implications. Argues that using *tutoring* to refer to the work done in writing centers is limiting and, possibly, detrimental to the centers, their employees, and their students. Suggests replacing *tutor* with *writing assistant, consultant, or fellow* and replacing *tutoring* with *consulting*.

0902. Ryan, A. Leigh Keller. "An Investigation and Description of Some Relationships Between Tutorial Assistance in a Writing Center and the Writing Apprehension of Freshman Composition Students." Diss. U of Maryland College Park, 1986. *DAI* 47-08A (1986): 2930. Claims that tutorial writing centers committed to individual instruction and to composing as a process offer students immediate and individual assistance at all stages of writing. Concludes that "students can learn more about the composing process, particularly their own, with the help of a tutor."

0903. Scharton, Maurice, and Janice Neuleib. "The Gift of Insight: Personality Type, Tutoring, and Learning." *The Writing Center: New Directions*. Ed. Ray Wallace and Jeanne Simpson. New York: Garland, 1991. 184-204. Provides an overview of the basic personality types identified by the Myers-Briggs Type Indicator and suggests ways that being aware of personality type may assist in day-to-day operations of the writing center, including tutor-client interaction.

0904. Scott, Paulette. "Tutor-Student Conferences: Theories and Strategies." *Writing Lab Newsletter* 12.3 (1987): 8-12. Examines three primary patterns of tutor-student conferences as defined by Thomas J. Reigstad and Donald A. McAndrew): tutor-centered, student-centered, and collaborative. Discusses strengths, weaknesses, and other aspects of these styles and illustrates their differences through tutor-student dialogues.

0905. Seckendorf, Margaret Hess. "Writing Center Conferences: An Analysis." Diss. State U of New York at Albany, 1986. *DAI* 47-08A (1987): 3024. Examines the nature of the interaction in writing conferences through audiotapes and observations of 19 conferences with two undergraduates in the State University of New York—Albany writing center. Finds that tutors and students differed on individual concepts of writing and of the writing conference. These differences result in conflict and dissonance. This dissonance, together with the manner in which it is or is not resolved, forms the basis of the interaction that structures the conversation.

0906. Severino, Carol. "The 'Doodles' in Context: Qualifying Claims about Contrastive Rhetoric." *The Writing Center Journal* 14.1 (1993): 44-62. Urges greater awareness of the complexities of the rhetorical strategies used by different cultures. Claims tutors tend to have overly simplistic views about the writing of ESL students and offers insights gleaned from contrastive rhetoric research. Narrative examples involve primarily Asian ESL students. Suggests a need for future research into contrastive rhetoric.

0907. Severino, Carol. "ESL and Native English Speaking Writers and Pedagogies—The Issue of Difference: A Review Essay." *The Writing Center Journal* 13.2 (1993): 63-70. A review essay of books on ESL teaching theory, relating the principles of contrastive rhetoric and process pedagogy to writing center theory.

0908. Shakespeare, William O. "Orienting the Student and Setting the Agenda in a Drop-In Writing Center." *Writing Lab Newsletter* 10.9 (1986): 10-13. Describes four types of students who commonly visit the writing center: the normal learner, the hostile learner, the apathetic learner, and the manipulator. Argues that effective tutoring requires the tutor to set the perimeters of writing center services, making clear to students that the writing center's focus is on collaborative *learning* rather than collaborative *writing*.

0909. Shamoon, Linda K., and Deborah H. Burns. "A Critique of Pure Tutoring." *The Writing Center Journal* 15.2 (1995): 134-51. Challenges nondirective tutoring orthodoxy, or "pure tutoring," and calls for a reexamination of writing center ideology. Points out weaknesses of expressivist and social constructionist viewpoints. Suggests that writing center scholars reexamine mentorship and directive tutoring, accommodating such practices if they make knowledge and achievement more accessible to students.

0910. **Shattuck, Randall S. "The Reciprocity of High and Low Order Concerns."** *Writing Lab Newsletter* **18.6 (1994): 13-14.** Argues that sentence structure, which Thomas J. Reigstad and Donald A. McAndrew list as a low-order concern, plays too integral a part in shaping high-order concerns to be considered distinct from them. Sees sentence structure as the preeminent concern.

0911. **Sheets, Rick A. "The Effects of Training and Experience on Adult Peer Tutors in Community Colleges." Diss. Arizona State U, 1994.** *DAI* **55-05A (1994): 1172.** Examines constructivism and metacognition as the theoretical foundation for tutor training. Finds that training in "active listening" and paraphrasing make a significant difference in the appropriateness of tutor responses. Previous experience as a tutor proves valuable.

0912. **Sherwood, Steve. "The Dark Side of the Helping Personality: Student Dependency and the Potential for Tutor Burnout."** *Writing Center Perspectives.* **Ed. Byron L. Stay, Christina Murphy, and Eric H. Hobson. Emmitsburg: NWCA Press, 1995. 63-70.** Warns of the dangers of tutors practicing neurotically unselfish behavior, pointing out its harmful consequences, including student dependency and tutor burnout.

0913. **Sherwood, Steve. "Discovering Order in Chaos: Fostering Meaning Without Crushing Creativity."** *Writing Lab Newsletter* **18.9 (1993): 4-6.** Contends that chaos theory offers writers new ways of creating and organizing ideas. Suggests writing center tutors ought to familiarize themselves with the implications of the theory to avoid stifling creativity in student writers.

0914. **Sherwood, Steve. "Fear and Loathing in the Writing Center: How to Deal Fairly with Problem Students."** *Writing Lab Newsletter* **16.8 (1992): 12-15.** Views fear as the cause of many interpersonal problems that impede writing and tutoring. Argues that, to help students overcome writer's block and other barriers, tutors must overcome their own and students' fears of failure, rejection, and meeting people.

0915. **Sherwood, Steve. "Humor and the Serious Tutor."** *The Writing Center Journal* **13.2 (1993): 3-12. Rpt. in 0008.** Cautions against clumsy or ill-timed humor but suggests that, used judiciously, humor can build tutor-student rapport, calm students' fears, soften criticism, and enhance creativity by generating unexpected connections between ideas.

Contends humor can help tutors create a setting in which productive collaboration can thrive.

**0916. Sherwood, Steve. "Tutoring and the Writer's 'Felt Sense': Developing and Safeguarding the Mind's Ear."** *Writing Lab Newsletter* **19.10 (1995): 10-14.** Argues the writer's "felt sense" places tutors at the interface of written and oral language, where they can help student writers make meaning. Urges directors to seek out tutors who already possess this quality and attempt to develop or fine-tune in it current staff members.

**0917. Shiffman, Betty Garrison. "Writing Center Instruction: Fostering an Ethic of Caring."** *Writing Lab Newsletter* **19.10 (1995): 1-5.** Argues the writing center is an ideal place to apply the principles of feminist teaching because of the balance of power between student and tutor. Discusses feminist teaching's emphasis on empowering the individual student, dialogue, subjectivity, collaboration, and establishing a caring relationship between tutor and student.

**0918. Shrofel, Salina. "Developing Writing Teachers."** *English Education* **23.3 (1991): 160-77.** Suggests ways of incorporating models of writing instruction based on writing center approaches (particularly individual tutorials) into classroom pedagogy.

**0919. Simard, Rodney. "Assessing a New Professional Role: The Writing Center Tutor."** *Writing Centers: Theory and Administration.* **Ed. Gary A. Olson. Urbana: NCTE, 1984. 197-205.** Claims the tutor differs in significant respects from the classroom teacher, a "generalist" rather than a "specialist" and capable of adapting quickly to a wide variety of clients.

**0920. Simard, Rodney. "The Graduate Student-Tutor in the Writing Center."** *CEA Forum* **12.3 (1982): 14-15.** Examines the position of the graduate student who tutors—as neither fully a student nor a professional—and suggests several methods to deal with this problematic status.

**0921. Simonian, Margaret Ann. "Tutors' Column: A Tutor Needs to Know the Subject Matter to Help a Student with a Paper: Agree_____ Disagree_____ Not Sure_____."** *Writing Lab Newsletter* **17.1 (1992): 9-10.** Responds to Susan M. Hubbuch (entry 0830). Argues that writing assistants who have little knowledge of a paper's subject matter can nevertheless help student writers compose clear, rhetorically effective papers.

0922. **Singley, Carol J., and Holly W. Boucher. "Dialogue in Tutor Training: Creating the Essential Space for Learning."** *The Writing Center Journal* **8.2 (1988): 11-22.** Places dialogue at the center of learning in writing center tutorials. Provides historical context for dialogue as a mode of learning and creativity. Suggests that the dialogic approach also be used in tutor training courses.

0923. **Slattery, Patrick J. "Using Conferences to Help Students Write Multiple-Source Papers."** *Dynamics of the Writing Conference: Social and Cognitive Interaction.* **Ed. Thomas Flynn and Mary King. Urbana: NCTE, 1993. 80-87.** Uses cognitive psychology to demonstrate how conferences can help students learn to reflect critically on contradictory views among their sources for a research paper. Illustrates by analyzing three student conferences about research papers.

0924. **Smiley, Janet. "Using Conferences to Teach Composition."** *Writing Lab Newsletter* **7.3 (1982): 1-2.** Uses Donald Murray's theories in *A Writer Teaches Writing* to argue that the pedagogy of the individual conference is the central teaching tool of writing center tutorials. Defines five charactcristics of conferencing ranging from the natural context of a communicative act to increased student involvement in the evaluation process.

0925. **Smith, Louise Z. "Family Systems Theory and the Form of Conference Dialogue."** *The Writing Center Journal* **10.2 (1990): 3-16. Rpt. in** *The Writing Center Journal* **11.2 (1991): 61-72.** Explores the psychosocial relationships, including dependency, that form during writing center conferences and contends that a knowledge of family systems theory can inform tutoring.

0926. **Smith, Sandy. "Ego States and the Writing Lab Staff."** *Writing Lab Newsletter* **9.2 (1984): 4-7.** Uses the principles of Transactional Analysis presented in Eric Berne's *Games People Play* and Thomas Harris's *I'm OK—You're OK* to claim that the ideas of the three ego states, Adult, Parent, and Child, can be applied beneficially in tutorials as a means of understanding and assisting student writers.

0927. **Smulyan, Lisa, and Kristin Bolton. "Classroom and Writing Center Collaborations: Peers as Authorities."** *The Writing Center Journal* **9.2 (1989): 43-49.** Describes problems high school writing assistants experienced in negotiating levels of perceived authority with students. Recounts how writing assistants learned to differentiate among various forms of collaboration to create an effective learning environment.

0928. Soliday, Mary. "Shifting Roles in Classroom Tutoring: Cultivating the Art of Boundary Crossing." *The Writing Center Journal* **16.1 (1995): 59-73.** Describes a project in which writing center tutors assisted students in composition classrooms. Indicates tutors successfully shifted between the traditionally separate roles of tutor and classroom teaching assistant. Argues the desirability of this hybrid approach.

0929. Spear, Karen I. "Promoting Cognitive Development in the Writing Center." *Writing Centers: Theory and Administration.* **Ed. Gary A. Olson. Urbana: NCTE, 1984. 62-76.** Describes basic writers in developmental terms and notes that writing centers teaching writing as a process aid such students; cautions that one-on-one tutorials may reinforce authority needs of dualistic thinkers and recommends using small group sessions for developmental learners.

0930. Taylor, David. "A Counseling Approach to Writing Conferences." *Dynamics of the Writing Conference: Social and Cognitive Interaction.* **Ed. Thomas Flynn and Mary King. Urbana: NCTE, 1993. 24-33.** Provides a model for moving conferences away from authority-driven, student-teacher model toward a more collaborative model that draws on the theories of Carl Rogers.

0931. Taylor, David. "A Counseling Approach to Writing Conferences." *Writing Lab Newsletter* **12.5 (1988): 10-11.** Urges tutors to structure and conduct meetings with students in ways that resemble the interview between a psychotherapist and his or her client. Divides the interview into five stages: preparing and entry, clarification, exploration, consolidation, and planning and termination.

0932. Taylor-Escoffery, Bertha. "The Influences of the Writing Center on College Students' Perceptions of the Functions of Written Language." **Diss. Indiana U of Pennsylvania, 1992.** *DAI* **53-11A (1993): 3885.** Examines the influences of the writing center on basic writing students' perceptions of the functions of written language. Finds that the writing center improved these perceptions in the "expressive" and the "transactional" domains. The writing center experience also reduced writing apprehension among basic writers by providing the necessary reinforcements to reduce this anxiety.

0933. Thompson, Thomas C. "Personality Preferences, Tutoring Styles, and Implications for Tutor Training." *The Writing Center Journal* 14.2 (1994): 136-49. Applies Myers-Briggs personality theory to tutor selection and training. Examines impact of personality type on tutoring and recommends training in personality theory to make tutors aware of why they prefer particular tutoring styles.

0934. Thompson, Thomas C. "'Yes, Sir!' 'No, Sir!' 'No Excuse, Sir!': Working with an Honor Code in a Military Setting." *Writing Lab Newsletter* 19.5 (1995): 13-14. Discusses the difficulties tutors face at The Citadel (SC), whose honor code prohibits cadets from receiving help on any graded assignment. Contends the policies of the writing center, where tutors "may use the Socratic method to lead students to discover their own conclusions" but cannot interpret literary passages for students or supply words to complete students' thoughts, help tutors avoid honor code violations.

0935. Trimbur, John. "Peer Tutoring: A Contradiction in Terms?" *The Writing Center Journal* 7.2 (1987): 21-28. Examines the apparent contradiction in terms between "peer" and "tutor." Acknowledges that a person selected as a tutor has skills above peers, thus differentiating the tutor and tutee; however, effective and informed tutor training courses can help eliminate this dichotomy by offering experiential co-learning as a model for future tutorials.

0936. Trimbur, John. "Peer Tutors and the Benefits of Collaborative Learning." *Writing Lab Newsletter* 7.9 (1983): 1-3. Argues that peer tutors become "more effective learners by becoming collaborative learners." Supports Kenneth Bruffee in recognizing that such tutoring, grounded in peer relationships, formalizes and builds upon informal structures such as "the unofficial study-groups, the self-help circles that students have always formed."

0937. Trimbur, John. "Students or Staff: Thoughts on the Use of Peer Tutors in Writing Centers." *WPA: Writing Program Administration* 7.1-2 (1983): 33-38. Acknowledges the power of peer influence but cautions that using peer tutors may reproduce old attitudes (including the stigma of remediation), replicate the structure of authority, and exploit student tutors. Recommends that writing program administrators treat tutors as students (not staff), focusing on their development as learners and writers.

0938. Veit, Richard C. "Basic Writer: Lab or Tutor? The Case for Tutors." *Improving Writing Skills.* Ed. Thom Hawkins and Phyllis Brooks. New Directions for College Learning Assistance 3. San Francisco: Jossey-Bass, 1981. 9-14. Discusses two philosophies of writing center instruction: self-instructional (materials-based) and humanistic (tutor-based). Discusses the advantages and disadvantages of each and favors "tutoring over workbooks and machines" because of "students' real needs and the limitations of materials."

0939. Wallace, Ray. "Towards Heuristic Use Later in the Writing Process: The Role of the Writing Center Tutor." *Focuses* 1.2 (1988): 19-26. Argues the use of heuristics in teaching writing has been limited primarily to classroom instruction in invention. Claims that returning heuristics to greater overall importance in the writing process rests with "the individualized instruction" offered by writing centers because tutors work with students in all stages of their writing.

0940. Wiener, Harvey S. *The Writing Room: A Resource Book for Teachers of English.* New York: Oxford UP, 1981. Devotes brief portion of book (pages 196-204) to writing centers, "typically understaffed and overworked" places that provide individual instruction. Lists 10 "touchstones for tutoring apprentice writers," focusing on the interpersonal relations of tutors and writers and professional conduct of tutors.

0941. Williams, Sharon. "Body Language: The Non-Verbal Path to Success in the Writing Center." *Writing Lab Newsletter* 16.4-5 (1992): 6-7. Views body language as an important source of information about a student writer's attitudes, attention level, and emotional state. Contends a tutor's attention to a writer's nonverbal cues can increase the odds of having a successful conference.

0942. Winterowd, W. Ross, and James D. Williams. "Cognitive Style and Written Discourse." *Focuses* 3.1 (1990): 3-23. Discusses the implications of cognitive learning styles and of brain theory—especially hemisphericity—upon tutors' understanding of how people experience, perceive, and write. Presents the results of a study of the cognitive styles and writing performances of 350 students in grade levels 6, 9, 10, and 12.

0943. Wolcott, Willa. "Talking It Over: A Qualitative Study of Writing Center Conferencing." *The Writing Center Journal* 9.2 (1989): 15-29. Indicates gender and ethnicity have little to do with how students approach tutorials. Claims that tutors generally see themselves as in authority and that the focus (on surface errors or global issues) of each conference hinges on the course the student is taking. Concludes conferences have similarities, but "each experience and each outcome are different."

0944. **Young, Virginia H. "Politeness Phenomena in the University Writing Conference." Diss. U of Illinois at Chicago, 1992. *DAI* 53-12A (1993): 4236.** Examines videotape of writing conferences to analyze the relationship of student comfort to manifestations of politeness phenomena in the teacher's comments. The data suggest strong cultural differences in students' preferences and also that, during writing conferences, subtle interactional mismatches can occur with the potential to impact negatively upon culturally non-mainstream students' short and long-term opportunities.

0945. **Zakaluck, B. "Peer Tutoring." *Encyclopedia of English Studies and Language Arts*. Ed. Alan Purves. New York: Scholastic, 1994. 902-03.** Provides a theoretical, historical, and practical overview of peer tutoring practices in a number of disciplines.

# Tutor Training

0946. Ackley, Elizabeth. "Training Peer Tutors for the Secondary School Writing Center." *The High School Writing Center: Establishing and Maintaining One.* Ed. Pamela B. Farrell. Urbana: NCTE, 1989. 65-72. Describes a week-long, 20-hour peer tutor training course that takes place in summer, detailing topics covered.

0947. Adams, Ronald, Robert Child, Muriel Harris, and Kathleen Henriott. "Training Teachers for the Writing Lab: A Multidimensional Perspective." *The Writing Center Journal* 7.2 (1987): 3-19. Argues that a multiplicity of perspectives from the prospective tutor, the experienced tutor, the writing teacher, and the writing lab director should be taken into account in training new tutors and in designing and assessing tutor training programs.

0948. Aleo, Cynthia. "Tutors' Column: Does a Comma Splice Have Horns?" *Writing Lab Newsletter* 17.9 (1993): 9. Points out that tutors are never fully trained but undergo continual on-the-job training, learning to adapt to the needs and style of each new student.

0949. Allen, Chad, and Greg Lichtenberg. *Harvard University Writing Center Training Manual.* Cambridge: Harvard, 1986. A widely available in-house training manual, detailing ways of working with students, providing a checklist for critical papers, and outlining approaches for dealing with common problems in writing.

0950. Amato, Katya. "Pluralism and Its Discontents: Tutor Training in a Multicultural University." *Writing Lab Newsletter* 17.4 (1992): 1-6. Looks at the difficulties of training tutors to work with multicultural students. Cautions tutors against stereotyping along cultural lines.

Suggests analyzing the patterns of ESL students' errors may provide a key to helping the students acquire English skills.

0951. **Anspach, Marlene. "A Paradoxical Approach to Training Tutors: A Theory of Failure."** *Writing Lab Newsletter* **13.2 (1988): 14-16.** Ironically presents a list of activities tutors should practice in order to invite failure. Suggests that focusing on failure can lead, paradoxically, to success.

0952. **Arkin, Marian. "Using the Journal and Case Study to Train Writing Peer Tutors."** *Teaching English in the Two-Year College* **9.2 (1983): 129-34.** Describes two techniques that can be used to train peer tutors, using journals and case studies to help students examine their practices as tutors.

0953. **Arkin, Marian, and Barbara Shollar.** *The Tutor Book.* **New York: Longman, 1982.** A textbook for instructing tutors to work effectively in a number of settings with varied populations, including people with learning disabilities, the physically challenged, those with different cultural backgrounds, and adult learners. Also deals with the counseling dimensions of tutoring.

0954. **Bannister-Wills, Linda. "Developing a Peer Tutor Program."** *Writing Centers: Theory and Administration.* **Ed. Gary A. Olson. Urbana: NCTE, 1984. 132-43.** Surveys several tutor training programs then articulates a general six-part model for training that can be adapted to varied settings.

0955. **Bell, Elizabeth. "The Peer Tutor as Principal Benefactor in the Writing Center Or It's Not Just for English Teaching Any More."** *Writing Lab Newsletter* **9.9 (1985): 10-13.** Points out that writing centers fail to capitalize on an outstanding feature of peer tutor training—that working as a tutor is a valuable skill that tutors can apply later in life in a range of settings and professional careers.

0956. **Benson, Kirsten F. "Assessment and Development in Graduate Tutor Training."** *Focuses* **3.1 (1990): 24-36.** Contends that discussions of training graduate tutors have been eclipsed by those focusing on training peer tutors. Claims that a great potential for misunderstanding and miscommunication exists in this situation because of the differences in levels of intellectual and cognitive development between graduate tutors and peer tutors. Suggests ways to train and assess graduate tutors.

0957. **Birdsall, Mary Pat. "Using Response Journals for Problem-Solving in the Writing Center."** *Writing Lab Newsletter* **17.8 (1993): 12-16**. Recommends using response journals to facilitate communication between the writing center director and writing consultants who work at different times. Such journals give consultants a sense of belonging, heighten awareness of the writing center mission, offer consultants a chance to share concerns and techniques, build morale, and help consultants work through problems.

0958. **Bishop, Wendy. "We're All Basic Writers: Tutors Talking About Writing Apprehension."** *The Writing Center Journal* **9.2 (1989): 31-42**. Reviews research on writing apprehension and its impact on students. Indicates tutors tend to use apprehension to generate creative tension that helps them approach difficult writing tasks constructively. Suggests that talking and writing about writing apprehension will help tutors deal with other students' writing apprehensions.

0959. **Bishop, Wendy. "The Writing Center Through Writers' Eyes."** *Writing Lab Newsletter* **14.3 (1989): 3-7**. Uses narratives students wrote about their visits to a writing center to help tutors see how students perceive them. Contends such narratives can help identify strengths and weaknesses of the tutoring staff and lead to improvements in tutoring and tutor training.

0960. **Bowden, Darsie. "Inter-Activism: Strengthening the Writing Conference."** *The Writing Center Journal* **15.2 (1995): 163-75**. Describes the Writing Center Conference Diagnostic (WCCD) process used by the writing center at DePaul University (IL) for training and evaluating tutors. Claims WCCD's interview format enhanced communication between student and tutor, reduced tutors' fear of evaluation, and improved writing and tutoring.

0961. **Broder, Peggy F. "Writing Center and Teacher Training."** *WPA: Writing Program Administration* **13.3 (1990): 37-45**. Argues that the writing center is especially effective as a practical training ground for writing teachers because tutors learn two key lessons: to view writing as a process and to see the value of paying close attention to individual students' ideas and papers. Sees the tutors' varied experiences in the writing center as vital preparation for humane and productive classroom teaching.

0962. **Carino, Peter. "Posing Questions for Collaborative Evaluation of Audio Taped Tutorials."** *Writing Lab Newsletter* **14.1 (1989): 11-13**.

Contends taping tutorials can help tutors evaluate the amount of talking they do, the quality of their rapport with students, and whether they provide too much or too little support.

0963. **Carmusin, Amy. "Let the Students Help." *Writing Lab Newsletter* 9.1 (1984): 10-11.** Tells of a peer tutoring course in which students are divided into committees on administration, advertising, and a speaker series. Claims that this course prepared the peer tutors to participate in writing center management and urges directors to allow peer tutors to assist in designing and implementing a center's offerings.

0964. **Child, Robert. "Tutor-Teachers: An Examination of How Writing Center and Classroom Environments Inform Each Other." *The Writing Center: New Directions.* Ed. Ray Wallace and Jeanne Simpson. New York: Garland, 1991. 169-83.** Investigates effect of training for tutoring on classroom practices of six teachers who had received tutor training at various stages of their career. Those who began in the classroom found their teaching strategies enhanced by their tutoring experience, whereas those who went from tutoring to classroom teaching felt more frustration in applying their tutoring experience to the classroom.

0965. **Clark, Beverly Lyon. *Talking about Writing: A Guide for Tutor and Teacher Conferences.* Ann Arbor: U of Michigan P, 1985.** A practical guide for tutors, providing detailed information on topics likely to arise in a tutoring session, such as the writing process, grammar and mechanics, specialized writing genres, and plagiarism. Also examines the interpersonal dimensions of tutoring, including effective roles the tutor might assume and ways of "reading" the client's attitudes and feelings.

0966. **Clark, Cheryl, and Phyllis A. Sherwood. "A Tutoring Dialogue: From Workshop to Session." *The Writing Center Journal* 1.2 (1981): 26-32.** Tutor trainer describes training workshop presenting theories, strategies, and techniques of tutoring; student tutor reports applying that information in tutorial sessions.

0967. **Clark, Irene L. *Writing in the Center: Teaching in a Writing Center Setting.* 2nd ed. Dubuque: Kendall/Hunt, 1992.** Designed for training writing center tutors, covers theoretical underpinnings and common tutoring concerns, including interpreting writing assignments, working with non-native and dialect speakers, and using computers in writing instruction. Includes bibliographies and experience-based exercises.

0968. Clark, Irene Lurkis. "Dialogue in the Lab Conference: Script Writing and the Training of Writing Lab Tutors." *The Writing Center Journal* 2.1 (1982): 21-33. As part of training asks students to write dialogues demonstrating how they would talk with a student about a given paper. Concerns emerging from the process were defining and facilitating productive student-tutor interactions, determining the focus of a session, deciding which composing strategies to discuss, and identifying directions for further work with the same student.

0969. Clark, Irene Lurkis. "Hypothetical Dialogues and the Training of a Lab Staff." *Writing Lab Newsletter* 7.4 (1982): 7-8. Claims that having tutors write hypothetical dialogues of tutoring sessions is an effective component of tutor training because tutors learn to focus on the interpersonal interactions, behaviors, and composing strategies that facilitate tutorial instruction.

0970. Clark, Irene Lurkis. "Preparing Future Composition Teachers in the Writing Center." *College Composition and Communication* 39.3 (1988): 347-50. Contends that the writing center is an ideal, if often overlooked, training ground for new composition teachers because of the insights into writing and thinking processes they can gain by coming into direct contact with students immersed in the writing process.

0971. Clark, Roger. "Using Flowcharts to Train Lab Tutors." *Writing Lab Newsletter* 8.4 (1983): 8-9. Claims that using flowcharts of a writing lab's organization, location of materials, and "general instructional cycle" can help new tutors avoid confusion and insecurity about whether they are "doing things right."

0972. Cobb, Loretta. "Practical Techniques for Training Tutors to Overcome Defensive Blocks." *The Writing Center Journal* 3.1 (1982): 32-37. Recommends using values clarification training to help tutors empathize with students who have difficulty in writing and to discover ways to overcome those students' resistance.

0973. Cogie, Jane. "Resisting the Editorial Urge in Writing Center Conferences: An Essential Focus in Tutor Training." *Writing Center Perspectives*. Ed. Byron L. Stay, Christina Murphy, and Eric H. Hobson. Emmitsburg: NWCA Press, 1995. 162-67. Describes ways tutor training can be carried out to help tutors overcome the tendency to dominate a tutoring session by editing the students' papers.

0974. Collins, James L. "Training Teachers of Basic Writing in the Writing Laboratory." *College Composition and Communication* 33 (1982): 426-33. Describes six-week summer course combining college basic writers with secondary teachers and university graduate teaching assistants in a writing lab approach. Through interaction with students, teachers began to learn ways to move writers from the equivalent of written-down talk to more polished writing.

0975. Collins, Norma Decker. "The Role of a Writing Center in a Teacher Education Program." *Writing Lab Newsletter* 18.4 (1993): 6-7. Explores the benefits of training education students in the writing center. Contends that working as tutors in a middle school writing center not only gave prospective teachers valuable student contact but led them to seek out research on the teaching of writing. Concludes that tutors, as a result of their experience, began to see themselves as teachers.

0976. Comins, Suzanne. "To the 'Manner' Born: A Rebuttal." *Writing Lab Newsletter* 8.3 (1983): 3-4. Responds to Peter A. Lyons's procedure of asking prospective tutors to evaluate a sample essay and not choosing those who focus on mechanical errors first (see entry 0511). Claims this approach is naive and counterproductive because good tutors are not "born" but have to be trained. Offers a different set of techniques for interviewing and selecting tutors.

0977. Croft, Mary. "Test Your Tutorship." *Writing Lab Newsletter* 7.6 (1983): 9-10. Provides a 30-question test on tutoring skills for tutors to take after they have completed training and to be used as a basis for group discussions.

0978. Denton, Thomas. "Peer Tutors' Evaluations of the Tutor Training Course and the Tutoring Experience: A Questionnaire." *Writing Lab Newsletter* 18.3 (1993): 14-16. Presents results from questionnaire that indicate lessons peer tutors learned in a tutor training course about collaborative, student-centered instruction inspired many to become teachers. Suggests such courses, combined with experience in the writing center, provide a rich educational experience for tutors.

0979. Dossin, Mary. "To: New Writing Tutors." *Writing Lab Newsletter* 11.5 (1987): 6. Suggests that new tutors learn from tutorials that go poorly. Offers a three-part, problem solving framework for self-criticism and self-examination, consisting of observation, analysis, and judgment.

**0980.** **Draper, Virginia. "Teaching Peer Tutors: Respect, Response, Insight."** *Writing Lab Newsletter* **6.7 (1982): 6-7.** Describes a tutor training course that focuses on creating an attitude of respect for the composing process and for freshman writers as a prerequisite to training in theories of tutoring.

**0981.** **Edwards, Suzanne. "Tutoring Your Tutors: How to Structure a Tutor-Training Workshop."** *Writing Lab Newsletter* **7.10 (1983): 7-9.** Discusses a six-hour workshop for training tutors by familiarizing them with writing lab policies and the support materials available to them, offering practical suggestions about tutoring techniques, and interpersonal skills, such as responding to the student writer's self-image.

**0982.** **Freehafer, Nancy. "Tutors' Essays: A Partial Record of a Tutor Training Class."** *Writing Lab Newsletter* **5.10 (1981): 8.** Discusses the use of journals kept by tutors about their individual tutoring sessions as one means of training tutors in a course titled "The Writing Tutor: Theory and Practice."

**0983.** **Gadbow, Kate. "Teachers as Writing Center Tutors: Release from the Red Pen."** *Writing Lab Newsletter* **14.4 (1989): 13-15.** Sees the writing center as a valuable retraining ground for classroom teachers. Contends that tutoring leads to better teaching by helping teachers develop respect for students, see flaws in writing assignments, be sensitive in evaluating students' writing, and realize how difficult it can be to interpret marginal comments.

**0984.** **Garrett, Marvin P. "Toward a Delicate Balance: The Importance of Role Playing and Peer Criticism in Peer-Tutor Training."** *Tutoring Writing: A Sourcebook for Writing Labs.* **Ed. Muriel Harris. Glenview: Scott, Foresman, 1982. 94-100.** Warns of danger of peer tutors' assuming an extreme role (directive teacher or sympathetic but uncritical listener); recommends role playing during training that requires peer tutors to assume part of tutor, tutee, or observer-commentator for both the tutoring and writing processes.

**0985.** **Gaskins, Jake. "Using 'Process Recordings' to Train Tutors."** *Writing Lab Newsletter* **19.2 (1994): 14-15.** Urges having tutors record the events of a tutorial in one column, an analysis of it in a second, and their emotional reaction in a third. This training tool helps tutors explore aspects of their work they might otherwise miss.

0986. Glasgow, Jacqueline N. "Training Tutors for Secondary School Writing Centers." *Writing Lab Newsletter* 20.3 (1995): 1-6. Discusses a model for training high school tutors by focusing on three areas of the one-to-one conference: establishing rapport, giving positive reader response, and describing the text.

0987. Glassman, Susan. "Training Peer Tutors Using Videos." *Writing Center Journal* 5.2/6.1 (1985): 40-45. Discusses how tutors plan, write, and act in a video script for training new tutors and offers advice on benefits and pitfalls of this approach.

0988. Glassman, Susan. "Tutor Training on a Shoestring." *Tutoring Writing: A Sourcebook for Writing Labs.* Ed. Muriel Harris. Glenview: Scott, Foresman, 1982. 123-29. Describes development of a recruiting and training program that operates efficiently within limitations of a specific institutional setting.

0989. Goggin, Maureen Daly. "Training Tutors to Work with Student Writers." *Writing Lab Newsletter* 12.7 (1988): 8-11. Provides a detailed look at the writing center's multifaceted tutor training program at Northeastern University (MA).

0990. Hain, Bonnie. "Training Tutors to Read Technical Writing." *Writing Lab Newsletter* 18.9 (1993): 15. Suggests various ways to help peer tutors overcome their anxiety about helping students with technical and scientific papers.

0991. Harris, Jeanette. "The Handbook as a Supplement to a Tutor Training Program." *Writing Centers: Theory and Administration.* Ed. Gary A. Olson. Urbana: NCTE, 1984. 144-51. Suggests that creating an in-house tutor manual containing writing center policies and other information can be a valuable supplement for traditional training and outlines typical sections of such a manual.

0992. Harris, Jeanette. "Handbook for Tutors." *Writing Lab Newsletter* 3.3 (1978): 4. Discusses the value of developing a handbook on writing center information and policies as one means of training tutors, especially those hired later in the year and unable to participate in orientation sessions.

0993. Hutto, David. "Scenarios for Tutor Training." *Writing Lab Newsletter* 14.6 (1990): 1-3. Discusses the use of case studies, or scenarios, in tutor training. Benefits include introducing tutors to difficult or unpleasant tutoring experiences and giving tutors practice in solving specific problems.

0994. **Jacoby, Jay. "Training Writing Center Personnel to Work with International Students: The Least We Need to Know."** *Writing Lab Newsletter* **10.2 (1985): 1-6.** Argues that tutors need to acquire some knowledge about teaching English as a second language in order to help international students. Describes a "minimalist" course in TESOL one writing center offers its tutors. Includes a list of selected readings, useful exercises, and advice on soothing international students' fears.

0995. **Johnson, Candice, and Linda Houston. "Effective Writing Lab Tutors—Collaboration is the Key."** *Writing Lab Newsletter* **18.5 (1994): 4-5.** Describes a tutor training course that helps tutors gain self-awareness through such tools as the Myers-Briggs Type Indicator, gain awareness of adult learners, and develop interpersonal and communication skills. Sees course as key in improving the quality of tutoring at the university's writing center.

0996. **Kail, Harvey, and Ronda Dubay. "Texts for Tutors and Teachers."** *Writing Center Journal* **5.1 (1984): 14-29.** Discusses and reviews books for training tutors through collaborative methods.

0997. **Kilborn, Judith. "Selecting and Training Peer Tutors for Business Writing."** *Writing Lab Newsletter* **8.4 (1983): 4-7.** Describes a program of graduate student mentors and undergraduate peer tutors in which the mentors trained the peer tutors in the requirements of business writing so that a writing lab could better meet the demands for its services by business students.

0998. **Koskinen, Patricia S., and Robert M. Wilson.** *A Guide for Student Tutors.* **New York: Teachers College, 1982.** A brief manual for students working with other students. Contains simple background information on the place of tutoring in education and specific suggestions for tutoring and dealing with common problems. Like other books in this series, this guide is geared to elementary grade language arts activities.

0999. **Koskinen, Patricia S., and Robert M. Wilson.** *Tutoring: A Guide for Success.* **New York: Teachers College, 1982.** Designed to assist adults who want to tutor in schools, this guide outlines qualifications for successful tutoring, specific strategies for tutoring effectively, and ways of dealing with common problems and special tutoring situations.

Although the authors point out that the general information contained here applies to almost all tutoring situations, the illustrations are confined largely to the elementary grades.

1000. **Kulkarni, Diane. "The Personal Literacy History: A Great Jumping-Off Place."** *Writing Lab Newsletter* **20.1 (1995): 7-8.** Advocates beginning the training of peer tutors by having them write a personal literacy history detailing their development as writers. Contends that such an assignment helps sensitize tutors "to the impact that literacy histories have on all writers."

1001. **Laque, Carol Feiser, and Phyllis A. Sherwood.** *A Laboratory Approach to Writing.* **Urbana: NCTE, 1977.** Provides an approach to writing instruction for either the writing lab or the traditional classroom. Provides a course of study for (re)training teachers. Includes chapters devoted to diagnosis and evaluation, teaching the writing process, and teacher/tutor self-evaluation.

1002. **Larson, Deborah. "Role Playing Emotions in Tutor Training."** *Writing Lab Newsletter* **11.1 (1986): 10-13.** Recommends using role playing to train tutors to deal with emotionally manipulative or demanding students. Contends such training helps tutors see students as people, not as writing problems, and helps supervisors screen tutor candidates to discover who will most effectively cope with the interpersonal demands of tutoring.

1003. **Leahy, Richard. "Using Audiotapes for Evaluation and Collaborative Training."** *Writing Lab Newsletter* **18.5 (1994): 1-3.** Argues that audiotaping tutoring sessions is a valuable training method. Suggests ways to avoid pitfalls and make good use of session tapes.

1004. **Loschky, Lynne. "The State of Peer Tutor Training: What We Are Presently Doing."** *Writing Lab Newsletter* **8.1 (1983): 1-6.** Reports the result of a survey on how college writing programs select, train, and use peer tutors. Finds that previous writing performance and recommendations from teachers are the two major factors in tutor selection. Tutors are most often trained through exchange sessions with veteran tutors. Tutors generally work with students from all disciplines, not just those in English classes.

1005. **Luce, Henry. "On Selecting Peer Tutors: Let's Hear it for Heterogeneity."** *Writing Lab Newsletter* **10.9 (1986): 3-5.** Argues that recruiting peer tutors from multiple disciplines has a number of advantages over recruiting tutors exclusively from the English department. Benefits include greater willingness by instructor in other disciplines to refer students to the center, a richer atmosphere, based on shared learning, and having tutors act as ambassadors from the writing center to their various departments.

1006. **Lyons, Greg. "Writing Activities for Writers."** *Writing Lab Newsletter* **15.7 (1991): 14-16.** Discusses the pedagogical value of having tutors keep journals, read and annotate scholarly articles, and write a semester report on their experiences in the writing center. Suggests that such writing provides tutors with valuable learning opportunities and introduces them to the profession.

1007. **MacDonald, Ross B.** *The Master Tutor: A Guidebook for More Effective Tutoring.* **Williamsville: Cambridge Stratford Study Skills Institute, 1995.** Serves as a general introduction to tutoring by focusing on such topics as the tutor's role in promoting independent learning and facilitating the tutee's insights into learning processes. Other topics include the tutoring cycle from greeting to closing, the tutor's options in a tutorial, and tutoring multiculturally.

1008. **Magnuson, Robin. "Preventing Writing Wrecks: The Role of the Writing Lab in Teacher Preparation."** *Writing Lab Newsletter* **10.8 (1986): 11-14.** Because many students who seek help are victims of poor teaching, contends that writing labs should help train teachers. Discusses three types of student victims and suggests that providing teachers with tutor training might help prevent these problems.

1009. **Meyer, Emily, and Louise Z. Smith.** *The Practical Tutor.* **New York: Oxford UP, 1987.** A textbook for tutor training that provides detailed coverage of many aspects of tutoring: establishing rapport with writers; helping writers generate, shape, and revise ideas; dealing with specific common errors; tutoring writing assignments in various disciplines; and working with computers.

1010. **Miller, Shelley. "Dodging the Pundit: The Prevention of Pedagogy in the Writing Center."** *Writing Lab Newsletter* **11.7 (1987): 1-4.** To avoid the problems created when a peer tutor assumes the role of writing expert, suggests training tutors to ask open-ended questions, refrain from setting themselves up as experts, let students do the majority of the talking, and avoid making evaluative statements.

1011. Mohr, Ellen. "Employing Undergraduate Students as Peer Tutors."
      *Writing Lab Newsletter* 10.6 (1986): 3-5. Describes the process one
      director uses in recruiting, hiring, and training peer tutors. Contends peer
      tutors not only provide a type of feedback that professional tutors
      cannot, but that their various "advantages far outweigh any
      disadvantages."

1012. Moore, Elizabeth. "The Tutor Test: Basis for Hiring." *Writing Lab
      Newsletter* 10.5 (1986): 11-12. Recommends giving a screening test
      when hiring tutors. Describes one center's test, which consists of three
      parts: writing a short essay, evaluating the strengths and weaknesses of
      sample papers, and detecting and correcting logical fallacies. Argues that
      the test is a valuable tool for tutor selection.

1013. Mulvihill, Peter, Keith Nitta, and Molly Wingate. "Into the Fray:
      Ethnicity and Tutor Preparation." *Writing Lab Newsletter* 19.7
      (1995): 1-5. Discusses a training seminar at Colorado College designed
      to make tutors aware of the ramifications of ethnicity on student and
      tutor attitudes during tutorials. Attempts to root out covert racism by
      using James Banks's six-stage typology of emerging ethnic identity to
      increase tutors' awareness. Describes multiethnic education program,
      including the assignment of an essay on the tutors' own ethnic identity.

1014. Neuleib, Janice, Maurice Scharton, Julia Visor, and Yvette Weber-
      Davis. "Using Videotapes to Train Tutors." *Writing Lab Newsletter*
      14.5 (1990): 1-3, 8. Shows how a writing center uses a video camera to
      give tutors an honest look at their performance in tutorials. Suggests that
      tutors can use videotapes to self-evaluate (and improve) their body
      language, the ratio of talking to listening, their tone of voice, and their
      treatment of students.

1015. North, Stephen M. "Training Tutors to Talk about Writing." *College
      Composition and Communication* 33 (1982): 434-41. Describes five
      tactics used in training: trainees play the role of tutor, play the role of
      student, observe sessions, watch videotape of their own tutoring, and
      study anecdotal accounts of sessions. Calls for research to evaluate
      tutoring effectiveness as the most effective response to dismissals of
      writing center work.

1016. Nugent, Susan. "The Library Information Aide: Connecting
      Libraries, Writing Centers, and Classrooms." *Writing Lab Newsletter*
      14.7 (1990): 13-15. Describes the creation of a library information aide

program that trains tutors to help students integrate research into writing projects.

1017. **Paolucci, Mary. "Journal Articles Reviewed by Writing Lab Staff at the University of Akron."** *Writing Lab Newsletter* **3.5 (1979): 2-3.** Discusses the value to tutor training of having graduate students who work in the writing center for one semester as part of their M.A. program summarize individually and discuss as a group journal articles on writing center theory and practice.

1018. **Patten, Stan. "Peer Professionals."** *Writing Lab Newsletter* **12.9 (1988): 1-4.** Describes a training course used to develop "peer professionals," a hybrid term for undergraduate tutors who are "peers" in age but "professional" in knowledge.

1019. **Podis, Leonard A. "Training Peer Tutors for the Writing Lab."** *College Composition and Communication* **31.1 (1980): 70-75.** Describes a tutor training program to make peer tutors knowledgeable about writing and instill the interpersonal techniques they will need to be effective helpers. Emphasizes balancing criticism and encouragement and seeks to avoid turning tutors into Kenneth Bruffee's "little teachers."

1020. **Posey, Evelyn. "An Ongoing Tutor-Training Program."** *Writing Center Journal* **6.2 (1986): 29-35.** Describes ways to continue writing center tutors' training by including them in the daily administration of the writing center, using a writing process worksheet while tutoring, and establishing writing workshops in which they share their writing and views on writing.

1021. **Reigstad, Thomas J., and Donald A. McAndrew.** *Training Tutors for Writing Conferences.* **NCTE Theory and Research into Practice Ser. Urbana: ERIC/NCTE, 1984.** Outlines a 15-week tutor training program, including information on theory and research supporting one-to-one collaboration in writing.

1022. **Rings, Sally, and Rick A. Sheets. "Student Development and Metacognition: Foundations for Tutor Training."** *Journal of Developmental Education* **15.1 (1991): 30-32.** Recommends that tutor training programs draw on two useful theoretical models: student development theory and metacognitive theory. The first model can help tutors help students become autonomous individuals, and the second model can help tutors involve students in more conscious formulation and achievement of goals.

1023. Rizzolo, Patricia. "Peer Tutors Make Good Teachers: A Successful Writing Program." *Improving College and University Teaching* 30.3 (1982): 115-19. Discusses one writing center's use of peer tutors trained in the techniques of questioning, explanation, and constructive criticism.

1024. Robins, Adrienne. "Teaching the Conferencing Strategies that Improve Students' Writing." *Writing Lab Newsletter* 15.10 (1991): 1-4. Describes a training process aimed at helping writing advisors develop their own conferencing strategies rather than imposing generic approaches on them. Emphasizes the development of communication skills, in both writers and advisors, rather than competence in writing.

1025. Rouse, Joy. "Tutor Recruitment and Training at Miami University." *Writing Lab Newsletter* 14.8 (1990): 1-3. Describes tutor recruitment and training program at Miami University (OH), which begins by assessing a tutor's writing and interpersonal abilities through a tutor test, interviews, role playing, and recommendations from professors. A tutor training course covers such topic as interpreting nonverbal communication, asking effective questions, giving feedback, and summarizing students' ideas.

1026. Ryan, Leigh. *The Bedford Guide for Writing Tutors.* Boston: Bedford-St. Martin's, 1994. Separate chapters provide information for training tutors about the general stages of the writing process, the dynamics of the tutoring session, ways of helping students through the writing process, various student populations frequently encountered in writing centers, formats and content expectations for papers in specific fields, and difficult tutoring situations. Includes exercises and an annotated bibliography.

1027. Sams, Ed. "The Weekly Tutor Meeting." *Writing Lab Newsletter* 15.9 (1991): 1-4. Recommends that the writing center director hold regular meetings with peer tutors to augment lessons taught in a tutor training course, get past the teacher/student relationship, and allow for in-depth discussion of issues, ideas, and experiences.

1028. Samuels, Shelly. "Using Videotapes for Tutor Training." *Writing Lab Newsletter* 8.3 (1983): 5-7. Claims that videotapes of actual tutoring sessions offer an excellent opportunity to train tutors by showing them models of effective and ineffective techniques and interpersonal interactions.

1029. Simpson, Jeanne. "Defining the Status of Writing Center Tutors." *Writing Lab Newsletter* 9.6 (1985): 4-6. Discusses training methods and philosophies, such as "problem-of-the-week sessions" and readings in professional journals, as ways of training graduate students as tutors and as future writing teachers. Also states that the tutor training program is the only place graduate students receive any instruction in "professional ethics and demands" at her university.

1030. Skerl, Jennie. "Training Writing Lab Tutors." *WPA: Writing Program Administration* 3.3 (1980): 15-18. Outlines preliminary instructions given to tutors in a voluntary, drop-in writing lab, including a procedure in which praising some element of the student's paper is followed by raising questions about it and then developing a plan of action.

1031. Smith, Mark. "Two Suggestions for Training Peer Tutors." *Writing Lab Newsletter* 5.8 (1981): 9. Suggests that analyzing sample student essays and role playing are valuable aids in tutor training.

1032. Sollisch, James W. "The Eternal Rough Draft: A Metaphor for Training Peer Tutors." *Writing Lab Newsletter* 10.4 (1985): 12-14. Sees advantages in peer tutors' lack of polish as writers. Claims they can empathize with student writers' problems and recall helpful strategies for invention and composing that professional tutors may have forgotten. Builds these assumptions into a tutor training course.

1033. Spellman-Trimble, Lisa. "Tutors' Column: A Knot of Questions: An Exercise in Training Tutors." *Writing Lab Newsletter* 12.9 (1988): 7-8. Examines the role of questions in the tutorial and offers a list of ten model questions for tutoring.

1034. Sullivan, Patrick. "Training Peer Tutors: Providing Tutors with a Basic Procedure." *Writing Lab Newsletter* 8.4 (1983): 1-2. Describes steps in tutor training, such as offering a student encouragement, getting the student thinking rather than just listening, isolating problematic areas in papers, and giving guidelines on what overall aspect of his or her writing a student needs to improve.

1035. Sullivan, Patrick. "Writing Lab Tutors Design a Tutor Training Program." *Writing Lab Newsletter* 9.1 (1984): 11-12. Presents 20 suggestions peer tutors offered for what they would like to include in a tutor training program. Suggestions range from a discussion on how thesis statements can be developed to what a tutor should do if the student doesn't respond to leading questions.

1036. Trevathan, Debby. "The Selection and Training of Peer Tutors." *Writing Lab Newsletter* 8.2 (1983): 1-5. Suggests faculty recommendations as the basis for selecting peer tutors. As part of tutor training courses advocates providing theoretical readings from such authors as Kenneth Bruffee, Peter Elbow, Marcia Silver, Mina Shaughnessy, and others as an introduction to the field.

1037. Weglarz, Mike. "Better Tutoring Through Peer Tutor Interaction." *Writing Lab Newsletter* 9.6 (1985): 9. States that allowing beginning tutors to work with and observe more experienced tutors is beneficial to training. Discusses a training course and also the possibility of allowing tutors to serve on committees that help administer the writing center as central aspects of tutor training.

1038. Werder, Carmen, and Roberta R. Buck. "Assessing Writing Conference Talk: An Ethnographic Method." *Writing Center Perspectives*. Ed. Byron L. Stay, Christina Murphy, and Eric H. Hobson. Emmitsburg: NWCA Press, 1995. 168-78. Describes a year-long, four-stage assessment strategy that allows tutors to take increasing part in their own evaluation and the implications of that procedure.

1039. Wright, Anne. "Training of Professional Staff." *The High School Writing Center: Establishing and Maintaining One*. Ed. Pamela B. Farrell. Urbana: NCTE, 1989. 73-76. Describes summer workshop for teachers who operate the writing center in a metropolitan high school, emphasizing the importance of planning to meet specific goals.

1040. Zander, Sherri. "The H.O.T. T.U.B. Method: How Other Tutors Teach Us Better." *Writing Lab Newsletter* 9.5 (1985): 11-12. Discusses how having tutors tutor each other and respond to a set of questions about the tutorials serves as an effective means of initiating discussion and beginning the training process in tutor training sessions or courses.

1041. Zander, Sherri. "Tutor Training: The Sharing of Perspectives within a Department." *Writing Lab Newsletter* 15.4 (1990): 12. Describes a two-day tutor training workshop in which members of the English Department's composition faculty participate. Contends that department involvement benefits tutors, faculty members, and the writing center itself because of the exchange of ideas and the goodwill the cooperative effort fosters.

**1042. Zaniello, Fran. "Using Video-tapes to Train Writing Lab Tutors."** *Writing Lab Newsletter* **3.10 (1979): 2-3.** Discusses the benefits of creating a videotape of tutor/student interactions that illustrates some of the things tutors should and should not do in the writing lab. Claims that taping peer tutors is an excellent way to evaluate their performance and develop strengths.

# Tutoring

1043. Addison, Joanne. "A Reader Responds .... Tutoring Students with Learning Disabilities: Working from Strengths." *Writing Lab Newsletter* 19.5 (1995): 12. Urges tutors not to see students with learning disabilities as "problems to be fixed." Suggests that tutors draw on students' existing strengths to help them enhance their writing skills.

1044. Alexander, Joan. "Some Tutoring Guidelines." *Writing Lab Newsletter* 4.4 (1979): 5. Offers a list of "do's and do not's" for tutors that ranges from being supportive to never making negative comments about instructors or assignments.

1045. Allen, Nancy. "Developing an Effective Tutoring Style." *Writing Lab Newsletter* 15.3 (1990): 1-4. Compares tutoring processes for writing and computer programming. Sees similarities in tutor-student relationships and the need to cope with complexities of syntax, style, and unfamiliar terminology.

1046. Along, Julie, and Beverly Lyon Clark. "A Tutor Tutors Spelling." *Writing Lab Newsletter* 6.4 (1981): 3-4. Contends discussing rules for syllabification with students can be an aid to teaching spelling in tutorials.

1047. Ameter, Brenda, and Coralyn Dahl. "Coordination and Cooperation: A Writing Center Serves a Hearing Impaired Student." *Writing Lab Newsletter* 14.6 (1990): 4-5. Describes how a writing center consulted linguistics and speech impairments specialists to help a hearing-impaired student improve his writing.

**1048. Amigone, Grace Ritz. "Writing Lab Tutors: Hidden Messages That Matter."** *The Writing Center Journal* **2.2 (1982): 24-29.** Outlines various kinds of nonverbal communication, particularly body language, and discusses their impact in writing center conferences. Also touches on effect of color on writing center clientele.

**1049. Anderson, Denise M. "Co-Authorship as a Tutoring Technique."** *Writing Lab Newsletter* **19.5 (1995): 15-16.** Lauds tutor-student co-authorship as a way to help students break through writer's block, teach them that writing can be fun, and cement the bond between tutor and student.

**1050. Babcock, Matthew. "Tutors' Column: Leggo My Ego."** *Writing Lab Newsletter* **19.5 (1995): 10-12.** Discusses the role of ego in writing tutorials and a failed attempt, by one peer tutor, to bypass ego problems by referring to the tutor as "the reader" and the student as "the writer."

**1051. Baker, Richard. "Tutors' Column: The Payoff."** *Writing Lab Newsletter* **17.7 (1993): 9.** Recounts a tutor's revelation about the joys of helping a basic writer improve her skills.

**1052. Baker, Tracey. "LD College Writers: Selected Readings."** *Writing Lab Newsletter* **19.3 (1994): 5-7.** Offers information and a brief bibliography on college students with learning disabilities. Suggests writing centers will need to cope with growing numbers of such students.

**1053. Barrios, Aimee. "Tutors' Column: When Writing is Not the Issue."** *Writing Lab Newsletter* **17.6 (1993): 9-10.** Discusses emotional problems that arise during tutorials. Claims tutors have a duty to help students cope with emotional difficulties in order to cope with academic challenges. Cautions that in some situations assuming the role of counselor can do more harm than good.

**1054. Bartelt, Margaret. "Am I a Good Tutor?"** *Writing Lab Newsletter* **19.6 (1995): 8.** Reminds self-doubting tutors that their primary duty is to help students reduce "writing avoidance" behaviors and cope with writing anxiety.

**1055. Bartosenski, Mary. "Color, Re-Vision, and Painting a Paper."** *The Writing Center Journal* **12.2 (1992): 159-73.** Presents a case study of a student with a learning disability who mastered writing by mastering revision. Recounts how the student learned to use colored markers and notebook dividers to identify various parts of essays, allowing her to create and present "her meaning 'like a painting.'"

1056. **Bartosenski, Mary. "Diagramming Connections for Essay Exams."** *Writing Lab Newsletter* **17.4 (1992): 14-15.** Demonstrates how a tutor helped a student learn to make logical connections between her knowledge and essay exam questions.

1057. **Bartosenski, Mary. "Spellbound by a Clean Page."** *Writing Lab Newsletter* **18.3 (1993): 8-9.** Illustrates how some students become too tied to their words to revise. Urges tutors to "break the spell" of the paper by deflecting the students' attention from surface language and toward underlying ideas.

1058. **Beaty, Sandra. "Writing Apprehension and Assurance."** *Writing Lab Newsletter* **11.4 (1986): 12-13.** Sees helping students cope with writing anxiety as a primary function of writing center tutors. Argues even strong writers often suffer from anxieties that get in the way of good writing and need the assurance tutors can give.

1059. **Benton, Kay Hutchison. "Writing Without Pain (Or at Least Less of It)."** *Writing Lab Newsletter* **8.6 (1984):8-9.** Shows how positive feedback from writing lab tutors helped an ESL student progress in her English skills.

1060. **Bishop, Wendy. "Opening Lines: Starting the Tutoring Session."** *Writing Lab Newsletter* **13.3 (1988): 1-4.** Explores connotations of the opening lines student writers use on coming to the writing center (e.g., "I need a paper proofread" or "my teacher sent me"). Suggests responses tutors might make to each statement and discusses the impact each response can have on the success of the tutorial.

1061. **Bishop, Wendy. "Slow Cooking and Fast Food: Balancing Tutoring Options in the Writing Center."** *Writing Lab Newsletter* **13.1 (1988): 10-12.** Compares benefits of two approaches to tutoring: a relationship formed between tutor and student over a number of sessions and a relationship consisting of a short, single meeting between tutor and student.

1062. **Black, Melissa. "Tutors' Column: Seeing the Possibilities."** *Writing Lab Newsletter* **19.7 (1995): 9-10.** Discusses tutoring's potential for helping students develop confidence in their ability to express their ideas in writing.

1063. **Blackmarr, Amy. "Tutors' Column: Stepping Out: From Tutoring to Business (Learning Business Skills in the Writing Center)."** *Writing Lab Newsletter* **20.1 (1995): 9-11.** Claims writing and communications skills peer tutors learn in the writing center will transfer to the business world. Marketable skills include problem solving, critical thinking, and communication abilities.

1064. **Bonfiglio, Anne D. "Essay C/Fourth Draft/May 24, 1982."** *Writing Lab Newsletter* **3.1 (1982): 23-26.** Recounts tutor's experience, reflecting on the ways her training and experience changed her attitudes toward tutoring and writing. Included in Cynthia Onore's "In Their Own 'Write'" (entry 0888).

1065. **Bosco, Jay J. "Tutor's Corner: The Experience of a Peer Tutor."** *Writing Lab Newsletter* **9.5 (1985): 13-14.** Narrates one peer tutor's discovery that the best comfort and help he can offer other students is that he, too, has gone through the same difficulties, demands, anxieties, writing courses, and ups and downs that they are going through.

1066. **Boswell, Rebecca. "Tutors' Column: Leaders Making Leaders."** *Writing Lab Newsletter* **13.5 (1989): 9-10.** Discusses the terrible silences following the presentation of essays to a freshman workshop group and how the students gradually learned to comment on one another's work.

1067. **Brainard, David. "Tutoring and Learning Disabilities."** *Writing Lab Newsletter* **17.9 (1993): 15-16.** Argues students with learning disabilities think in individual languages only they can decode. Contends tutors can help most effectively by offering encouragement, patience, and sensitivity.

1068. **Brannon, Lil. "On Becoming a More Effective Tutor."** *Tutoring Writing: A Sourcebook for Writing Labs.* **Ed. Muriel Harris. Glenview: Scott, Foresman, 1982. 105-110.** Points out necessity of tutors' being aware of how their personalities affect tutoring sessions and describes several general styles of approaching a tutorial.

1069. **Branscomb, H. Eric. "Types of Conferences and the Composing Process."** *The Writing Center Journal* **7.1 (1986): 27-35.** Discusses three types of conferences—process, content, and skills—and considers how each is beneficial and can be used to maximum efficiency in a writing center tutorial.

1070. **Brendel, Gail. "Tutors' Column: Professional Intimacy."** *Writing Lab Newsletter* **18.2 (1993): 11-12.** Discusses difficulties peer tutors face in building and maintaining a professional relationship that allows for a measure of intimacy.

1071. **Bridges, Jean Bolen. "Dialect Interference: A 'Standard' Barrier."** *Writing Lab Newsletter* **8.10 (1984): 9-12.** Claims that dialectic differences create problems for tutors trained in "standard" English but not trained to be sensitive to regional, sub-regional, racial, and ethnic variants. Gives examples of dialectical differences, including an extensive comparison of black dialect and standard edited English forms.

1072. **Brinkley, Ellen H. "Types of Student Clients."** *The High School Writing Center: Establishing and Maintaining One.* **Ed. Pamela B. Farrell. Urbana: NCTE, 1989. 81-84.** Argues that all students benefit from using a writing center—not only the two extremes (highly motivated students who seek out help to succeed and "basic" writers) but those between as well.

1073. **Brooks, Phyllis. "Peer Tutoring and the ESL Student."** *Improving Writing Skills.* **Ed. Thom Hawkins and Phyllis Brooks. New Directions for College Learning Assistance 3. San Francisco: Jossey-Bass, 1981. 45-52.** Claims that not all students referred to a writing center with ESL problems are true ESL students. Many are native speakers who can benefit from the same tutoring focus an ESL student would receive in language, editing, and composing processes.

1074. **Brostoff, Anita. "An Approach to Conferencing."** *Writing Lab Newsletter* **4.7 (1980): 7-8.** Discusses methods for establishing rapport with students as a basis for conferencing and as an aid to diagnostic assessment.

1075. **Brostoff, Anita. "The Writing Conference: Foundations."** *Tutoring Writing: A Sourcebook for Writing Labs.* **Ed. Muriel Harris. Glenview: Scott, Foresman, 1982. 21-26.** Suggests ways to approach initial writing conference and establish an atmosphere of mutual trust and professionalism.

1076. **Cai, Xiaomin. "Behavioral Characteristics of Oriental ESL Students in the Writing Center."** *Writing Lab Newsletter* **18.8 (1994): 5-6.** Explains cross-cultural differences of Oriental ESL students. Points out Oriental students' sense of "nonself," facesaving approach to social interaction, need to establish a warm relationship with a tutor, and tendency to become dependent on the tutor. Cautions against overemphasizing cultural differences.

1077. Calabrese, Marylyn. **"Will You Proofread My Paper?: Responding to Student Writing in the Writing Center."** *Writing Lab Newsletter* **15.5 (1991): 12-15.** Contends most students who request proofreading do not understand what they are asking for. Advises tutors to emphasize their roles as readers, not editors, to help students understand the tutors' role and learn to make more appropriate requests for assistance.

1078. Campbell, Elizabeth, and Kristine Webb. **"Tutoring Techniques for Students in the Oral Tradition."** *Writing Lab Newsletter* **12.2 (1987): 5-9.** Discusses difficulties faced by students who speak nonstandard dialects and how writing center tutors can help. Suggests tutors can affirm students' experiences, help them express their ideas in an appropriate diction, and help them detect systematic editing errors.

1079. Castellucci, Karen. **"Tutors' Column: Getting to Know You ... Building Relationships as a Tutor."** *Writing Lab Newsletter* **16.1 (1991): 9-11. Also in 0006.** Explores the difficult, yet important, stage of the tutorial during which the tutor and writer build a relationship of trust.

1080. Chapman, David. **"Out of the Dragnet and into the Writing Center."** *Writing Lab Newsletter* **13.4 (1988): 11-12.** Takes a humorous look at tutoring grammar by parodying *Dragnet*'s Sgt. Joe Friday.

1081. Chapman, David. **"What If We Stopped Writing Drafts and Started Drafting Writers?"** *Writing Lab Newsletter* **15.1 (1990): 4-5.** Envisions a fantasy world in which society values tutors as much as professional athletes. Presents the concept of a professional tutor draft in the form of a short play.

1082. Chapman, David W. **"High Noon at the Writing Corral: A Tale of the West."** *Writing Lab Newsletter* **12.4 (1987): 1-2.** Parodies a writing center tutorial with a particularly difficult student as a meeting between a pair of gunfighters.

1083. Chappell, Virginia A. **"Hands Off: Fostering Self-Reliance in the Writing Lab."** *Writing Lab Newsletter* **6.6 (1982): 4-6.** Discusses focusing, diagnosing, and teaching as ways tutors can strike a balance between teaching students about composition and merely helping them get a paper written."

1084. Chavez, Flavio. "The USW Method." *Writing Lab Newsletter* 17.3 (1992): 15. Outlines the "Use the Same Word" method for keeping student writers on track during essay exams by having them repeat the wording of the essay question in their thesis statement.

1085. Chiteman, Michael D. "Helping Students Write in Response to Literature: One Tutor's Approach." *Writing Lab Newsletter* 10.5 (1986): 6-8. Discusses difficulties students face in writing about literature: trying to cover too much, unfamiliarity with the type of assignment, and trying "to impose personal experiences where they don't belong." Suggests how tutors can help students overcome these difficulties.

1086. Cohen, Andrew D. "Reformulation: Another Way to Get Feedback." *Writing Lab Newsletter* 10.2 (1985): 6-10. Describes the "reformulation technique" as useful in helping ESL students learn to revise in English. Students write a short text, native writers revise the text, then the ESL students analyze and discuss the changes of vocabulary, syntactic structures, cohesive links, and discourse functions.

1087. Crisp, Sally. "'Aerobic' Writing: A Writing Practice Model." *Writing Lab Newsletter* 12.9 (1988): 9-12. Recommends having students write aerobically—in sustained, regular exercises—in order to break through writer's block, overcome writing anxiety, and attain greater proficiency.

1088. Crisp, Sally. "Our Bill of Writes." *Writing Lab Newsletter* 15.5 (1991): 8. Lists several dozen slogans and puns involving the term *write* that writing centers could use on T-shirts and bumper stickers.

1089. Croft, Mary K. "'I Would Prefer Not To': A Consideration of the Reluctant Student." *Writing Centers: Theory and Administration*. Ed. Gary A. Olson. Urbana: NCTE, 1984. 170-81. Offers five heuristic questions for investigating source of student reluctance and suggests ways of dealing with resistant students.

1090. Cross, Vanessa B. "Tutors' Column: Peer Tutoring: A Contact Sport for the '90s." *Writing Lab Newsletter* 19.4 (1994): 9. Draws an analogy between tutoring and football, based on the images of teacher as coach, tutor as quarterback, and student as player all striving as a team to reach the goal (becoming a better writer).

1091. Crouch, Mary Lou. "The Writing Place at George Mason University." *The Writing Center Journal* 2.2 (1982): 33-35. Traces series of conferences with one student to show how his confidence had to be won before he could begin making gradual improvement in his writing.

1092. Crump, Eric. **"Voices from the Net: Feeling Prepared to Help Learning Disabled Writers."** *Writing Lab Newsletter* **17.9 (1993): 10-12.** Presents a WCenter exchange about tutoring students with learning disabilities. Particular concerns involve the identification of students with learning disabilities, providing special services, and overcoming particular writing problems.

1093. Crump, Eric. **"Voices from the Net: Lifting the Veil from Writing Anxiety."** *Writing Lab Newsletter* **17.4 (1992): 10-12.** Discusses the problem writing anxiety and some possible solutions suggested by correspondents on WCenter.

1094. Crump, Eric. **"Voices from the Net: 'Swords Might be Safer: The Question of Pens in Tutorials.'"** *Writing Lab Newsletter* **19.4 (1994): 6-7.** Excepts WCenter point-counterpoint debate on whether tutors should bring a pen to tutorials. Includes opinions from several researchers, most of whom acknowledge that the question is far more complex than it first appears.

1095. Crump, Eric. **"Voices from the Net: Talk About Talk in the Writing Center."** *Writing Lab Newsletter* **17.7 (1993): 10-11.** Excerpts WCenter discussion of the best way to help a student referred to a writing center because of problems with spoken grammar. Participants advised the tutor to help the student understand that her dialect is not wrong but that standard spoken English is a dialect more appropriate to certain situations.

1096. Crump, Eric. **"Voices from the Net: Weird (?) Topics: A Pressure Point in the Negotiation of Student Authority."** *Writing Lab Newsletter* **18.4 (1993): 8-9.** Presents a WCenter discussion on why students use the authority shared with them by their composition teachers to choose inappropriate or "weird" writing topics.

1097. Cullen, Roxanne. **"Writing Centers as Centers of Connected Learning."** *Writing Lab Newsletter* **16.6 (1992): 1-4.** Views the writing center as the ideal setting for teaching students how to personalize—or make individually relevant—information they learn in classes. Endorses the "midwife" metaphor for tutoring.

1098. David, Carol, Margaret Graham, and Anne Richards. "Three Approaches to Proofreading." *Writing Lab Newsletter* 13.2 (1988): 10-14. Offers advice on how to teach proofreading to three populations of clients: walk-in students, assigned students, and ESL students.

1099. Davis, Candice. "Tutors' Column: Qualities of a Good Writing Assistant." *Writing Lab Newsletter* 15.5 (1991): 9-10. Contends good writing assistants are good listeners, offer meaningful feedback, gear their advice to individual students, and guide writers toward, as opposed to giving them, ideas. Emphasizes communications skills.

1100. Davis, Kevin. "Responding to Writers: A Multi-Variate Approach to Peer Interaction." *The Writing Center Journal* 10.2 (1990): 67-73. Argues peer tutors' inflexibility prevents their taking a writer-centered approach to tutoring. Suggests tutors change their conversational focus, methodological approach, and interactive style to fit each student's situation. Discusses the effects of changing each variable.

1101. Dean, Ruth. "What is the Assignment?" *Writing Lab Newsletter* 11.4 (1986): 10-12. Discusses the difficulty some students have in understanding and satisfying writing assignments. Suggests tutors must often explain assignments by defining and clarifying key terms used in the assignment.

1102. Deutsch, Lucille. "The Research Paper: How the Tutor Can Help." *Writing Lab Newsletter* 6.2 (1981): 1-2. States that tutors can assist students writing research papers by asking them central questions about their thesis, organization, documentation, and the reliability of their resource materials.

1103. Devet, Bonnie. "Five Years on the Hotline: Answering a Writer's Hotline." *Writing Lab Newsletter* 12.4 (1987): 12-14. Discusses the nature of questions callers asked and the lessons tutors learned during a writing hotline's first five years of operation.

1104. Devet, Bonnie. "Laundry Day at the Writing Center." *Writing Lab Newsletter* 15.5 (1991): 16. Illustrates that the intimate relationship developed during tutoring sometimes carries over into other aspects of students' lives.

1105. Devet, Bonnie. "A New Tutor's Role in a College Writing Center." *CEA Forum* 12.3 (1982): 12-13. Examines the relationship of students and tutors. Tutors must know their relationship to the teacher who referred a particular student, their relationship to that student, and their feelings about themselves.

1106. Devet, Bonnie, Ericka Burroughs, Lydia Hopson, Donna Kenyon, Trisha Martin, Cheryl Sims, Hope Norment, Liz Young, Sylvia Gamboa, and Kathy Haney. "The Hurricane and the Writing Lab." *Writing Lab Newsletter* 14.7 (1990): 5-6. Describes the emotion-charged atmosphere in a writing center following Hurricane Hugo. Illustrates the difficulty of maintaining an emotional balance while helping students write papers about traumatic experiences.

1107. Dillingham, Dan. "The Tutor's Corner: A Peer Tutor's Views on the Group Tutorial." *Writing Lab Newsletter* 10.2 (1985): 11-12. Contends small group tutoring can work well if tutors establish a relaxed environment and encourage involvement by all members.

1108. Dillingham, Daniel. "The Outline: A Strategy for Dyslexic Writers." *Writing Lab Newsletter* 12.7 (1988): 5-6. Recommends having dyslexic students construct a detailed outline before attempting to write an essay. Claims outlining keeps dyslexic students on track.

1109. DiPardo, Anne. "'Whispers of Coming and Going': Lessons from Fannie." *The Writing Center Journal* 12.2 (1992): 125-44. Rpt. in 0007 and 0008. Profiles the development of Fanny, a Native American student, over several writing center tutorials. Explores the corresponding development of Morgan, a peer tutor, as she struggles with the collaborative techniques she tries to apply while tutoring Fanny. Urges tutors to be sensitive to other cultures, to question their assumptions about students, and to continually seek clues to the "hidden corners" of a student's past, personality, and methods of learning.

1110. Dornsife, Robert. "Establishing the Role of Audience in the Writing Center Tutorial." *Writing Lab Newsletter* 18.8 (1994): 1-2. Claims tutors begin at a "pedagogical and rhetorical disadvantage" when they must rely on the students' often vague concept of a target audience for their writing. Sees the audience awareness as vital to an effective tutorial.

1111. Dossin, Mary. "Helping Students to Proofread." *Writing Lab Newsletter* 11.2 (1986): 3-4. Contends tutors can and should teach students how to proofread their own papers. Suggests tutors train students to read their papers backward, sentence by sentence.

1112. **Dossin, Mary. "Untrained Tutors."** *Writing Lab Newsletter* **15.4 (1990): 11.** Describes the practices of untrained tutors as a surprising model of what tutors probably ought to do. Suggests that effective tutors arrange concerns hierarchically, group problems, and approach problems one by one, asking questions and listening carefully to the writer's answers rather than overwhelming the writer with advice.

1113. **Dossin, Mary M. "Getting Beyond the Typo: Effective Peer Critiquing."** *Composition Chronicle* **4.4 (1991): 4-5.** Identifies three steps in helping students see the value of peer critiques: instilling a commitment to drafting, learning to accept criticism, and focusing on higher-order concerns.

1114. **Dossin, Mary M. "The** *Sine Qua Non* **for Writing Tutors."** *Writing Lab Newsletter* **19.2 (1994): 5.** Argues that the two essential qualities of a tutor are energy and intellectual curiosity. Sees all other qualities as secondary.

1115. **Dossin, Mary M. "Something for Everyone."** *Writing Lab Newsletter* **18.6 (1994): 15.** Discusses the liberatory possibilities of the writing center, focusing on the difference between students who depend on tutors for basic writing competence and those who depend on tutors for feedback on ideas.

1116. **Downs, Virginia. "What Do English Teachers Want?"** *The Writing Center Journal* **2.2 (1982): 30-32.** On basis of marked papers seen at writing center, warns that some teachers' excessive requests for revision may be counterproductive.

1117. **Doxey, Carolyn. "Tutors' Column."** *Writing Lab Newsletter* **15.4 (1990): 9.** Describes several encounters with international students, all of which turned out to be positive, enriching experiences for student and peer tutor—a surprise to the tutor, considering the "war stories" fellow tutors had told her.

1118. **Droll, Belinda Wood. "Teacher Expectations: A Powerful Third Force in Tutoring Sessions."** *Writing Lab Newsletter* **17.9 (1993): 1-4.** Reminds tutors to factor the impact teacher expectations have on student writing into tutoring sessions. States that accounting for such expectations allows the tutor to tailor advice to the special needs of individual students.

1119. **Dukes, Thomas. "The Writing Lab as Crisis Center: Suggestions for the Interview."** *Writing Lab Newsletter* **5.9 (1981): 4-6.** Claims a primary responsibility of the writing lab tutor is to assist students in dealing with their feelings about writing—especially hostile or fearful emotions that impede their progress as writers.

1120. **Dyer, Patricia M. "Business Communication Meets in the Writing Center: A Successful Four-Week Course."** *Writing Lab Newsletter* **15.7 (1991): 4-6.** Describes an intensive course in business communication held in a university writing center. The class included one-to-one writing instruction and training in word processing.

1121. **Easley, Rex. "The Collaborative Writing Workshop and the Classroom Tutor."** *Writing Lab Newsletter* **17.10 (1993): 11, 14.** Discusses benefits of using tutors as workshop group leaders in basic writing classes. Claims students became more collaborative and formed bonds with tutors and other students. Also saw increase in tutor morale due to a greater sense of involvement with students and faculty members.

1122. **Edwards, Marcia H. "Expect the Unexpected: A Foreign Student in the Writing Center."** *Teaching English in the Two-Year College* **9.2 (1983): 151-56.** Examines differences between American and international students and looks at specific ways in which cultural differences may affect tutorials in writing conferences.

1123. **Eggers, Tilly. "Reassessing the Writing Center: Helping Students See Themselves as Writers."** *CEA Forum* **12.3 (1982): 3-7.** Outlines a simple pattern that helps students begin to see and describe themselves as writers by discussing their beliefs about writers, including their actions, attitudes, and language.

1124. **Enfield, Susan. "Tutors' Column: Tutoring: The Antidote to the Closed Mind."** *Writing Lab Newsletter* **15.8 (1991): 9-10.** Reveals lessons in tolerance a grammar-bigoted peer tutor learned by working closely with a highly motivated minority student.

1125. **Ewald, Helen Rothschild. "Using Error-Analysis in the Writing Lab for Correctness and Effectiveness."** *Writing Lab Newsletter* **8.5 (1984): 6-8.** Discusses how tutors can use error analysis, which "seeks to discover the hypotheses or assumptions underlying mistakes in a writer's text," as a means of assisting students in tutorials.

1126. **Faerm, Elizabeth. "Tutors' Column: Tutoring Anne: A Case Study."** *Writing Lab Newsletter* **17.1 (1992): 9-10.** Describes tutor's experience in helping a hearing-impaired student understand John Donne's poetry. Suggests student's inability to "hear" the poem's tone and rhythm presented the greatest barrier to detecting the meaning of the poem.

1127. **Fanning, Patricia. "Posing Questions: The Student-Centered Tutorial Session."** *Writing Lab Newsletter* **14.4 (1989): 1-2, 11.** Discusses the value of asking heuristic questions to foster a student-centered tutorial. Contends the approach encourages students to find their own solutions to writing problems.

1128. **Farrell-Childers, Pam. "A Good Laugh is Sunshine in a House or a Writing Center."** *Writing Lab Newsletter* **18.4 (1993): 5-6.** Sees humor as a vital aspect of writing center practice because it creates a sense of warmth, promotes the sharing of ideas, and releases tension.

1129. **Fayer, Dina. "Tutors' Column: Orthodoxy and Effectiveness."** *Writing Lab Newsletter* **18.5 (1994): 13. Also in 0006.** Argues that the nondirective methods taught in tutor training must be modified with each student, illustrating from her experience need or respond better to a more authoritative approach.

1130. **Fink, Darlynn. "Help! How Do I Tutor the International Student?"** *Writing Lab Newsletter* **15.1 (1990): 14-16.** Discusses tutors' problems in assisting international students due to language barriers, differing agendas, and a perceived lack confidence in peer tutors. Suggests ways to train tutors to solve these problems and work more effectively with international students.

1131. **Fishbain, Janet. "Listening: To Establish Rapport, to Comprehend Students' Perceptions, to Hear an Essay, to Check a Students' Perceptions."** *Writing Lab Newsletter* **18.1 (1993): 10-12.** Argues creative listening allows tutors to bridge social gaps with students, understand the students' perspectives on the act of writing, interpret student writing in meaningful ways, and make useful comments.

1132. **Fitzgibbons, Elaine. "The Tutor's Corner: Prejudice: How to Cope When You're Not Sure What to Do About It."** *Writing Lab Newsletter* **11.2 (1986): 9-10.** Cautions tutors not assume that student aloofness or skepticism results from prejudice against the tutor's age or gender, but suggests that tutors "clear the air" by asking if students are uncomfortable being tutored by someone younger or of a different gender.

uncomfortable being tutored by someone younger or of a different gender.

1133. **FitzRandolph, Susan. "The Tutor's Corner: My Internship: A Unique Learning Experience."** *Writing Lab Newsletter* **11.8 (1987): 7-9.** Describes a peer tutor's personal growth as a result of working in the collaborative setting of the writing center, including gains in knowledge about computers, composition, and how her own personality affected the learning of others.

1134. **Fleming, Susan. "The Text as Authority Figure."** *Writing Lab Newsletter* **18.2 (1993): 15-16.** Examines the reluctance of some students, particularly women, to challenge the authority of texts and how this feeling prevents their expressing their own views.

1135. **Friedlander, Alexander. "Meeting the Needs of Foreign Students in the Writing Center."** *Writing Centers: Theory and Administration.* **Ed. Gary A. Olson. Urbana: NCTE, 1984. 206-14.** Provides a very brief overview of special needs of ESL students and ways to respond to those needs within the framework of the writing center.

1136. **Friedmann, Thomas. "A Blueprint for Writing Lab Exercises."** *Writing Lab Newsletter* **8.5 (1984): 1-4.** Tells of faculty members' efforts to develop a series of grammar exercises for basic writers after traditional fill-in and multiple choice questions in grammar textbooks proved ineffective. Offers six general principles for developing effective exercises.

1137. **Fulwiler, Toby. "Provocative Revision."** *The Writing Center Journal* **12.2 (1992): 190-204. Rpt. in 0008.** Advocates teaching writing as re-writing. Suggests writing center tutors help students learn to revise by taking them through a process of "limiting, adding, switching, and transforming." Seeks to make writing "generative, liberating, and fun" and gives tutors an easily digested lesson on the composing process.

1138. **Gadbow, Kate. "Foreign Students in the Writing Lab: Some Ethical and Practical Considerations."** *Writing Lab Newsletter* **17.3 (1992): 1-5.** Examines problems one writing center faced in trying to meet the increasing needs of international students. Offers advice on tutoring ESL students and where to find additional information about non-native speakers and writers.

1139. **Galskis, Angelique. "Tutors' Column: The Painless Writing Sample."** *Writing Lab Newsletter* **14.7 (1990): 9-10.** Recommends beginning a tutorial by determining a student's attitude toward writing. Claims merely asking a student "How do you feel about writing?" may uncover valuable clues to his or her attitude.

1140. **Gamboa, Sylvia H., and Angela W. Williams. "Writing Centers on the ROPES: Using a Wilderness Lab for Discovery."** *The Writing Center Journal* **11.2 (1991): 29-40.** Describes lessons tutors learned about communication, teamwork, self-confidence, group problem-solving strategies, the value of diversity, and the need to take risks by taking part in an outdoor challenge course. Discusses resulting changes in writing center practices.

1141. **Garbowsky, Maryanne. "The 'Cutting' Edge: Working in the Writing Center."** *Writing Lab Newsletter* **16.9-10 (1992): 19-20.** Contends a primary advantage to working in the writing center is seeing students as individuals rather than simply as members of a class. Emphasizes the need to repair student self-esteem and confidence before beginning work on their writing.

1142. **Giger, Tim. "Tutors' Column: Zen and the Art of Prewriting."** *Writing Lab Newsletter* **20.2 (1995): 9.** Applies a Zen archery principle (of concentrating on the archer's fluidity of motion, rather than the target) to prewriting. Claims focusing on thoughts rather than putting words on the page helps writers to avoid censoring themselves.

1143. **Gills, Paula. "A Reader Responds."** *Writing Lab Newsletter* **9.8 (1985): 6-8.** Presents the current thinking and research on dyslexia and considers ways tutors can work most effectively with dyslexic students.

1144. **Gills, Paula. "The Troubleshooter."** *Writing Lab Newsletter* **14.3 (1989): 12-13.** Presents brief bibliography about students with learning disabilities and discusses emotional impact such disabilities often have on students.

1145. **Gills, Paula. "The Troubleshooter."** *Writing Lab Newsletter* **14.6 (1990): 12-13.** Offers advice on helping students with learning disabilities improve as writers. Recommends tutors provide as much structure as possible, allow students to make mistakes without penalty, and be patient and flexible.

1146. Gills, Paula. "The Troubleshooter Column." *Writing Lab Newsletter* 13.8 (1989): 4-5. Discusses laws, evaluation methods, academic accommodations, and tutoring techniques that apply to students with learning disabilities.

1147. Glenn, Coral Lou. "Tutors' Column: Mother vs. Tutor." *Writing Lab Newsletter* 14.9 (1990): 9. Relates how a peer tutor learned to limit her altruistic urge to help students too much.

1148. Goldberg, Susan H. "To: *Writing Lab Newsletter* Readers/ From: Bill Stull, Director of Writing (University of Hartford)/ Subject: Learning Skills Center in Action." *Writing Lab Newsletter* 5.8 (1981): 4-5. Uses the description of a successful tutoring session with a student to demonstrate the principles of a learning skills center in action and its contributions to learning enrichment on a campus.

1149. Goldberg, Susan H. "The Tutor-Teacher System." *Writing Lab Newsletter* 5.7 (1981): 1-2. Discusses a method for working closely with teachers of freshman English in designing tutorials that responded to the needs of the teachers' assignments and course goals.

1150. Goldsby, Jackie. *Peer Tutoring in Basic Writing: A Tutor's Journal.* Classroom Study No. 4. Berkeley: University of California Bay Area Writing Project, 1981. Describes one peer tutor's experiences in the writing center at the University of California—Berkeley. Narratives illustrate why certain tutorials are more successful than others.

1151. Gordon, Helen H. "Controlled Composition: Putting Grammar in Context." *Writing Lab Newsletter* 11.2 (1986): 12-14. Recommends using controlled composition in teaching grammar. Students copy short passages (of about 200 words) while changing the tense or some other aspect and being sure to adhere to correct usage. Sees this method as especially useful for students overwhelmed by large numbers of errors.

1152. Green, Sharon, and Mary Gorman. "Tutoring Non-Traditional Students: Blending Writing and Informal Counseling." *Writing Lab Newsletter* 12.8 (1988): 2-3. Discusses the writing-related affective problems of nontraditional students and advises tutors on how to help students overcome these problems.

1153. Griffin, Tammy. "Tutors' Column." *Writing Lab Newsletter* 15.7 (1991): 9-11. Recounts a tutorial during which a tutor used gardening metaphors to explain aspects of composition to a returning student.

Recommends tutors explain concepts in nonthreatening language and avoid using words that can trigger anxiety.

1154. **Griffith, Jeannie. "Tutors' Column: Helping Students Know What Their Professors Want."** *Writing Lab Newsletter* **19.9 (1995): 11-12.** Provides various strategies for interpreting a professor's assignment for a student. Suggests that such clarification is a key part of tutoring.

1155. **Grinder, Kim. "Process and Processing in a Middle School Writing Lab."** *Writing Lab Newsletter* **14.2 (1989): 11-12.** Describes practices of a middle school writing center intended to help students overcome writing fears and approach writing as a process.

1156. **Grise, Sue. "Getting the Picture: Dramatization as a Tutoring Tool."** *Writing Lab Newsletter* **19.3 (1994): 8-9.** Suggests dramatization (using illustrative anecdotes) helps tutors convey difficult writing lessons and is a sophisticated writing technique that can help students improve their writing.

1157. **Haas, Teri. "Conversation Workshops for Second Language Learners."** *Writing Lab Newsletter* **12.10 (1988): 8-10.** Suggests ESL students gain fluency in a second language and insight into the culture through casual conversations with tutors in the writing center. Describes conversation workshops one writing center sponsored.

1158. **Haas, Teri. "The Unskilled Writer and the Formula Essay: Composing by Rules."** *The Writing Center Journal* **3.2 (1983): 11-21.** Describes a ten-day workshop designed to help writers who have failed a freshman composition entrance exam, detailing how these writers learned to move from making superficial corrections in formulaic writing to seeing writing as a process subject to substantial revision.

1159. **Hall, Marina. "Tutors' Column: Tutoring Teaches Tutors Too."** *Writing Lab Newsletter* **15.1 (1990): 9.** Illustrates lessons peer tutors learn by working on other students' writing. Argues tutors often gain more from the experience than the student writer.

1160. **Hall, Phil. "Tutor's Corner: Giving Silliness a Chance."** *Writing Lab Newsletter* **9.9 (1985): 7-8.** Discusses the value of having tutees write on highly imaginary topics that invite humor and silliness as a way of breaking the ice and overcoming the tutees' anxieties and resistances.

1161. Hamilton, David. "Writing Coach." *College Composition and Communication* **28.2** (1977): **154-58.** Uses the sports coach as a metaphor for the writing teacher. Emphasizes the use of "assistant coaches" as tutors to assist the "coach" in focusing campus-wide and community involvement for the improvement of "new recruits" as writers.

1162. Hangartner, Patricia. "Applying Learning Principles in Developmental Writing." *Writing Lab Newsletter* **7.9** (1983): **3-5.** Discusses how writing labs for students in basic writing courses can best serve this population, with suggestions ranging from making the lab easily accessible, to scheduling required appointments, to allowing students to learn at their own pace.

1163. Hansen, Jolene. "Closing the Gap." *Writing Lab Newsletter* **18.9** (1993): **9.** Advocates using journals and response writing to help students "close the gap" between their knowledge and their teachers' requirements. Finds journals especially useful in helping students "discover what they already know."

1164. Harris, Muriel. "Do We Need Materials for ESL and Engineering Students?" *Writing Lab Newsletter* **3.6** (1979): **2-3.** Discusses the development of course modules strategically targeted for ESL students and engineering students after the Purdue University Writing Lab realized that it was not meeting the needs of these two groups.

1165. Harris, Muriel. "Peer Tutoring: How Tutors Learn." *Teaching English in the Two-Year College* **15.1** (1988): **28-33.** Examines ways peer tutors learn more about writing through their work in a writing center, including not only grammar and mechanics but also audience awareness, information processing, and problem solving strategies.

1166. Harris, Muriel. "The Roles a Tutor Plays." *English Journal* **69.9** (1980): **62-65.** Outlines potential benefits of tutoring and describes three principal roles tutors fill: coach, commentator, and counselor.

1167. Harris, Vincent. "Tutor's Column: The Journey Continues." *Writing Lab Newsletter* **14.10** (1990): **9-10. Also in 0006.** Minority peer tutor examines the issue of race in tutoring, based on his own observations and experiences. Despite apparent progress, contends racial segregation and stereotyping still occur, even in writing centers.

1168. **Hartstein, Marc. "Tutor's Corner: Objectivity in Tutoring."** *Writing Lab Newsletter* **9.2 (1984): 9-10.** Argues tutors must maintain objectivity and emotional distance when working with student writers, even if those students present papers on subjects the tutor finds objectionable or strongly disagrees with.

1169. **Haynes, Jane. "Triage Tutoring: The Least You Can Do."** *Writing Lab Newsletter* **12.10 (1988): 12-13.** Takes an emergency room approach to tutoring students who come to the writing center for last minute help. Tutors assess essays based on purpose/unity, development, and grammar/mechanics/spelling, addressing only major strengths and weaknesses.

1170. **Healy, Dave. "Varieties of Apathetic Experience."** *Writing Lab Newsletter* **14.2 (1989): 5-8.** Discusses the various types of apathy students demonstrate during writing center tutorials and offers advice on how to overcome it. Divides apathetic students into twelve categories, among them students forced by their teachers to visit the center, students baffled by teachers' assignments, and students who "just plain don't give a *$#%@."

1171. **Hickman, Dixie Elise. "Non-Traditional Teaching Aids."** *Writing Lab Newsletter* **5.6 (1981): 1-2.** Urges tutors to be creative in designing nontraditional aids to instruction that emphasize and work with each student's learning interests.

1172. **Hobson, Eric. "The Writer's Journal and the Artist's Sketchpad."** *Writing Lab Newsletter* **15.1 (1990): 1-3, 7.** Demonstrates that writers and visual artists share creative tools and approach composition in similar ways. Argues that a tutor's knowledge of this overlap can open fruitful dialogues with students and facilitate learning.

1173. **Hoffman, Randi. "Working with ESL Students."** *Writing Lab Newsletter* **3.1 (1982): 27-28.** Reflects on ways experience tutoring an ESL student helped tutor realize that many tutoring strategies work equally well with native speakers and second-language writers. Included in Cynthia Onore's "In Their Own 'Write'" (entry 0888).

1174. **Holbrook, Jo Ann. "Tutors' Column."** *Writing Lab Newsletter* **14.5 (1990): 9-10.** Citing a case in which a tutor unwittingly crushed an adult student's ego, urges tutors to remember to be sensitive, thoughtful, and considerate when giving feedback.

1175. Holladay, Hilary. "Tutors' Column." *Writing Lab Newsletter* 19.6 (1995): 7. Offers advice on how to assist students in revising graduate school application essays. Suggests using active, concrete language, downplaying their weaknesses, focusing on relevant professional experiences, and giving the reader a sense of themselves as people.

1176. Holmes, Elizabeth. "Tutor's Corner: Individualized Instruction." *Writing Lab Newsletter* 9.8 (1985): 9-10. Argues that each tutor's personal style and the opportunity to respond to students individually are what make tutoring such a dynamic and beneficial process.

1177. Hooks, Rita Daly. "Tutors' Column: A Delighted Tutor." *Writing Lab Newsletter* 13.1 (1988): 9. Relates a tutor's satisfaction in helping nontraditional students at a junior college writing lab.

1178. Horn, Susanna. "Fostering Spontaneous Dialect Shift in the Writing of African-American Students." *Dynamics of the Writing Conference: Social and Cognitive Interaction.* Ed. Thomas Flynn and Mary King. Urbana: NCTE, 1993. 103-10. Points out that many African-American students "spontaneously" eliminate many dialect-associated errors from drafts once they feel secure about a paper's content. Urges tutors to allow time for bidilectal students to draw on their own knowledge to correct error.

1179. Horn, Susanna. "Tutoring Two Students at the Same Time." *Writing Lab Newsletter* 17.2 (1992): 14-15. Describes the advantages of one writing center's policy that each tutor work with two students during the same hour-long session.

1180. Hornibrook, Judy. "Tutors' Column: Learning from Teaching: A Study of Writing Tutors." *Writing Lab Newsletter* 12.5 (1988): 7-8. Survey of writing center tutors indicates tutors grew as both readers and writers as a result of their tutoring experience.

1181. Hurlow, Marcia. "Writing Labs and Linguistic Insecurity." *Writing Lab Newsletter* 9.8 (1985): 4-6. Discusses the author's research on writing anxiety, or "linguistic insecurity," and considers how knowledge of ways to minimize anxiety and reassure students can benefit tutors.

1182. Hunt, Doug. "Diagnosis for the Writing Lab." *Tutoring Writing: A Sourcebook for Writing Labs.* Ed. Muriel Harris. Glenview: Scott, Foresman, 1982. 66-73. Describes formal and informal means of diagnosing writing difficulties (without preferring one over the other) and suggests means of carrying out informal diagnosis during tutorials.

1183. **Hunt, Doug. "A Five-Minute Diagnostic for Writing Labs."** *Writing Lab Newsletter* 3.3 (1978): 3. Discusses a six-question, multiple choice diagnostic test of a student's understanding of grammar as a means tutors can have for a quick assessment of a student's technical proficiency.

1184. **Hunter, Linda. "Writing Anxiety: Connections Beyond the Writing Lab."** *Writing Lab Newsletter* 11.2 (1986): 4-6. Illustrates how one student learned to cope with her own unreasonable expectations through a combination of controlled risk taking and personal and academic counseling.

1185. **Huot, Brian. "Working with Charlotte: A Close Look at Tutoring the Special Learner."** *Writing Lab Newsletter* 13.3 (1988): 9-12. Describes a tutor's turbulent experiences with an epileptic student. Explores eventually successful attempts to help the student, despite her displays of temper and frustrating lack of progress. Argues tutors must carefully base expectations for student progress on a realistic assessment of the special learner's needs and abilities.

1186. **Jordan, Gillian. "Humor in Tutorials."** *Writing Lab Newsletter* 15.9 (1991): 8, 10. Contends tutors can use humor to soothe students' writing anxiety, create a benign environment for learning, and make writing fun. Cautions against laughing at a student's ideas or language.

1187. **Kalister, Rose Ann. "The Adult Learner in the Writing Center: Teaching Techniques."** *Writing Lab Newsletter* 7.7 (1983): 4-6. Finds adult students particularly want instruction in grammar and are often unrealistic in their workloads and expectations. Discusses how writing centers can respond to the needs of adult students through minicourses and instructional materials.

1188. **Kamanya, Ella. "Tutors' Column: The Non-Native English Writer."** *Writing Lab Newsletter* 12.10 (1988): 7-8. Discusses strategies for helping non-native English speaking students in the writing center, in particular how to respond constructively to these students' defense mechanisms.

1189. **Kari, Daven M. "Revitalizing Clichés: A Workshop Strategy."** *Writing Lab Newsletter* 11.7 (1987): 8-10. Discusses positive aspects of clichés, seeing them as rich with potential meaning and useful language strategies. Urges tutors to help students understand how to revivify tired expressions by expanding on, partially rewriting, inverting, combining, and poking fun at clichés.

1190. **Karuri, Wangeci JoAnne. "Must We Always Grin and Bear It?"** *Writing Center Perspectives.* **Ed. Byron L. Stay, Christina Murphy, and Eric H. Hobson. Emmitsburg: NWCA Press, 1995. 71-83.** Examines shortcomings of the two most common responses of tutors to papers with offensive content or ideology (confrontation or evasion). Recommends that the tutor become a "supportive researcher" who tries to understand the context and intent of the writer.

1191. **Keane, Ellen. "Tutors' Column: Perceptions of Tutors and Students Differ."** *Writing Lab Newsletter* **16.9-10 (1992): 10.** Questionnaire on tutoring strategies indicates tutors and students differ in their perception of the effectiveness of paraphrasing and using charts and diagrams to illustrate points.

1192. **Kennedy, Barbara L. "Non-Native Speakers as Students in First-year Composition Classes with Native Speakers: How Can Writing Tutors Help?"** *The Writing Center Journal* **13.2 (1993): 27-38.** Applies an information-processing perspective to tutoring ESL students. Identifies problems ESL students have with reading and writing, including decoding, summary writing, accessing information from their native language, recognizing cultural preferences in rhetorical organization, and understanding culture-bound texts. Suggests tutoring strategies that might provide solutions.

1193. **Kennedy, Karen Sue. "Tutors' Column: What's in a Name?"** *Writing Lab Newsletter* **18.1 (1993): 13.** Makes distinctions between the terms *writing consultant* and *tutor*, focusing on differences in purpose, expertise, and character of relationship formed with students.

1194. **Kilborn, Judith. "Lefse, Popovers, and Hot Cross Buns: Observations about Three Tutors."** *Writing Lab Newsletter* **13.1 (1988): 1-4, 12.** Uses baking metaphors to describe the attributes and personalities of three tutors. Suggests writing center directors must exercise caution and flexibility in selecting tutors.

1195. **Klaczak, Jacqueline. "Peer Tutoring: A Holistic Approach."** *Writing Lab Newsletter* **18.7 (1994): 15-16.** Argues peer tutors are most effective if they look at the motivations, fears, and thinking skills that cause a student's writing problems.

1196. Kleist, David. "Tutors' Column: The Weltschmerz of Prescriptive Grammar." *Writing Lab Newsletter* 14.1 (1989): 9-10. Relates the frustrations a peer tutor feels in trying to teach grammar to students who are not habitual readers.

1197. Klooster, David. "Tutee Training, or It Takes Two to Collaborate." *Writing Lab Newsletter* 13.4 (1988): 1-4. Contends the effectiveness of tutoring often depends on how well a writing center has educated student writers about what goes on during tutorials. Offers advice on how to train students to contribute ideas, energy, and conversation to the tutorial.

1198. Klosterman, Nancy. "Tutors' Column: The Writing Center: Friend or Foe." *Writing Lab Newsletter* 18.3 (1993): 11-12. Offers lessons learned on the job about writing and tutoring by a freshman peer tutor.

1199. Knepper, Marty. "Learning at the Learning Center: A Personal Reflection on Nine Years 'At the Lab.'" *Writing Lab Newsletter* 12.3 (1987): 13-14. Reflects on the close relationship between writing and learning, the interpersonal aspects of tutoring, and the knowledge tutors gain by assisting students from all disciplines.

1200. Knight, Susan J. "Tutor's Corner: The Peer Tutor as Counselor." *Writing Lab Newsletter* 9.10 (1985): 7-9. Contends peer tutors help students solve writing problems and deal with frustrations about writing.

1201. Konstant, Shoshana Beth. "Multi-Sensory Tutoring for Multi-Sensory Learners." *Writing Lab Newsletter* 16.9-10 (1992): 6-8. Rpt. in 0008. Provides background information on learning disabilities and the information processing styles of multisensory learners. Argues tutors need to tailor information to fit students' "perceptual channels."

1202. Kraft, Eugene. "Percentage Writing." *Writing Lab Newsletter* 11.2 (1986): 7-8. Advocates "percentage" writing, in which students take a commonsense approach to structuring essays, supported by extensive intervention and modeling by the tutor or teacher. Stresses relaxation and mutual trust—on the part of student and tutor—as key elements of this approach.

1203. Krapohl, Cheryl. "Tutors' Column: Late Night at the Writing Center: Service Station or Oasis?" *Writing Lab Newsletter* 14.2 (1989): 9. Examines attitudes of students who come to the writing center not to learn but to guarantee an A in a course.

1204. **Kucsma, Alexander J. "The Silent Tutor: Using Patterns to Teach Writing."** *Writing Lab Newsletter* **17.7 (1993): 4-5.** Recommends writing centers maintain a file of model responses to rigidly patterned writing assignments, such as book reviews, for students to consult. Argues such patterns act as "silent tutors."

1205. **Kulkarni, Diane. "If I Could Only Burn My Bra Now."** *Writing Lab Newsletter* **17.2 (1992): 15.** Looks humorously at a situation in which a tutor delves more deeply into a writer's ideas than the writer is willing to go.

1206. **Kulkarni, Diane. "Tutors' Column: Writing to Discover."** *Writing Lab Newsletter* **15.3 (1990): 9.** Recounts a peer tutor's personal revelation that writing, though sometimes painful, is a dynamic process of discovery.

1207. **Kussrow, Paul G. "Faculty Writers and the Writing Center."** *Composition Chronicle* **4.1 (1991): 4-5.** Graduate faculty member who sought help at the writing center argues that faculty members, despite initial reluctance to experience criticism, should take advantage of the assistance available on the writing center's "neutral turf." Among benefits, cites a personal increase in appreciation of other disciplines, a better publication record, and a heightened awareness of language.

1208. **Lamb, M.E. "Just Getting the Words Down on Paper: Results for the Five-Minute Writing Practice."** *The Writing Center Journal* **2.2 (1982): 1-6.** Describes a strategy used to help writers write recursively without interference from editing or procedural concerns.

1209. **Lance, Robert. "Using Analogies to Overcome Jargonistic Teaching."** *Writing Lab Newsletter* **6.7 (1982): 3.** Claims students are often confused or put off by the heavy use of jargon in a tutorial to describe grammar or organizational problems. Urges tutors to use analogies drawn from the student's major or fields of interest as a way of making concepts clearer and of engaging the student more fully in the tutorial.

1210. **Lang, Frederick K. "A Substitute for Experience."** *The Writing Center Journal* **7.1 (1986): 19-25.** Claims asking developing writers to cite personal experience as support for an essay is counterproductive because they often lack or cannot readily access relevant personal experience. Sees this inability as an unfair disadvantage, especially in essay competency exams. Suggests teaching writers to fabricate narrative experiences—in short, to lie—to tap into "inner" experience.

1211. **Larkin, Marnie. "Tutors' Column."** *Writing Lab Newsletter* **17.3 (1992): 9.** Bemoans the negative attitudes of some student writers but claims tutors have a duty to show these students that writing can be exciting and creative.

1212. **Laskowski, Briget. "'Hands-Off' in the Writing Center."** *Writing Lab Newsletter* **18.3 (1993): 12.** Suggests tutors resist the urge to intervene directly in students' work and to keep their hands off computer keys and manuscripts.

1213. **Lauby, Jacqueline. "Note: This Writing Center Will** *Not* **Correct Your Dangling Modifiers, Teach You Comma Rules, Or Have You Underline Nouns Once, Verbs Twice."** *Writing Lab Newsletter* **9.1 (1984): 8.** Tells of the author's experience with the writing center to which she came for assistance with mechanics but even far greater help when the tutor refocused the tutorial onto issues of organization, clarity, and audience.

1214. **Lavely, Marcia M. "Tutors' Column: The Fruits of Tutoring."** *Writing Lab Newsletter* **13.6 (1989): 9-10.** Discusses the benefits of one-to-one and small group tutoring. Describes the diversity of students served by writing centers and the range of services they offer.

1215. **Leahy, Richard. "Clustering: A Not-Quite Case History."** *Writing Lab Newsletter* **10.8 (1986): 6-7.** Shows how a tutor's use of the clustering technique helped a student learn how to revise. Suggests the possibility that, even in one tutorial, students can learn techniques that will have a lasting impact on their writing.

1216. **LeBlanc, Diane. "Teaching Creative Writing in Writing Centers."** *Writing Lab Newsletter* **19.9 (1995): 1-4.** Relates how a writing center works with creative writers, including acting as an audience for individual writers and organizing fiction and poetry workshops. Suggests sponsoring open readings and creative writing contests.

1217. **Leeson, Lea Ann. "All of the Answers or Some of the Questions? Teacher as Learner in the Writing Center."** *The Writing Center Journal* **2.2 (1982): 18-29.** Describes conferences with students in which misunderstanding occurs because students are not allowed to express their own goals and strategies.

1218. **Leitzel, Danelle. "Tutors' Column: Manami and Me."** *Writing Lab Newsletter* **20.4 (1995): 9.** Uses the narrative example of her tutorials with an ESL student to relate to students' struggles with anxieties and the need for encouragement because she herself has had similar emotional experiences in her life.

1219. Leslie, Charles J. **"Learning a Lesson in the Writing Lab."** *Writing Lab Newsletter* **16.1 (1991): 12-13.** Discusses the dangers of encouraging novice writers to take stylistic risks that an accomplished writer might find difficult.

1220. LeTourneau, Mark S. **"Typical ESL Errors and Tutoring Strategies."** *Writing Lab Newsletter* **9.7 (1985): 5-8.** Provides extended examples and classification of the more common grammar errors made by ESL students and offers strategies of response for tutors.

1221. Lichtenstein, Gary. **"Super Tutor!"** *Writing Lab Newsletter* **8.1 (1983): 9-10.** Describes a naive tutor's realization that "tutoring can be a slow, arduous process" that mocks the "unrealistic expectations" the tutor originally had.

1222. Lidh, Todd M. **"Tutors' Column: Nothing to Fear But Fear Itself."** *Writing Lab Newsletter* **17.4 (1992): 9.** Sees the anxiety and doubt tutors sometimes feel as potentially positive forces.

1223. Linden, Myra J. **"Dear Editor: I'd Just Like to Say That ...: A Letter to the Editor BW Assignment."** *Writing Lab Newsletter* **8.2 (1983): 9-10.** Tells of how basic writing students assigned to a sub-freshman writing course in an academic skills center wrote letters to the editors of local newspapers as a way of developing their writing skills.

1224. Linehan, Marion. **"Don't Make Me Think!"** *Writing Lab Newsletter* **18.9 (1993): 14.** Discusses the problems of tutoring frazzled students who come to the writing center an hour before their papers are due. Poses larger questions as to what motivates such students.

1225. Livesey, Matthew. **"Tutors' Column: Ours *Is* to Wonder Why."** *Writing Lab Newsletter* **15.2 (1990): 9-10. Also in 0006.** Illustrates a peer tutor's use of questions to teach a student to clarify and organize her ideas.

1226. Logan, Junius. **"The Tutor's Corner: Literaria Bohemia Nervosa."** *Writing Lab Newsletter* **12.1 (1987): 11-12.** Takes a humorous look at the image of writing center tutors as saviors. Parodies the tutor as a gun-toting rescuer of wayward students.

1227. **Lynch, Kelly. "Tips for the Writing Center Assistant."** *Writing Lab Newsletter* **6.7 (1982): 7-8.** Encourages tutors to display a positive and nonjudgmental attitude to students and, rather than lecture, provide books and manuals that explain important points.

1228. **Lyons, Chopeta C. "Spelling Inventories."** *Writing Lab Newsletter* **6.4 (1981): 2-3.** Describes a method in which the tutor keeps a "spelling inventory" of a student's misspelled words, determines patterns of error, and discuss them with the student.

1229. **Malbec, Toby W. "Tutor's Corner: Using Interview Techniques."** *Writing Lab Newsletter* **8.10 (1984): 5-6.** Focuses on the value of "open-ended questions" as an interviewing technique for new tutors seeking a way to structure beneficial tutorials.

1230. **Malikowski, Steve. "Tutors' Column: Have You Heard What Your Students Have Been Saying?"** *Writing Lab Newsletter* **15.6 (1991): 9-10.** Emphasizes the importance of good listening skills in facilitating effective writing center tutorials.

1231. **Mapp, Larry G. "Thinking About Thinking: Pedagogy and Basic Writers."** *A Sourcebook for Basic Writing Teachers.* **Ed. Theresa Enos. New York: Random House, 1987. 579-83.** Demonstrates how a lack of classroom and time constraints in a writing center allowed a tutor and basic writer to generate concrete detail through repeated questioning and discussion over a series of sessions.

1232. **Marek, Margaret-Rose. "Right Brain Processing and Learning Disabilities: Conclusions Not to Reach in the Writing Center."** *Writing Lab Newsletter* **16.4-5 (1992): 14-18.** Critiques an article by Mary Jane Schramm (entry 1296) containing a checklist of symptoms of students with learning disabilities. Claims those symptoms could as easily identify students who process information with the right hemisphere of the brain. Cautions tutors against attempting to diagnose learning disabilities.

1233. **Marmorstein, Donna. "The Tutor as Hard Laborer."** *Writing Lab Newsletter* **17.7 (1993): 8.** Illustrates the emotionally taxing aspects of writing center work, comparing the rigors tutors undergo to those of hard physical labor.

1234. **Marron, Peggy. "Tutoring a Deaf Student: Another View."** *Writing Lab Newsletter* **17.5 (1993): 15-16.** Examines the difficulties and rewards of tutoring a hearing-impaired student. Among other benefits, cites the tutor's learning to use sign language and her fresh awareness of the need to adapt tutoring strategies to meet the needs of individual students.

1235. **Martin, Kathy. "A Quick Check and Cure for Fragments."** *Writing Lab Newsletter* **8.6 (1984): 4.** Claims that telling if a single sentence is a fragment is usually not difficult for tutors; offers a technique tutors can use for identifying fragments in paragraphs.

1236. **Mattison, Anne. "The Tutor's Corner: Applying the Thinking-Writing Connection."** *Writing Lab Newsletter* **10.6 (1986): 7.** Offers peer tutors strategies for getting students to think about their writing. Contends students too often let tutors do the thinking for them.

1237. **McCallum, Paul. "The Tutor's Corner: Confessions of a Tutor."** *Writing Lab Newsletter* **11.10 (1987): 7.** Characterizes the peer tutor as "an authority figure conspicuously lacking in authority." Reveals a peer tutor's apprehensions about failing to satisfy students and reflecting badly on the center. Concludes tutors must make clear that students themselves must take responsibility for their performance as writers.

1238. **McDonald, James C. "Tutoring Literature Students in Dr. Frankenstein's Writing Laboratory."** *The Writing Center Journal* **12.2 (1992): 180-89.** Draws analogy from *Frankenstein* to describe tutoring literature students in the writing center. Claims students' misreadings of literary works are, like Frankenstein's monster, often "more complex, alive, and human" than the accepted readings of the literary community (the frightened townspeople). Urges tutors to help students learn from the differences between their interpretations and their professors'.

1239. **McGrath, Susan. "Tutor's Corner: Drawing the Line."** *Writing Lab Newsletter* **9.4 (1984): 9-10.** Argues that tutors will have fewer difficult tutorials if they make clear to the student at the beginning what services the writing center can and cannot offer.

1240. **Medress, Tammy. "Tutors' Column: Patience and Persistence Please."** *Writing Lab Newsletter* **16.6 (1992): 9-10. Also in 0006.** Illustrates one tutor's realization of the value of patience and persistence in dealing with students who come to writing center tutorials unprepared to share the workload.

1241. **Mills, Helen. "Diagnosing Writing Problems and Identifying Learning Disabilities in the Writing Lab."** *Tutoring Writing: A Sourcebook for Writing Labs.* **Ed. Muriel Harris. Glenview: Scott, Foresman, 1982. 74-83.** Provides a step-by-step procedure for conducting individual conferences and determining needs of clients; includes a general description of several learning disabilities.

1242. **Mills, Helen. "Writing Lab Programs for the Learning Disabled and Handicapped."** *Writing Lab Newsletter* **5.3 (1980): 3-5.** Describes the development of instructional materials and tutorial programs for students with learning and/or physical disabilities. Claims such students can prosper in the flexible instructional environment of a writing lab.

1243. **Mills, Nina. "Tutors' Column."** *Writing Lab Newsletter* **13.8 (1989): 9-10.** Relates how a nontraditional student found help and employment at a university writing center.

1244. **Mohr, Ellen. "Daring to Deal with Diversity."** *Writing Lab Newsletter* **20.3 (1995): 7-8.** Discusses methods of tutoring three populations: the returning adult, the ESL student, and the underprepared student. Provides tutoring strategies for working with writers at different levels of expertise and relates these to tutor training.

1245. **Mongeon, J.E. "It's that Time of Year."** *Writing Lab Newsletter* **18.2 (1993): 14.** Discusses how approaches to tutoring change during the holiday rush, when demand for tutoring goes up. Suggests tutors with limited time can still effectively help students by looking at thesis, development, and structure of essays.

1246. **Moody, Pam. "Tutors' Column: A Slight Case of Plagiarism."** *Writing Lab Newsletter* **17.5 (1993): 9-11. Also in 0006.** Narrates the lessons a peer tutor learned in working with a student whose dislike of English and writing culminated in his plagiarism of a literature paper.

1247. **Morreale, Susan E. "Let's Talk."** *Writing Lab Newsletter* **17.4 (1992): 16.** Demonstrates the value of having students talk their way through an idea they have trouble writing down.

1248. **Morris, Karen. "Closed Mouth, Open Ears: Listening in the Tutorial."** *Writing Lab Newsletter* **15.2 (1990): 7-8, 14.** Says tutors do too much talking in tutorials and too little listening. Contends that good listening encourages students to take responsibility for their own work, helps establish good interpersonal relationships, and facilitates effective collaboration.

1249. **Morris, Karen L. "Hats and Feathers: Roles and Attributes of Tutors."** *Writing Lab Newsletter* **12.4 (1987): 10-11.** Discusses the various roles tutors must play during tutorials, including coach, commentator, counselor, listener, diagnostician, observer, demonstrator, "dumb bunny," and explainer. Contends tutors must often simultaneously play several different roles.

1250. **Morrow, Diane Stelzer. "Tutoring Writing: Healing or What?"** *College Composition and Communication* **42.2 (1991): 218-29.** Examines the therapeutic possibilities of tutoring, on the basis of the author's experiences as both a family practice physician and a writing tutor. Draws parallels and discusses differences in the physician and tutor roles.

1251. **Morse, Phillip. "Using Communication Skills in the Writing Conference."** *Writing Lab Newsletter* **14.1 (1989): 1-6.** Claims good tutoring often depends on the tutor's sensitivity to the writer's ideas, feelings, and intentions. Offers counseling techniques that can improve tutoring by heightening tutors' sensitivity and enhancing interpersonal communication.

1252. **Mullin, Anne E. "Improving Our Abilities to Tutor Students with Learning Disabilities."** *Writing Lab Newsletter* **19.3 (1994): 1-4.** Explores the writing center's role in meeting requirements of the Americans with Disabilities Act. Focuses primarily on how to recognize students with learning disabilities and how to improve the delivery of writing center services to these students.

1253. **Nairn, Lyndall. "A Workshop on Note-Taking: How to Manage Information."** *Writing Lab Newsletter* **13.7 (1989): 7-8.** Describes a writing center workshop on note taking that emphasizes listening skills, two types of note taking methods, and reviewing notes before exams.

1254. **Neff, Julie. "Learning Disabilities and the Writing Center."** *Intersections: Theory-Practice in the Writing Center.* **Ed. Joan A. Mullin and Ray Wallace. Urbana: NCTE, 1994. 81-95.** Points out that most writing center literature does not address special needs of writers with learning disabilities and uses a series of case studies to illustrate how writing center tutors can work collaboratively with these writers to help them become independent through self-cuing.

1255. **Neth, April. "The Tutor's Corner: The Writing Tutor Bicycle."** *Writing Lab Newsletter* **12.2 (1987): 11-12.** Compares tutoring to learning to ride a bicycle, focusing on the need to learn a complicated process and take risks.

1256. **Newbill, Mary Susan. "Tutors' Column: Speaking Football."** *Writing Lab Newsletter* **12.7 (1988): 7-8.** Discusses the problems created by a student's use of slang in an academic essay.

1257. **Noonan, Brendan. "Tutoring and Intuition."** *Writing Lab Newsletter* **3.1 (1982): 29-31.** Reflects on ways tutoring an ESL student helped tutor realize that tutoring is like conversation and that standardized tutoring strategies will not fit all conferences. Included in Cynthia Onore's "In Their Own 'Write'" (entry 0888).

1258. **Noppen, Mick. "The Tutor's Corner: Speaking of Writing."** *Writing Lab Newsletter* **10.1 (1985): 9-10.** Emphasizes the need for basic writers to talk their way through the early stages of writing. Suggests tutors are especially suited for helping them arrive at a workable topic.

1259. **Olson, Candace J. "'From Invention to Congratulations': The Writing Center as an Example of the Recursive Process."** *Writing Lab Newsletter* **19.4 (1994): 14-16.** Examines the role of the recursive process in invention, writing, tutoring, and revision. Argues that the recursive process not only forms the heart of writing center practice but is a key ingredient in creativity.

1260. **Olson, Gary A., and John Alton. "Heuristics: Out of the Pulpit and into the Writing Center."** *The Writing Center Journal* **2.1 (1982): 48-56.** Reports favorable outcome of providing tutors with heuristic models designed to be used in prewriting. Tutors selected suitable models for individual students having difficulty with invention.

1261. **O'Mealy, Joseph, and James Register. "Editing/Drilling/Draft-Guiding: A Threefold Approach to the Services of a Writing Workshop."** *College Composition and Communication* **35 (1984): 230-33.** Offers a general guide for those new to drop-in writing centers. Suggests editing as an appropriate response to "expert" writers, drill for writers with a limited set of problems, and a series of meetings with writers with more extensive difficulties.

1262. **Oram, Virginia White. "The Writing Center: Business or Therapy?"** *Writing Lab Newsletter* **10.8 (1986): 1-2.** Contrasts businesslike writing centers with "humane" centers that double as counseling services. Portrays tutoring as "a sacred rite" and the tutor as "go-between and confessor."

1263. **Oye, Paula M. "Writing Problems beyond the Classroom: The Confidence Problem."** *Dynamics of the Writing Conference: Social and Cognitive Interaction.* **Ed. Thomas Flynn and Mary King. Urbana: NCTE, 1993. 111-19.** Examines the situation of the often-neglected C-level student, who writes competent but dull or superficial papers. Argues that such students' writing often reflects their lack of confidence. Illustrates how one student's writing improved as she gained confidence.

1264. **Paddock, Mark. "Tutors' Column."** *Writing Lab Newsletter* **16.8 (1992): 9-10.** Describes lessons a peer tutor learned in trying to ease an international student's struggle with organizing and expressing his ideas about English literature.

1265. **Parbst, John R. "Off-Topic Conversation and the Tutoring Session."** *Writing Lab Newsletter* **19.1 (1994): 1-2, 5.** Recommends tutors use off-topic conversation to relax anxious students and, by opening apparently unrelated avenues of thought, to stimulate creativity.

1266. **Parry, Robyn. "Techniques for Assisting Adult Students Returning to Formal Education."** *Writing Lab Newsletter* **15.6 (1991): 13-16.** Argues writing centers can ease adult students' often difficult transition from work to school by helping them cope with writing anxiety, update composition skills, deal with grammar errors, and learn to write on computers.

1267. **Patton, Vicki. "Mini Course: How to Use the Dictionary."** *Writing Lab Newsletter* **8.8 (1984): 1-4.** Discusses a minicourse a writing lab developed for ESL students on how to use the dictionary and find information of help in writing papers.

1268. **Peloquin, Linda G. "Tutors' Column: Relinquishing Responsibility."** *Writing Lab Newsletter* **18.10 (1994): 13-14.** Proposes relinquishing responsibility for students' work and success as a strategy for dealing with two types of problem students—those who chronically procrastinate and those who refuse to engage in the tutoring session.

1269. **Pendleton, William. "You've Got to Please Yourself or Writing is a Garden Party."** *Writing Lab Newsletter* **12.5 (1988): 1-2.** Examines the problems student writers have in aiming their writing at a particular audience. Suggests students put themselves in the place of the target audience, in effect writing for their alter-ego.

1270. **Perkins, Lorraine. "An Approach to Organization."** *Writing Lab Newsletter* **2.4 (1977): 2.** Discusses a method for teaching essay organization to student writers.

1271. **Pitts, Sandra K. "The Reading/Writing Lab: A First-Aid Station for Every School."** *Reading Horizons* **25 (1985): 227-32.** Discusses how two academic support units—a tutoring center and a reading/writing lab—offered assistance to inspire underprepared students and enabled them to succeed in mainstream English courses.

1272. **Piva, Penny. "Tutors' Column: Tutoring Days."** *Writing Lab Newsletter* **19.8 (1995): 9.** Provides anecdotal support for the notion that being a peer tutor can change a student's outlook and career choice.

1273. **Pobo, Kenneth. "The Writing Center Meets English 102: Truth, Consequences, and Other Stuff."** *Writing Lab Newsletter* **16.9-10 (1992): 3-5.** Discusses the anxiety students often bring to writing and reading tasks, especially when confronting powerful works of literature. Sees such fear as a potential opportunity to help students grow.

1274. **Pote, Carlene. "Tutors' Column: What Do You Mean, 'There is No Writing Fairy?'"** *Writing Lab Newsletter* **19.2 (1994): 13.** Illustrates one peer tutor's realization that the seemingly magical aspects of her writing style were actually stages of an identifiable process and shows how this lesson improved her tutoring.

1275. **Prabhu, Lalita. "My Aunt, My School to Come, Loves. A Tutoring Program for the Advanced ESL Student."** *Writing Lab Newsletter* **10.3 (1985): 10-12.** Examines the complexity of assisting ESL students in the writing center. In particular, alerts tutors to the fact that Asian students often arrange English sentences as they would in their own language—subject, object, predicate, rather than subject, predicate, object. Suggests strategies tutors may find useful in working with ESL students.

1276. *A Program for the Creation of an Individualized, Goal-Oriented Freshman English Curriculum.* **Washington, D.C.: National Center for Educational Research and Development, Regional Research Program, 1973.** Discusses the benefits of personalized approaches to instruction and describes a program in which senior English majors serve as tutors in assisting instructors to identify and reinforce the strong points of a student's writing with a secondary emphasis on the targeting of errors.

1277. **Rabuck, Donna Fontanarose. "Giving Birth to Voice: The Professional Writing Tutor as Midwife."** *Writing Center Perspectives.* **Ed. Byron L. Stay, Christina Murphy, and Eric H. Hobson. Emmitsburg: NWCA Press, 1995. 112-19.** Offers midwife as metaphor for describing work of tutors; also describes a program designed for minority and economically disadvantaged students (the Writing Skills Improvement Program at the University of Arizona).

1278. **Raum, Elizabeth. "The Magic of Conferences."** *Writing Lab Newsletter* **11.7 (1987): 11-13.** Explores the strengths of the individual writing conference in teaching specific aspects of composition and editing skills.

1279. **Reed, Cheryl. "'Industrial Strength Tutoring': Strategies for Handling 'Customer Complaints.'"** *Writing Center Perspectives.* **Ed. Byron L. Stay, Christina Murphy, and Eric H. Hobson. Emmitsburg: NWCA Press, 1995. 94-103.** Offers solutions from industrial/business psychology for dealing with difficulties that arise in tutoring sessions, illustrating with several scenarios. Includes annotated bibliography on industrial/business psychology.

1280. **Reeves, Ramona C. "The Tutor's Corner: The Second Language Student."** *Writing Lab Newsletter* **12.3 (1987): 7-8.** Recounts an experience with an international student during which the peer tutor established effective communication, found a way to motivate the student through her "Seven Commandments of Writing" (e.g., "Thou shalt not be lazy ..."), and guided the student away from the use of technical jargon and other practices that confused the reader.

1281. **Renaud, Judith. "Tutors' Column: The Writing Center Story."** *Writing Lab Newsletter* **15.7 (1991): 11-12.** Describes a tutor's encounter with a student who refuses to examine her essay topic deeply, does so at the tutor's urging, and uncovers painful emotions toward her mother. Suggests such "human dramas" form a subplot to the "writing center story."

1282. **Reynolds, Irene. "The Tutor's Corner."** *Writing Lab Newsletter* **11.6 (1987): 7.** Relates how one peer tutor discovered the virtue of laziness, learning that both she and the student benefitted when she let the student do most of the work.

1283. **Ridpath, Sandra. "The Use of Computers in the Tutoring Process: Overcoming Communication Obstacles Between the Tutor and the ESL Student."** *Writing Lab Newsletter* **17.3 (1992): 7-8.** Recommends having ESL students compose at a computer while the tutor looks on, acting as audience. Claims this approach bypasses problems created by oral language barriers or illegible handwriting and focuses attention on important aspects of composition.

1284. **Roberts, Patricia. "A Peer Tutor Assesses Her Teaching Ability."** *Improving Writing Skills.* **Ed. Thom Hawkins and Phyllis Brooks. New Directions for College Learning Assistance 3. San Francisco: Jossey-Bass, 1981. 39-40.** A personal reflection on the value of being a tutor. Claims that one of her strengths as a tutor is that writing has never come easily to her and that she can help other struggling writers by sharing this experience.

1285. **Robertson, Elizabeth. "Moving from Expressive Writing to Academic Discourse."** *The Writing Center Journal* **9.1 (1988): 21-28.** Through a case study, demonstrates how a tutor can lead a student from personal journal writing to the morc objective academic paper. Stresses the lessons the student learned about gaining knowledge through writing. Suggests using this technique makes the academic world more accessible to students.

1286. **Roderick, John. "Problems in Tutoring."** *Tutoring Writing: A Sourcebook for Writing Labs.* **Ed. Muriel Harris. Glenview: Scott, Foresman, 1982. 32-39.** Describes ways tutors can deal with problems common to student writers, such as low self-esteem, lack of focus, and consistent patterns of error.

1287. **Roger-Hogan, Nicole. "The Tutor's Corner: Twenty Minutes in the Life of Bob the Tutor."** *Writing Lab Newsletter* **11.5 (1987): 7-8.** Drawing on observations of two quite different tutorials, illustrates that flexibility is one of the key traits of an effective tutor.

1288. **Roques, Merri-Lynn. "Tutors' Column: Getting Started."** *Writing Lab Newsletter* **20.3 (1995): 9.** Presents a narrative example of a recalcitrant student to discuss strategies for getting tutorials started and to avoid having writers play the role of passive listeners.

1289. Salsbury, Sylvia. "Helping Writers Get Hold of Their *Self* with Mediational Questions." *Writing Lab Newsletter* 17.7 (1993): 1-3. Applies principles of psychological mediation to writing center tutorials, in which the tutor asks questions to help a student discover what he or she thinks about a given topic and choose an approach. Emphasizes good listening skills on the tutor's part and personal reflection on the student's.

1290. Samuels, Shelly. "Emphasizing Oral Proofreading in the Writing Lab: A Multi-Function Technique for Both Tutors and Students." *Writing Lab Newsletter* 9.2 (1984): 1-4. Claims that oral proofreading facilitates tutoring by shortening the time it takes to diagnose grammar and syntax problems, providing the student a means for editing his or her work, and demonstrating to the student the interconnections among speech, reading, and writing.

1291. Sanchez, Claudia, Camilla Foltz, Jennifer Smith, Teresa Renaker, and Elizabeth Huyck. "The Tutor's Corner: Voices from Mt. Holyoke's Writing Center." *Writing Lab Newsletter* 10.10 (1986): 9-10. Describes peer tutors' most challenging experiences, including helping clarify ideas, how to accept criticism of their tutoring, learning how to avoid editing student papers, encouraging young women to empower themselves, and helping ethnic students cope with "proper" grammar.

1292. Satre, Kay, and Valerie Traub. "Non-Directive Tutoring Strategies." *Writing Lab Newsletter* 12.8 (1988): 5-6. Attempts to define the role and describe specific strategies of the non-directive tutor. Argues that the non-directive tutor's primary jobs are to help the writer make use of already existing communication skills and to share knowledge of writing conventions.

1293. Scanlon, Leone C. "A Reader Responds ... Learning Disabled Students in the Writing Center." *Writing Lab Newsletter* 9.5 (1985): 9-11. Points out that traditional tutoring techniques of asking leading questions often create feelings of anxiety, frustration, and intimidation for students with learning disabilities. Suggests more beneficial approaches tutors can implement.

1294. Schmitzer, Thomas C. "Looking for Clues." *Dynamics of the Writing Conference: Social and Cognitive Interaction.* Ed. Thomas Flynn and Mary King. Urbana: NCTE, 1993. 59-61. Describes a conference in which a seemingly intrusive phrase in a student's draft allowed student and tutor to explore ideas that proved highly useful in revision.

1295. **Schramm, Mary Jane. "Labels: Are They Necessarily Evil? A Response to a Response."** *Writing Lab Newsletter* **16.4-5 (1992): 18-19.** Responds to Margaret-Rose Marek's critique (entry 1232) of "Just Like Joe" (entry 1296), stating the article and its accompanying checklist were not intended for diagnosing learning disabilities. Contends the designation "learning disabled" can help writing centers address individual problems.

1296. **Schramm, Mary Jane. "Tutors' Column: Just Like Joe."** *Writing Lab Newsletter* **15.10 (1991): 9-10.** Narrates a tutor's experiences in assisting a student with learning disabilities. Offers tutors a checklist of characteristics evinced by students with learning disabilities.

1297. **Schuette, Lynn M. "Tutors' Column: Tutor? Why Should I?"** *Writing Lab Newsletter* **14.8 (1990): 9-11. Also in 0006.** Contends that tutoring benefits the tutor by increasing her humility, reflection on writing, effectiveness as a writer, and emotional equilibrium.

1298. **Scott, Jean Bruce. "Tutors' Column: Getting it On the Page."** *Writing Lab Newsletter* **19.1 (1994): 11.** Illustrates how a tutor tailored various forms of freewriting to fit students needs.

1299. **Seiger, Karen. "Tutors' Column: Bumps, Charmers, and Perfect Ones."** *Writing Lab Newsletter* **13.2 (1988): 9, 16.** Divides students into three categories that describe their behavior during tutorials.

1300. **Sherwood, Phyllis. "What Should Tutors Know?"** *Tutoring Writing: A Sourcebook for Writing Labs.* **Ed. Muriel Harris. Glenview: Scott, Foresman, 1982. 101-04.** Describes some affective factors that come into play in tutorials and provides several strategies for eliciting responses from students.

1301. **Sickbert, Virginia. "The Tutor's Corner: For Next Year."** *Writing Lab Newsletter* **11.9 (1987): 5.** Veteran peer tutor argues tutors should remember not to correct papers, to listen carefully, to let the student do the writing, and to offer students at least two alternative strategies for revising.

1302. **Simmons, Heidi. "Tutors' Column: Welcome to My Web."** *Writing Lab Newsletter* **18.6 (1994): 9.** Recounts one peer tutor's experiences with a student who subtly coaxed her, through praise and helplessness, into doing too much of the work.

1303. Simpson, Steven. "Tutors' Column." *Writing Lab Newsletter* 17.8 (1993): 9. Records one peer tutor's experiences with, and lessons learned from, tutoring a close friend in the writing center.

1304. Simson, Rennie. "Where's Professor Adjunct?" *Writing Lab Newsletter* 15.4 (1990): 7. Describes a peer tutoring program aimed at providing tutorial support for students taking courses from adjunct professors. Contends these low-paid faculty members often have little time to spend helping their students one-to-one and suggests tutors can fill this need.

1305. Smethers, Paul E. "The Tutor's Corner: Initial Intern Observations of Writing Center Operations." *Writing Lab Newsletter* 10.5 (1986): 5-6. Recounts the benefits of having worked for a semester in a writing center, including mastering the rules of grammar and style and learning how to help other students achieve their potential as writers.

1306. Smith, Erin. "Tutors' Column: A College Try." *Writing Lab Newsletter* 13.4 (1988): 9-10. Discusses the tutor's role in encouraging students to persevere in solving writing problems and prevent their ultimately failing.

1307. Smith, Jane Bowman. "A Tutorial Focusing on Concrete Details: Using Christensen's Levels of Generality." *The Writing Center Journal* 10.2 (1990): 59-66. Illustrates the use of Francis Christensen's principles on the levels of generality to teach students to develop their essays with concrete detail. Cites a particular student's case in depth.

1308. Smith, Janet. "Tutors' Column: The Seduction of a Schoolmarm." *Writing Lab Newsletter* 13.9 (1989): 9-10. Chronicles a peer tutor's rejection of authority and acknowledgment that she does not have all the answers.

1309. Sollisch, James. "From Fellow Writer to Reading Coach: The Peer Tutor's Role in Collaboration." *Writing Center Journal* 5.2/6.1 (1985): 10-14. Argues tutors and students are aware of their roles as writers in the collaborative process but also need to acknowledge their roles as readers since assuring a reader's comprehension of a text is the essence of good writing.

1310. Spilman, Isabel B. "Tutors' Column: Tutoring Five on Five." *Writing Lab Newsletter* 13.10 (1989): 9-10. Describes how a writing center divided freshman writing classes into peer response groups of ten students each. Contends that group tutoring provides students with a real audience of peers, assurance that they write on nearly the same level as the other members, and increasing confidence in their ability.

1311. Stebbins, Peter J. "Tutor's Corner: The Journal as a Sounding Board." *Writing Lab Newsletter* 9.7 (1985): 11. Peer tutor discusses how he improved his skills as a tutor by using a journal to record his responses to tutorials and what he learned from each session.

1312. Stephenson, Denise. "Audience Reconsidered: Focusing on Peers." *Writing Lab Newsletter* 19.6 (1995): 1-3. Urges tutors to become more aware of audience in student writing. Contends that an awareness of a specific audience governs nearly every form of "real world" writing but is too often ignored in the classroom.

1313. Stevenson, Steve. "Tutors' Column." *Writing Lab Newsletter* 19.10 (1995): 9. Humorously conveys how a technophobe came to terms with computers in the writing center. Asserts that computer literacy learned in the writing center will make even English majors attractive on the job market.

1314. Stoffel, Judy. "Editing for Style *à la* Joseph Williams." *Writing Lab Newsletter* 10.1 (1985): 12-14. Contends that Joseph Williams's *Style: Ten Lessons in Clarity and Grace* can help students learn to write clear, efficient prose. Recommends that tutors teach students to eliminate passive voice, revise nominalizations, trim verbal fat, reduce the number of *and*, *who* and *which* clauses, and be more specific.

1315. Strickland, Judy. "Tutors' Column: Working with International Students." *Writing Lab Newsletter* 16.3 (1991): 9-10. Relates how one graduate student tutor learned to work effectively with international students.

1316. Sullivan, Sally. "From Thought to Word: Learning to Trust Images." *The Writing Center Journal* 3.1 (1982): 11-19. Describes series of ongoing tutorials with a student working to add concrete detail to her writing. Provides sample exercises used to help student.

1317. Tanner, Martha. "The Tutor's Corner: Confessions of a Writing Center Tutor: How Fear Almost Kept Me from Getting Involved."

*Writing Lab Newsletter* 11.4 (1986): 9-10. Examines the fears a peer tutor experienced during tutorials, primarily a fear of meeting new people and being unable to help student writers. Shows how the tutor coped with her fears.

1318. Taylor, David. "Beyond Howdy Doody." *Writing Lab Newsletter* 11.2 (1986): 1-2. Drawing on the medic-patient metaphor for tutoring, advises tutors to draw up a "composing profile" on each student writer. Divides questions tutors might ask into four categories: matters of fact, the student's writing background, the writing process, and the assignment.

1319. Taylor, David. "Invasion of the Gremlins." *Writing Lab Newsletter* 12.3 (1987): 1-3. Discusses the trouble students have in dealing with comma errors and offers a self-assessment test students can use to identify and strengthen their grammar weaknesses.

1320. Taylor, David. "Listening Skills for the Writing Center." *Writing Lab Newsletter* 12.7 (1988): 1-3. Contends tutors have the power to change student writers through sympathetic listening. Analyzes five specific skills that enhance listening and tutoring abilities.

1321. Taylor, David. "Peer Tutoring's Hidden World: The Emotional and Social Issues." *Writing Lab Newsletter* 13.5 (1989): 1-5. Examines the emotional pressures peer tutors undergo as part of their jobs. Contends that tutors find opportunities for personal and professional growth by learning through training and experience to cope with such pressures.

1322. Tegan, Mary Beth. "Tutors' Column." *Writing Lab Newsletter* 19.3 (1994): 10. Recounts how one tutor realized she had jumped to the wrong conclusion about a student's work and therefore given faulty advice. Suggests tutors must guard against snap judgments and give the student credit for knowing what he or she wants to do with a piece of writing.

1323. Thaiss, Christopher J., and Carolyn Kurylo. "Working with the ESL Student: Learning Patience, Making Progress." *The Writing Center Journal* 1.2 (1981): 41-46. Describes tutoring sessions with two ESL students, demonstrating ways of encouraging students to develop realistic long-term goals and strategies for achieving them.

1324. Thompson, Melinda Rainey. "Imitation and Explanation." *Writing Lab Newsletter* 13.2 (1988): 5-8. Contends that, in working with international students, tutors should use a three-part strategy combining reformulation of ideas and sentences, controlled composition, and traditional drill with extensive tutor-student dialogue.

1325. Thonus, Terese. "Tutors as Teachers: Assisting ESL/EFL Students in the Writing Center." *The Writing Center Journal* 13.2 (1993): 13-26. Examines the plight of tutors attempting to help ESL students pass the Test of English as a Foreign Language (TOEFL). Alerts tutors to pitfalls and misconceptions they might confront in tutoring international students. Suggests tutors can effectively tutor ESL students if they learn more about ESL pedagogy.

1326. Topel, Lissa. "Tutors' Column: Confessions of a Terrified Tutee." *Writing Lab Newsletter* 15.4 (1990): 9-10. Describes the fear a student felt upon entering the writing center for the first time. Illustrates how a tutor calmed her, helped her, and eventually inspired her to become a peer tutor herself.

1327. Trelka, Mary E. "The Tutor's Corner: The Tutor as Mother Confessor." *Writing Lab Newsletter* 11.1 (1986): 9-10. Urges tutors to maintain a "semi-professional" distance to avoid getting too deeply involved in students' emotional difficulties. Recommends sending distressed students to the campus counseling center.

1328. Tubbs, Gail Lewis. "A Case for Teaching Grammar to Writers." *Writing Lab Newsletter* 15.7 (1991): 1-3. Argues for making grammar instruction part of the tutorial even in writing centers that focus on process. Suggests writing centers may be the last place student writers confront grammar since most are not learning it as part of their English studies.

1329. Tultz, Melissa. "Tutors' Column: Tutoring: Using Your Noodle by Using Your Major." *Writing Lab Newsletter* 18.8 (1994): 9. Urges tutors to draw on the writing strategies of their major field of study to help students. Recounts personal experience in successfully applying the scientific method of inquiry to a student's writing project.

1330. Upton, James. "'Talking to Myself ...': A Writing Self-Help Worksheet." *Writing Lab Newsletter* 16.7 (1992): 7-8. Offers worksheet aimed at helping high school students become independent writers and critics.

1331. Upton, James. "Toward Independence." *Writing Lab Newsletter* 11.1 (1986): 13-14. Recommends "Praise-Question-Polish" approach in training students to become independent writers. Instructor teaches students to ask tutors the following questions: "What do you like about my paper?" "What questions do you have about my paper?" and "What suggestions do you have to improve my revision of this paper?"

1332. Upton, James. "A 'WALK' in the Writing Center." *Writing Lab Newsletter* 13.9 (1989): 15-16. Describes the Writing Assignment List of Keys (WALK), a method of diagnosing and talking about writing problems. Contends that WALK is an effective writing and tutoring tool.

1333. Upton, James. "What's Old is New; What's New is Old: Models for Conferences." *Writing Lab Newsletter* 19.6 (1995): 14-15. Discusses three patterns of writing conferences in one high school writing center. Lists specific questions tutors can ask to keep a tutorial on track.

1334. Upton, Jim. "A Center Sharing: 'A Tutor's Dozen.'" *Writing Lab Newsletter* 19.9 (1995): 5. Lists a dozen assumptions about the role of the writing center tutor, ranging from the need for empathy to the need to continually reevaluate methods of instruction.

1335. Veinot, Cynthia. "Tutors' Column: What is a Peer Tutor?" *Writing Lab Newsletter* 13.3 (1988): 7. Seeks to define the roles, duties, and limits of the peer tutor. Discusses differences between the peer tutor and the classroom teacher. Contends tutors are especially suited for helping students explore possible responses to writing assignments.

1336. Wack, Michael. "The Tutor's Corner: Tutoring in a Technical College." *Writing Lab Newsletter* 11.3 (1986): 7. Discusses techniques useful in working with science and engineering students, among them using a "graphical" approach to accommodate the scientific mind-set of students.

1337. Walker, Amy, and Gail Corso. "Tutoring Ties." *Writing Lab Newsletter* 14.7 (1990): 7-8, 11-12. Transcribes a dialogue between a student and a tutor, including commentary from the tutor's inner voice, designed to illustrate the complex dynamics of the tutorial.

1338. Walker, Kristin. "Difficult Clients and Tutor Dependency: Helping Overly Dependent Clients Become More Independent Writers." *Writing Lab Newsletter* 19.8 (1995): 10-14. Provides several approaches tutors can use to help dependent student writers attain independence. Urges tutors to use a heuristic worksheet to help students focus attention on their own writing and revision processes.

1339. Wallace, David L. "Using Peer Tutors to Overcome Writer's Block." *Research & Teaching in Developmental Education* 3.2 (1987): 32-41. Discusses how peer tutors can help students overcome writer's block. Emphasizes the tutor's interpersonal skills, a relaxed interaction between tutor and student, and clear communication.

1340. Ware, Elaine. "Visual Perception Through 'Window Proofreading.'" *Writing Lab Newsletter* 9.9 (1985): 8-9. Describes a proofreading technique with which tutors can help students identify their own errors.

1341. Weiner, Sandor. "In Search of Goals: Theses for the Tutorial Session." *Writing Lab Newsletter* 6.7 (1982): 1-2. States that agreeing with the student upon a goal, or thesis, for each tutorial before the session begins makes objectives clear and allows tutorial time to be used more efficiently.

1342. Weller, Rebecca. "Tutors' Column: Authorizing Voice: Pedagogy, Didacticism and the Student-Teacher-Tutor Triangle." *Writing Lab Newsletter* 17.2 (1992): 9-11. Also in 0006. Discusses harm to a writer's self-esteem when her instructor commented only on her errors. Explores the tutor's role as mediator between instructor and student. Documents the writer's improvement after the tutor's intervention, when the instructor agreed to suspend judgment until the second draft.

1343. West, Joyce Anderson. "The Writing Lab: An Undergraduate's Viewpoint." *Writing Lab Newsletter* 4.8 (1980): 2-3. Describes an undergraduate's first experiences as a peer tutor and her reflections on what she learned.

1344. Weythman, Sara. "Things to Do in the Writing Center." *Writing Lab Newsletter* 15.10 (1991): 11. Lists 38 activities tutors and students can do in the writing center.

1345. White, Linda F. "Spelling Instruction in the Writing Center." *The Writing Center Journal* 12.1 (1991): 34-47. Discusses theories behind the teaching of spelling as part of the writing process. Explains why poor spelling is often due not to low intelligence or laziness but to the writer's method of deciphering and making meaning.

1346. Wilcox, Brad. "Conferencing Tips." *Writing Lab Newsletter* 18.8 (1994): 13. Advises tutors how to structure a writing conference. Offers the five-stage WRITE process: Watch, Respect, Involve, Teach, and Encourage.

1347. Williams, Sharon. "Sentence Errors in the Writing Conference: The Little Red Caboose." *Writing Lab Newsletter* 18.2 (1993): 13-14. Offers a handout one writing center developed on revising common sentence errors. Suggests that tutors should focus more attention on such errors.

1348. Wolcott, Willa. "The Use of Structured Modules in Writing Center Classes." *Writing Lab Newsletter* 6.5 (1982): 6-8. Describes a one-credit writing lab course required for special admission students. Uses modules that guide students through a series of prewriting steps that culminate in a first draft of an essay.

1349. Wong, Xia. "Tutoring Across Cultures." *Writing Lab Newsletter* 19.1 (1994): 12-15. Offers insights into tutoring students from other, primarily Asian, cultures. Examines three tutor/student relationships (American tutor/Asian student, Asian tutor/American student, and Asian tutor/Asian student) and discusses the potential problems and benefits of each.

1350. Woo, Helen. "Tutors' Column: Expectations of a Tutor." *Writing Lab Newsletter* 18.4 (1993): 13, 12. Also in 0006. Peer tutor discusses her motivation to become a tutor. Also reveals her frustrated expectations as a tutor when students did not always react as she had hoped.

1351. Yancey, Kathleen Blake. "Finding the Key Idea in Topic Sentence." *Writing Lab Newsletter* 2.8 (1978): 2. Describes how tutors can use the concept of "key ideas" to help students progress from the thesis statement, to key ideas, to topic sentences/ideas.

1352. Yardas, Mark. "Tutors' Column: Achieving Rapport with Quiet Students." *Writing Lab Newsletter* 16.2 (1991): 9-10. Also in 0006. Recounts lessons learned from an extraverted tutor's difficulty in establishing clear communication with an introverted student, including the need to pace a tutorial according to the student's needs and the value of silence.

1353. Young, Virginia Hudson. "Exploiting the Writing-Speaking Relationship in the Writing Center." *Writing Lab Newsletter* 12.2 (1987): 1-5. Explores the connections between oral and written communication and their ramifications for tutoring.

1354. Zimmerman, Jesse. "The Tutor's Corner." *Writing Lab Newsletter* 10.3 (1985): 9. Recounts the lessons a peer tutor learned on the job, among them that tutoring carries with it a responsibility to help boost the confidence of student writers.

1355. **Zimmerman, Nancy. "Tutors' Column: Foiling Your Tutor: A Process Analysis for Tutees."** *Writing Lab Newsletter* **12.6 (1988): 7-8.** Ironically suggests ways students can deliberately prevent effective tutoring and avoid improving their writing.

# Ethics

1356. Behm, Richard. "Ethical Issues in Peer Tutoring: A Defense of Collaborative Learning." *The Writing Center Journal* 10.1 (1989): 3-12. Addresses charges that the help given to students by writing center tutors amounts to plagiarism. Examines the principles of collaborative learning, as well as its weaknesses and strengths. Concludes that collaborative learning is ethical and, indeed, essential to the education of writing students.

1357. Clark, Ircne Lurkis. "Collaboration and Ethics in Writing Center Pedagogy." *The Writing Center Journal* 9.1 (1988): 3-12. Rpt. in 0008. Validates a tutor's active collaboration with a student—including proofreading when necessary. Cites the benefits of modeling writing tasks for students—and the role of imitation in learning—and questions the pedagogical soundness of unilaterally forbidding tutors to correct errors or rephrase passages. Advocates collegial collaboration, not letting tutors "do the preponderance of the student's work."

1358. Coleman, Karen W. "'Quick Fix' vs. 'Instruction.'" *Writing Lab Newsletter* 11.9 (1987): 3-4. Discusses the appropriateness of running a grammar hotline, focusing primarily on the issue of whether such a service constitutes a "band-aid" or teaching approach. Acknowledges that most callers simply want a quick answer, but suggests some clients nevertheless learn from the interchange.

1359. Crump, Eric. "Voices from the Net: Sharing Records, Part II: Political Considerations." *Writing Lab Newsletter* 18.3 (1993): 6-7. Discusses the ethics of furnishing information on writing center tutorials to instructors who request it. Opinions vary from seeing few problems with giving out information to refusing to reveal anything about a student's experience at the center.

1360. **Crump, Eric. "Voices from the Net: Sharing Records: Student Confidentiality and Faculty Relations."** *Writing Lab Newsletter* **18.2 (1993): 8-9.** Presents an E-mail conversation that originally appeared on WCenter about the dilemma facing writing center directors as to whether to share information about students' tutorials with faculty members. Indicates that some writing centers maintain strict confidentiality of student records while others open their records to instructors.

1361. **Crump, Eric. "Voices from the Net: The Causes and Consequences of Writing Center Dependency."** *Writing Lab Newsletter* **17.10 (1993): 12-14.** Presents a WCenter discussion in which correspondents debate the problem of student dependency on the writing center. Focuses primarily on the issue of whether some dependency—seen as communal interdependency—is actually healthy.

1362. **Freed, Stacey. "Subjectivity in the Tutorial Session: How Far Can We Go?"** *The Writing Center Journal* **10.1 (1989): 39-43.** Discusses the ethical dilemmas tutors confront when students voice opinions the tutors find morally, ethically, or politically repugnant. Grants the need to use tact but concludes that tutors have a duty to challenge the opinions of students, if only to "check them on the validity of their arguments."

1363. **George, Claire. "Response to Writing Center Ethics."** *Writing Lab Newsletter* **17.8 (1993): 7-8.** Debates the issue of whether, and to what degree, a tutor should intervene when she suspects a professor is treating a student unfairly. Through a specific example, shows how intervention accomplished little and may have aggravated the problem.

1364. **Haynes-Burton, Cynthia. "Intellectual (Proper)ty in Writing Centers: Retro Texts and Positive Plagiarism."** *Writing Center Perspectives.* **Ed. Byron L. Stay, Christina Murphy, and Eric H. Hobson. Emmitsburg: NWCA Press, 1995. 84-93.** Argues that technological developments make definitions of plagiarism increasingly difficult and urges that writing centers reexamine and redefine their conceptualization of collaboration and their place in the (print) economy that jealously guards intellectual property rights.

1365. **Herek, Jennifer, and Mark Niquette. "Ethics in the Writing Lab: Tutoring Under the Honor Code."** *Writing Lab Newsletter* **14.5**

**(1990): 12-15.** Discusses the ramifications of a university honor code on ethical practices in the writing center. Contends that the code makes tutors more sensitive to, and less likely to cross, the ethical boundaries they encounter during tutorials.

1366. **Jacoby, Jay. "'The Use of Force:' Medical Ethics and Center Practice."** *Intersections: Theory-Practice in the Writing Center.* **Ed. Joan A. Mullin and Ray Wallace. Urbana: NCTE, 1994. 132-47.** Raises ethical question of extent to which a tutor may intervene in a student's writing and suggests that the concept of informed consent in medical ethics provides a model for dealing with the dilemma.

1367. **Jessop, Anne. "Tutors' Column."** *Writing Lab Newsletter* **15.9 (1991): 9-10.** Relates a tutor's experience in helping a student with a racist paper. Poses the dilemma tutors sometimes face in working with students whose opinions they find politically or morally distasteful. Argues that tutors should not let their own politics prevent them from calmly discussing the issue.

1368. **King, Mary. "Ethics and Good Teaching."** *Writing Lab Newsletter* **5.4 (1980): 3-4.** Recognizes that students often want writing lab tutors to side with them in grade disputes and offers ways by which tutors can defuse this situation and still offer assistance to these students.

1369. **Lichtenstein, Gary. "Ethics of Peer Tutoring."** *Writing Center Journal* **4.1 (1983): 29-34.** Claims that peer tutors provide students with a model of independent learning. Presents six principles, or ethics, that provide the foundation for the various thinking processes tutors model within collaborative learning.

1370. **O'Connor, Aisha. "Tutors' Column: Whose Paper Is It, Anyway?"** *Writing Lab Newsletter* **13.7 (1989): 9-10.** Relates a peer tutor's struggle with the issue of how much help to give in improving a student's paper.

1371. **Pemberton, Michael. "Writing Center Ethics."** *Writing Lab Newsletter* **18.4 (1993): 10, 12.** Briefly discusses the dilemma tutors often face of whether to voice opinions in the face of student essays they find ethically or morally repugnant. Does not attempt to resolve the dilemma.

1372. **Pemberton, Michael. "Writing Center Ethics: Questioning Our Own Ethics."** *Writing Lab Newsletter* **19.5 (1995): 8-9.** Discusses how writing centers can armor themselves against budget cuts by anticipating and countering the arguments for their elimination. Also announces the column's upcoming exploration of the top ten reasons why writing centers are unethical.

1373. **Pemberton, Michael. "Writing Center Ethics: Undermining the System."** *Writing Lab Newsletter* **19.7 (1995): 15-16.** Discusses two common myths about writing centers, namely that they "undermine academic systems that evaluate students on the basis of individual achievement" and "undermine instructors' goals." Contends that since writing centers' central concern is helping students learn to write better, they do not undermine the evaluation process in "any meaningful way."

1374. **Pemberton, Michael A. "Writing Center Ethics."** *Writing Lab Newsletter* **17.5 (1993): 14-15.** Briefly discusses the need for an ethics column and some of the issues the new column will address in future installments.

1375. **Pemberton, Michael A. "Writing Center Ethics."** *Writing Lab Newsletter* **17.7 (1993): 6-7.** Discusses the issue of dishonesty in the writing center. Argues that tutors often lie to themselves and their students for altruistic and pragmatic reasons. Concludes that such lying is not always unethical.

1376. **Pemberton, Michael A. "Writing Center Ethics."** *Writing Lab Newsletter* **17.8 (1993): 6-7.** Discusses the ethical quandaries a writing center director experiences when the interests of the center conflict with the interests of the institution it serves.

1377. **Pemberton, Michael A. "Writing Center Ethics."** *Writing Lab Newsletter* **17.9 (1993): 6-7.** Begins discussion of an ethical quandary posed to a writing center director when his tutors noticed that teaching assistants were issuing poor assignments and making few comments on papers. Involves the question of whether the director should reveal the names of individual TAs to their supervising professor.

1378. **Pemberton, Michael A. "Writing Center Ethics."** *Writing Lab Newsletter* **17.10 (1993): 15-16.** Further considers whether a writing center director should report the poor performance of graduate teaching assistants to the TAs' supervisor, who has requested this information. Concludes that such a report would violate confidentiality, influence the TAs' willingness to send their students to the center, and not come under the umbrella of the writing center's responsibilities.

1379. Pemberton, Michael A. "Writing Center Ethics." *Writing Lab Newsletter* 18.6 (1994): 10. Explores four scenarios in which a student asks for help with an angry letter the tutor finds ethically objectionable. Requests readers' commentary on the scenarios.

1380. Pemberton, Michael A. "Writing Center Ethics: Directive Non-Directiveness: Readers' Responses to Troublesome Scenarios." *Writing Lab Newsletter* 18.10 (1994): 15-16. Details readers' responses to scenarios of problematic tutoring sessions and discusses the dilemmas involved in "supportive" tutoring sessions that can be subtly directive and "upfront" directive tutoring sessions that can silence student voices.

1381. Pemberton, Michael A. "Writing Center Ethics: Drawing the Line Between Personal and Professional." *Writing Lab Newsletter* 19.2 (1994): 6-7. Discusses tutoring scenarios that demand primarily professional or primarily personal responses from tutors. Attempts to set boundaries for behavior in these scenarios.

1382. Pemberton, Michael A. "Writing Center Ethics: Equity, Opportunity, and Access." *Writing Lab Newsletter* 19.9 (1995): 15-16. Disputes a commonly held complaint that writing centers are unethical because they give some students (those who come for help) an unfair advantage over others (those who do not).

1383. Pemberton, Michael A. "Writing Center Ethics: Grammar Redeux, Redeux, Redeux." *Writing Lab Newsletter* 20.1 (1995): 5-6. Discusses the perennial problem of whether writing center tutorials should focus attention on grammar or "higher-order" problems. Concludes that in trying to settle this question for themselves, they should ask "What can I do to achieve the maximum benefit for a particular student ... in the amount of time I have available."

1384. Pemberton, Michael A. "Writing Center Ethics: Ignorance and the Unethical Writing Center." *Writing Lab Newsletter* 19.6 (1995): 13-14. Debunks the two commonly cited reasons why colleagues consider writing centers unethical (because tutors tell students how to write their papers or because tutors write students' papers for them).

1385. Pemberton, Michael A. "Writing Center Ethics: Responding (or Not) as Readers in Context." *Writing Lab Newsletter* 19.3 (1994): 15-16. Discusses a writing center tutor's options when students ask for help on papers the tutor finds politically or morally repugnant.

1386. Pemberton, Michael A. "Writing Center Ethics: 'Sharers and Seclusionists.'" *Writing Lab Newsletter* 20.3 (1995): 13-14. Discusses the ethics of reporting information about tutorials to professors. Divides directors into two categories: "sharers," who consider it their duty to provide such information, and "seclusionists," who consider confidentiality between student and tutor a higher priority.

1387. Pemberton, Michael A. "Writing Center Ethics: Teaching, Learning, and Problem-Solving." *Writing Lab Newsletter* 19.8 (1995): 15-16. Disputes a commonly held notion that writing centers are unethical because tutors do much of the problem solving (and therefore the learning) for the student writer. Claims that tutoring facilitates students' problem solving abilities.

1388. Pemberton, Michael A. "Writing Center Ethics: Telling Stories in and Out of School." *Writing Lab Newsletter* 18.2 (1993): 4. Questions the ethics of using anecdotes about real students to illustrate academic articles on writing centers. Poses the question of whether writing center tutors should write about their experiences with individual students but does not attempt to answer it here.

1389. Pemberton, Michael A. "Writing Center Ethics: The Ethics of Intervention: Part II." *Writing Lab Newsletter* 18.5 (1994): 8-9. Discusses the ethics of working to improve papers tutors find morally repugnant. Presents a scenario of a student arguing against Affirmative Action in racist terms. Asks for readers' advice on how to respond to the student.

1390. Pemberton, Michael A. "Writing Center Ethics: The Question of Expertise." *Writing Lab Newsletter* 19.10 (1995): 15-16. Explores and refutes reasons three and four in the "Top Ten Reasons Why Writing Centers are Unethical." Reason three challenges tutors' expertise as writing teachers. Reason four challenges tutors' ability to assist writers from other disciplines.

1391. Pemberton, Michael A. "Writing Center Ethics: The Three Laws of Tutoring." *Writing Lab Newsletter* 19.4 (1994): 13-14. Adapts Isaac Asimov's "Three Laws of Robotics" to tutoring in the writing center. In essence, the three revised laws provide a hierarchy of guidelines aimed at discouraging tutors from writing or revising students' work and encouraging students to learn to fend for themselves.

1392. Pemberton, Michael A. "Writing Center Ethics: Walls." *Writing Lab Newsletter* 20.4 (1995): 13-14. Discusses the ethical implications of whether writing centers—as physical spaces—should be "open" or "closed." Claims that this issue is an ethical one because it is tied to "assessments of relative pedagogical utility and value."

1393. Pemberton, Michael A. "Writing Center Ethics: Weirdoes, Wackos, and Writing Centers." *Writing Lab Newsletter* 20.2 (1995): 11-12. Discusses the dilemmas that arise when open conflict breaks out between faculty members and writing center personnel. Cites WCenter tales of difficulties with professors. Concludes that "finding a reasonable and ethical way to respond" to such challenges may "prove to be one of our most rewarding and self-affirming experiences."

1394. Sherwood, Steve. "White Lies in the Writing Center: The Fragile Balance Between Praise and Criticism." *English in Texas* 22.3 (1991): 29-32. Rpt. in *Writing Lab Newsletter* 18.4 (1993): 1-4. Examines ethics of lying in the writing center setting. Argues tutors sometimes need to tell white lies to spare feelings, encourage students to do better, or prevent students from giving up. Urges tutors to adopt a "presumption against lying" and to use white lies only as a last resort.

1395. Weaver, Patti. "Tutors' Column: Angel and the Devil's Advocate." *Writing Lab Newsletter* 17.10 (1993): 9. Uses a case study to examine whether tutors should help strengthen papers that express opinions they find offensive.

# Research

1396. **Bauman, Gail A. "A Case Study Examination of the Development of the Writing Process Behaviors of Kindergarten Children as Demonstrated in an Informal Classroom Writing Center." Diss. Florida State U, 1985. *DAI* 46-04A (1985): 889.** Describes the writing process behaviors of children in a public school kindergarten writing center. Analyzes prewriting, writing, rewriting, concepts of print, invented spelling, and accompanying language. Finds that (1) the language used while writing is predominantly interactional; (2) some children engage in consciously stated prewriting plans; and (3) topics, home, experience, and peers all influence kindergarten children's writing.

1397. **Bell, Elizabeth. "A Comparison of Attitudes Toward Writing." *Writing Lab Newsletter* 7.2 (1982): 7-9.** Reports on a survey of attitudes toward writing between two groups—developmental students in a basic writing course and upper-level students in a tutor training course. Found that both groups had anxieties about writing well but the tutors enjoyed writing and the challenge of perfecting their craft while the basic writers disliked writing and found it more threatening than challenging.

1398. **Bennett, James Louis. "The Effects of Instructional Methodology and Student Achievement Expectations on Writing Performance in Community College Composition Classes." Diss. U of Washington, 1988. *DAI* 49-09A (1988): 2512.** Examines the effects of required writing lab assignments on the writing performance of community college composition students. Concludes improvement did occur but criteria for significance were not met. Comments on the "inconclusive nature" of research into composition instruction and the evaluation of writing performance and calls for further research into the design of appropriate measurement instruments.

1399. **Bobys, Aline R. "Emerging Literacy in a Whole Language Kindergarten." Diss. U of South Dakota, 1994. *DAI* 55-10A (1994): 3146.** Conducted ethnographic research on the emerging literacy patterns of kindergarten students from diverse socioeconomic backgrounds. Investigated the students' participation in a writer's workshop/laboratory as well as their self-directed learning strategies. Found all students grew in their understanding of reading, writing, and thinking as reciprocal processes as they engaged in meaningful literacy activities.

1400. **Broder, Peggy. "Such Good Friends: Cooperation Between the English Department and the Writing Labs." *WPA: Writing Program Administration* 5.2 (1981): 7-11.** Survey of 25 writing center directors on the relationship of the writing lab to the English department found that (1) faculty did not understand the role of the writing lab in helping students with papers; (2) they disagreed with the lab on what skills should be taught; and (3) they questioned the qualifications of peer tutors. Offers suggestions for addressing these issues.

1401. **Callahan, Darragh Elizabeth. "The Effects of Variety and Complexity of Provisioning on the Development of Constructive Play of Preschool-age Children in Writing Centers." Diss. Boston U, 1994. *DAI* 55-04A (1994): 0859.** Uses Jean Piaget's theories that children learn through constructive play to study the development of writing skills in young children. Writing centers were used in this study to assess the impact of the environment on the child's "larger processes of knowledge construction." The writing centers were designed to "encourage experimentation and use by children in support of constructive play."

1402. **Cox, Bené Scanlon. "Priorities and Guidelines for the Development of Writing Centers: A Delphi Study." *Writing Centers: Theory and Administration*. Ed. Gary A. Olson. Urbana: NCTE, 1984. 77-84.** Uses Delphi technique to rank priorities of writing center directors and provide guidelines for designing and developing writing centers.

1403. **David, Carol, and Thomas Bubolz. "Evaluating Students' Achievement in a Writing Center." *Writing Lab Newsletter* 9.8 (1985): 10-14.** Discusses the pre- and posttesting of students who failed composition courses and were placed in the writing center to work on improving grammar skills. Contends that individualized instruction focused on error correction and an increased understanding of grammatical rules led to increased scores for students on the posttests.

1404. Davis, Kevin. "Improving Students' Writing Attitudes: The Effects of a Writing Center." *Writing Lab Newsletter* 12.10 (1988): 3-5. Presents the results of research into the effects of the writing center on student attitudes and improvement in writing abilities.

1405. Davis, Kevin. "What the Faculty Know About What We Do: Survey Results." *Writing Lab Newsletter* 17.5 (1993): 6-7. Indicates how little faculty members at East Central University (OK) knew about the purpose, policies, or practices of their writing center. None knew the location of the writing center, and nearly all believed it focused primarily on correcting mechanical errors.

1406. Davis, Kevin M., Nancy Hayward, Kathleen R. Hunter, and David L. Wallace. "The Function of Talk in the Writing Conference: A Study of Tutorial Conversation." *The Writing Center Journal* 9.1 (1988): 45-51. Examines the conversational transactions between tutors and students in four tutorials. Research variables included teacher/ writer ratios of structuring, soliciting, responding, reacting, and interrupting remarks. Findings indicate a blend between teacher (directive) and nonteacher (soliciting) talk on the part of tutors. Concludes that, although students occasionally direct the tutoring conversation, tutors are clearly in charge.

1407. Dyson, Anne Margaret Haas. "A Case Study Examination of the Role of Oral Language in the Writing Process of Kindergartners." Diss. U of Texas at Austin, 1981. *DAI* 47-06A (1986): 2001. Investigates, through case studies, the role of oral language in early writing by observing 22 children in a classroom writing center at a public school kindergarten. Among other research methodologies, examines audio recordings of the children's talk in the writing center and the children's written products. Finds that oral language functions during the children's composing processes and varies according to the individual child's writing purpose and his/her working knowledge of written language.

1408. Dziombak, Constance E. "Searching for Collaboration in the ESL Computer Lab and the ESL Classroom." Diss. Columbia U Teachers College, 1990. *DAI* 51-07A (1990): 2296. Reports the results of a study of types of collaboration in an ESL classroom and in a computer lab. Concludes that collaborative activities are important in second-language learning since they provide students with opportunities for meaningful communication and language practice.

1409. Hagemann, Julie. "Writing Centers as Sites for Writing Transfer Research." *Writing Center Perspectives.* Ed. Byron L. Stay, Christina Murphy, and Eric H. Hobson. Emmitsburg: NWCA Press, 1995. 120-31. Argues that writing centers are better sites than classrooms for studying how students transfer writing skills from one discipline to another, illustrating with a case study of a student enrolled in five courses in three disciplines.

1410. Hammar, Diane D. "The Effectiveness of Computer-Assisted Writing Instruction for Juniors Who Have Failed the Regents Competency Test in Writing." Diss. U of Rochester, 1986. *DAI* 47-11A (1986): 3962. Evaluates the Computer-Assisted Writing (CAW) Program developed by the Rochester City School District (NY) to help high school students who failed the New York State Regents Competency Test. Experienced classroom teachers and writing lab instructors worked with four experimental groups. Concludes CAW was slightly less effective than experienced classroom remediation teachers using traditional methods of instruction.

1411. Hardy, Patricia Sue. "Process, Product, and Concepts About Writing: A Study of Sixteen Children Ages Three Through Six." Diss. Texas Woman's U, 1981. *DAI* 42-08A (1982): 3504. Investigates the acquisition and use of writing by children ages three through six. Observation of writing center activities indicates that motor control, directionality in print, editing, and corrective behaviors improve with age. The data from the study support the conclusion that early writing attempts by preschool children appear to be highly personalized processes. Early writing was shown to be a self-motivated process encouraged by writing models in the home.

1412. Haynes, Carole Ann Schaum. "A Study of Learning Centers in Southeastern Two-Year and Four-Year Public and Private Colleges and Universities." Diss. U of Tennessee, 1989. *DAI* 50-11A (1989): 3463. Examines learning centers in two-year, four-year, public, and private colleges to determine the services offered to underprepared students and analyze the levels of success the learning centers achieved as perceived by students, faculty, and administrators. Examines seven major areas of learning centers, including tutoring in writing improvement.

1413. Hayward, Malcolm. "Assessing Attitudes Towards the Writing Center." *The Writing Center Journal* 3.2 (1983): 1-10. Reports results of survey showing that faculty and writing center staff generally agree upon the goals of writing courses but disagree on reasons for referring students to writing center, with faculty stressing matters of grammar and punctuation, whereas writing center staff listed matters of organization and paragraphing as primary. Suggests ways of improving communication between these groups, particularly ways to inform faculty of the ability of writing centers to deal with higher-order concerns.

1414. **Hert, Ronald Sterling. "A Study of One Computer-Driven Text Analysis Package for Collegiate Student Writers." Diss. U of North Texas, 1988. *DAI* 50-05A (1988): 1199.** Examines the effects of the text analysis program *WRITER'S WORKBENCH* on writing performance, writing apprehension, and students' attitudes toward the computer and using this program. Finds no significant improvement in writing between the students who used the program in a computer writing lab as part of a freshman composition course and those who did not.

1415. **Howard, Katrena Clabough. "Writing in the Reading Classroom: Teachers' Methods, Materials, and Beliefs." Diss. U of Georgia, 1987. *DAI* 48-03A (1987): 617.** Investigates the nature and extent of writing instruction in reading classrooms to determine teachers' beliefs about the incorporation of writing instruction in reading. Concludes that teachers include little writing instruction in their reading curriculum and that the district's writing center seemed to have little effect on the inclusion of writing or writing instruction in reading lessons. Participants believed that students received writing instruction in other classes, so writing need not be included in the reading curriculum.

1416. **Hurlow, Marcia. "Experts with Life, Novices with Writing."** *Dynamics of the Writing Conference: Social and Cognitive Interaction.* **Ed. Thomas Flynn and Mary King. Urbana: NCTE, 1993. 61-68.** Examines the writing of nontraditional students, finding a significant correlation between these students' insecurity about writing and the number of clause types and number of words per T-unit in their writing. Suggests older tutors are especially effective in dealing with such students' writing anxiety.

1417. **Jordan-Henley, Jennifer. "A Snapshot: Community College Writing Centers in an Age of Transition." *Writing Lab Newsletter* 20.1 (1995): 1-4.** Draws on the results of a nationwide survey to identify trends in community college writing centers, including mergers with learning centers and personnel issues.

1418. **Karnowski, Patricia Lee.** "Observational Study Describing the Composing Behaviors of 3-, 4-, and 5-Year-olds During the Writing Process." Diss. Miami U, 1985. *DAI* 46-10A (1985): 2915. Investigates the writing behaviors of 11 children through videotaped sessions at a preschool writing center. Examines the communication systems and the forms of writing children will attempt in a natural, unrestricted setting. Finds that (1) preschool children have much information about the form and function of print and are eager to demonstrate this knowledge; (2) the social atmosphere of a writing center is conducive to writing; and (3) in this social setting, "young children can provide spontaneous teaching engagements to further the thinking and understanding of another child."

1419. **Kiedaisch, Jean, and Sue Dinitz.** "Learning More from the Students." *The Writing Center Journal* 12.1 (1991): 90-100. Discusses a statistical analysis of student comments about tutoring sessions. Found first-year students were most satisfied by writing center services and students with learning disabilities least satisfied. Suggests other centers should do research to determine if their students have similar reactions.

1420. **Larrance, Anneke J., and Barbara Brady.** "A Pictogram of Writing Center Conference Follow-Up." *Writing Lab Newsletter* 20.4 (1995): 5-7. Presents the results of a survey of 171 writing centers to "discover the uses and patterns of writing center conference follow-up." Found a majority (65%) do follow-up conferences by sharing a written description or summary of the tutorial with faculty and/or writing center staff. Also, the majority communicate with faculty outside the center only with student consent.

1421. **Magolda, Marcia B. Baxter, and Judith L. Rogers.** "Peer Tutoring: Collaborating to Enhance Intellectual Development." *College Student Journal* 21.3 (1987): 288-96. Reports a research study carried out at Miami University (OH) to investigate the extent to which peer tutors experienced cognitive growth as a result of tutoring. The results did not show a significant difference between tutors interacting with tutees at different levels of frequency; the study did show that tutors conceived of collaboration differently because of their varying levels of intellectual development and their tutoring differed accordingly.

1422. **Masiello, Lea, and Malcolm Hayward.** "The Faculty Survey: Identifying Bridges Between the Classroom and the Writing Center." *The Writing Center Journal* 11.2 (1991): 73-79. Discusses the results of a survey aimed at identifying shared values and bridging differences with faculty. Argues writing center administrators should pay close attention to the center's relationship with faculty members, including their misperceptions about the center's mission.

1423. Matthews, Mike. "Student Perceptions of Writing Center Personnel: Degrees of Separation." *English in Texas* 25.3 (1994): 5-7. Discusses results of community college survey to ascertain if significant differences exist between users and nonusers of writing centers and if connections exist between how students feel about themselves as writers and what they think of writing center personnel.

1424. Neuleib, Janice. "Evaluating Writing Centers: A Survey Report." *Writing Lab Newsletter* 11.4 (1986): 1-5. Explores the methods some writing centers use to evaluate themselves, going beyond simple record keeping to conducting research on writing and tutoring. Provides results of a National Writing Centers Association survey on how writing centers around the nation evaluate their performance.

1425. Neuleib, Janice. "Research in the Writing Center: What to Do and Where to Go to Become Research Oriented." *Writing Lab Newsletter* 9.4 (1984): 10-13. Talks about the difficulty of conducting research in a writing center, especially when students only visit occasionally and patterns of use, need, and improvement are difficult to track. Presents guidelines for conducting research with particular types and groups of students and offers sample questions researchers can use to develop information and profiles.

1426. Nordberg, Beverly. "Descriptive Case Studies of Basic Writers in Grades Four Through Eight in a Writing Center Setting." Diss. U of Wisconsin—Milwaukee, 1986. *DAI* 48-01A (1987): 69. Examines 20 basic writers in grades four through eight in a writing center setting to address the question of why, as national studies show, dislike of writing grows as students progress through the grades. Finds that (1) prewriting and planning techniques were poorly used; (2) narrative writing was more interesting and successful than non-narrative writing; (3) students' composing processes affected their final product; (4) writing apprehension increased as students progressed through the grades; and (5) students were able, despite sometimes poor performance, to show objective knowledge of writing skills and to make perceptive comments about their own work.

1427. North, Stephen M. "Designing a Case Study Method for Tutorials: A Prelude to Research." *Rhetoric Review* 4 (1985): 88-99. Presents own difficulties in selecting appropriate research methodology and defining disciplinary knowledge as analogous to the situation of composition studies. Essay followed by North's letter defending his exploratory, personal approach to the subject.

1428. North, Stephen M. "Writing Center Research: Testing Our Assumptions." *Writing Centers: Theory and Administration*. Ed. Gary A. Olson. Urbana: NCTE, 1984. 24-35. Suggests moving beyond current research approaches (reflecting on experience, speculating, enumerating) by identifying and testing writing center assumptions. Illustrates how that might be done with examples of research studies on the tutorial relationship and the composing process.

1429. Powers, Suzanne. "What Composition Teachers Need to Know About Writing Centers." *Freshman English News* 19.2 (1991): 15-21. Survey of writing center directors indicates their strong concern that teachers view the writing center as a site for grammar remediation. Concludes such a view limits the writing center's potential to produce independent writers and to address writing issues beyond mechanics.

1430. Rabianski, Nancyanne. "Accommodating the IQ and Learning Style of a Student Writer." *The Writing Center Journal* 1.2 (1981): 13-25. Reviews literature on prewriting heuristics and reports research project to determine which heuristics (ranging from unstructured freewriting to highly structured approaches) are most effective. Research design requires identifying IQ and conceptual level of student, pairing student with a heuristic on that basis, planning lessons that require the student to use both freewriting and the selected heuristic, and then evaluating the results.

1431. Roberts, David H. "A Study of Writing Center Effectiveness." *The Writing Center Journal* 9.1 (1988): 53-60. Compares the effectiveness of credit-bearing courses offered by two writing centers to conventional classroom instruction. Considers such variables as writing quality, students' understanding of the writing process, and levels of writing apprehension. Determines that instruction in the writing center can be as effective as classroom instruction.

1432. Sadlon, John A. "The Effect of a Skills Center Upon the Writing Improvement of Freshman Composition Students." *Writing Lab Newsletter* 5.3 (1980): 1-3. Reports on the results of a research experiment focusing on students who attended a weekly or biweekly private, individualized tutorial in place of one hour of regular classroom instruction per week. Finds that all of these students did at least as well as composition students who received only classroom instruction, while many of the students in the research project did far better.

1433. **Scanlon, Bettye Bené. "Future Priorities for College and University Writing Centers: A Delphi Study." Diss. Peabody College for Teachers of Vanderbilt U, 1980. *DAI* 42-05A (1980): 1889.** Establishes guidelines for writing center development based on priorities crucial for writing center operations. Focuses on establishing a writing center philosophy of service, creating administrative policy, expanding services, and providing teaching and research models.

1434. **Severino, Carol. "The Writing Center as Site for Cross-Language Research." *The Writing Center Journal* 15.1 (1994): 51-61.** Proposes a research model for a multicultural writing center that blends a collaborative learning philosophy with concepts from applied linguistics and teaching English as a second language. Explores possible consequences of such a philosophical hybrid. Suggests that since ESL and native speakers already interact there, the writing center is an ideal site for such research.

1435. **Soven, Margot. "Curriculum-Based Peer Tutoring Programs: A Survey." *WPA: Writing Program Administration* 17.1-2 (1993): 58-74.** Presents survey results of 95 schools using curriculum-based peer tutoring programs (also called Writing Fellows or Writing Associates programs) in which peer tutors are assigned to individual classes across the discipline. Focuses on such issues as budgets, staffing, selecting peer tutors, training and supervision, and program evaluation.

1436. **Stay, Byron. "When Re-Writing Succeeds: An Analysis of Student Revisions." *Writing Center Journal* 4.1 (1983): 15-28.** Examines the types and quality of revision techniques of unskilled college writers composing in a writing center. Isolates the most troublesome kinds of skills for students to master and offers suggestions on how best to teach these skills in the classroom.

1437. **Steger, Paul. "An Analysis of Kindergarten Children's Use of a Word Processor in Their Print Literacy Development." Diss. Portland State U, 1988. *DAI* 49-10A (1988): 3002.** Investigated kindergartners' use of a word processor in a writing lab in which eight learning lessons on computers were available. The children improved in their cognitive and print literacy skills and intertwined print and technological behaviors and skills as they wrote with a word processor.

1438. **Sutton, Doris, and Daniel Arnold. "The Effects of Two Methods of Compensatory Freshman English."** *Research in the Teaching of English* **8 (1974): 241-49.** Compares instruction in classes and in a writing laboratory on grade point averages of students over a two-year period and finds students in the writing lab made significantly higher grade point averages in English and in all course work.

1439. **Thompson, Ralph W. "Ricks College Writing Lab Survey."** *Writing Lab Newsletter* **4.9 (1980): 2.** Presents the results of a survey conducted by Ricks College (ID) of 350 writing labs, focusing on the characteristics of successful and unsuccessful labs.

1440. **Trimbur, John. "Literacy Networks: Toward Cultural Studies of Writing and Tutoring."** *The Writing Center Journal* **12.2 (1992): 174-79.** Calls for research into the informal, self-sponsored writing and reading that students do for purposes of entertainment, networking, and mental health. Suggests the writing center is an ideal place to carry out such research because of the conversations already going on between tutor and student.

1441. **Van Dam, Denis Christian. "Effects of Writing Center Usage and Motivation on Academic Writing Performance." Diss. U of Southern California, 1985.** *DAI* **46-09A (1985): 2590.** Examines freshman composition students' use of the writing center at the University of Southern California to measure attitudes toward writing, improvement in writing, and attitudes toward the writing center. Concludes that "while writing centers are not panaceas to cure poor writing, they are useful tools in helping students to improve their narrative and expository writing in a university-level freshman composition course."

1442. **Watkins-Goffman, Linda Frances. "A Case Study of the Second Language Writing Process of a Sixth-Grade Writing Group." Diss. New York U, 1986.** *DAI* **47-08A (1987): 2932.** Focuses on a sixth-grade writing group of eight ESL students limited in English proficiency and in experience with expressive writing. The data for the study included audiotapes, videotapes of writing center sessions, the researcher's observational log, and the children's writings in English. Finds that writing can be a useful tool for language acquisition in that "it provides an opportunity for more immediate feedback and for the monitoring of output."

1443. **Wills, Linda Bannister. "Competency Exam Performance and the Writing Lab."** *Writing Lab Newsletter* **8.10 (1984): 1-4.** Presents the results of a study to determine the value of one-to-one, contextual instruction in a writing lab on the competency exam performance of 500 college freshmen. Found students increased their scores significantly on error-recognition types of exams.

1444. **Wilson, Barbara Hurd. "Prewriting Behaviors of Field Dependent and Field Independent Remedial Writers in a College Writing Center." Diss. U of Maryland College Park, 1984.** *DAI* **46-03A (1985): 605.** Examines and finds no significant differences between field dependent and field independent remedial writers' prewriting behaviors in a college writing center. Scores on the Group Embedded Figures Test determined field dependence-independence. Recommends researchers investigate the interaction between other specific prewriting behaviors and field dependence and between prewriting behaviors and other learning styles. Also recommends that ethnographic methods such as protocol analysis be used to explore the processes underlying prewriting behaviors.

1445. **Wolterbeek, Marc. "Writing Center Directors Speak."** *Writing Lab Newsletter* **15.8 (1991): 14-16.** Offers results of a survey of writing center directors in the Bay Area of San Francisco. Addresses such issues as inaccurate faculty perceptions of the writing center mission, tutor training, heavy student traffic, problems with facilities, and student/staff ratio.

1446. **Wright, Sharon. "Mapping Diversity: Writing Center Survey Results."** *Writing Lab Newsletter* **18.10 (1994): 1-4.** A survey of writing centers in the South Central region and of 14 selected writing centers nationwide on such issues as reporting lines, budgets, salaries, staffing, and daily operations indicates that writing centers are moving toward "greater sophistication, broader appeal, and wider access."

1447. **Zelenak, Bonnie, Irv Cockriel, Eric Crump, and Elaine Hocks. "Ideas in Practice: Preparing Composition Teachers in the Writing Center."** *Journal of Developmental Education* **17.1 (1993): 28-34.** Describes a study conducted at the University of Missouri to assess the influence of experience as writing center tutors upon teaching assistants' classroom teaching. Discovered these teachers focused on higher-order concerns, had increased empathy for students, and developed different views of the student-teacher relationship.

# Author Index

The numbers refer to entries, not to pages.

# Subject Index

The numbers refer to entries, not to pages.

Harris, Thomas, 0926
Harvard University (MA), 0005, 0949
Hazelwood High School (MO), 0225, 0226
hegemony, 0300
hemisphericity, 0942, 1232
heuristics, 0017, 0056, 0531, 0708, 0768, 0815, 0939, 1089, 1102, 1127, 1225, 1260, 1333, 1338, 1430
high school/university articulation programs, 0123, 0280, 0310, 0492, 0508
high schools, 0001, 0018, 0027, 0034, 0037, 0042, 0046, 0048, 0068, 0077, 0080, 0085, 0086, 0087, 0093, 0094, 0106, 0121, 0123, 0132, 0144, 0145, 0149, 0157, 0158, 0159, 0164, 0167, 0192, 0201, 0210, 0213, 0220, 0225, 0226, 0252, 0255, 0280, 0310, 0325, 0378, 0379, 0380, 0390, 0392, 0396, 0409, 0435, 0442, 0447, 0453, 0475, 0492, 0508, 0513, 0514, 0562, 0564, 0574, 0575, 0576, 0577, 0578, 0579, 0589, 0590, 0592, 0593, 0607, 0608, 0617, 0662, 0692, 0722, 0730, 0731, 0745, 0750, 0753, 0761, 0885, 0927, 0946, 0986, 1039, 1072, 1330, 1333, 1410
Highland Park High School (NJ), 0157
holistic theory, 0333, 0634, 1195
Hong Kong Baptist College, 0146
honor codes, 0934, 1365
honors programs, 0097, 0513
humanistic traditions, 0351, 0809, 0856
humor, 0915, 1128, 1160, 1186
Huntington High School (NY), 0159
hypercard, 0687
hypertext, 0680, 0687

*I'm Okay—You're Okay* (Harris), 0926
"Idea of a Writing Center, The" (North), 0291, 0346, 0376
ideology, 0878, 0909, 1190
Illinois Community College Board, 0160
Illinois Institute of Technology, 0700

Illinois State University, 0182, 0256, 0364, 0724
inappropriate topics, 0775, 1096
increasing use rates, 0064, 0391, 0526, 0528, 0546, 0554, 0588
independent learning, 0294, 1007, 1022, 1115, 1127, 1302, 1330, 1331, 1338, 1369, 1391
individualized instruction, 0022, 0026, 0030, 0031, 0034, 0044, 0049, 0077, 0098, 0149, 0150, 0152, 0160, 0168, 0180, 0181, 0193, 0222, 0263, 0268, 0271, 0285, 0289, 0290, 0293, 0448, 0527, 0537, 0551, 0578, 0580, 0585, 0695, 0712, 0722, 0738, 0765, 0803, 0817, 0818, 0819, 0842, 0851, 0902, 0924, 0939, 0940, 1099, 1141, 1171, 1176, 1234, 1276, 1298, 1403
inner speech, 0326, 0373, 0916, 1337
inner-city schools, 0101
institutional contexts, 0417, 0475, 0899
institutional models, 0005, 0067, 0076, 0151, 0179, 0256, 0267, 0268, 0269, 0270, 0273, 0303, 0315, 0317, 0322, 0323, 0346, 0368, 0476, 0560, 0595, 0596, 0698
institutional pressures, 0245, 0265, 0266, 0364, 0368, 0399, 1376
institutional roles, 0299, 0631, 0637
institutional status, 0239, 0243, 0245, 0260, 0272, 0289, 0441
instructional activities, 0321, 0440, 0998
instructional materials, 0129, 0130, 0164, 0165, 0183, 0227, 0381, 0439, 0454, 0459, 0466, 0467, 0485, 0505, 0524, 0534, 0548, 0552, 0578, 0586, 0628, 0629, 0656, 0725, 0728, 0747, 0767, 0850, 0938, 0971, 0981, 1136, 1164, 1171, 1187, 1204, 1227, 1242, 1267, 1314, 1316, 1330, 1338, 1347, 1348
Integrated Learning Model, 0820
intellectual curiosity, 1114
intellectual freedom, 0300
intellectual property, 0804, 1364
interdisciplinarity, 0615
interdisciplinary programs, 0055, 0614, 0637, 0658

student-centered instruction, 0060, 0273, 0336, 0555, 0772, 0837, 0978, 1127. *See also* individualized instruction
study centers, 0482
study clinics, 0088
study habits, 0042
study skills model, 0053
*Style: Ten Lessons in Clarity and Grace* (Williams), 1314
stylistics, 0090, 0300, 0588, 1219
subcultures, 0362
subjective knowledge, 0348
subjectivity, 0370, 0785, 0843, 0917, 1362
subversion, 0272, 0895, 1373
supplemental instruction, 0038, 0096, 0126, 0174, 0228, 0293, 0297, 0317, 0386, 0624, 0725, 0754, 0764, 0776, 0783, 0991
surface errors vs. global issues, 0301, 0808, 0943, 1057. *See also* editing/proofreading
surveys, 0052, 0089, 0151, 0224, 0234, 0236, 0238, 0240, 0350, 0391, 0433, 0554, 0576, 0611, 0665, 0724, 0774, 1004, 1180, 1397, 1400, 1405, 1413, 1417, 1419, 1420, 1422, 1423, 1424, 1429, 1435, 1439, 1445, 1446
"symbolic action," 0278. *See also* Burke, Kenneth
syntax, 1045, 1290

T-unit length, 1416
TA-TALKers, 0754
tagmemics, 0056
task orientation, 0810
teacher education/training, 0055, 0147, 0182, 0228, 0338, 0422, 0765, 0766, 0800, 0835, 0840, 0884, 0900, 0918, 0970, 0974, 0975, 0978, 0983, 1001, 1008, 1029, 1447
teacher-student relationship, 0804, 0818, 0880, 0897
teachers' assignments, 0141, 0201, 0224, 0269, 0394, 0421, 0453, 0531, 0558, 0589, 0617, 0628, 0638, 0645,

0649, 0659, 0662, 0666, 0667, 0687, 0730, 0731, 0794, 0830, 0893, 0900, 0934, 0967, 0983, 1000, 1009, 1013, 1044, 1085, 1101, 1118, 1149, 1154, 1163, 1170, 1204, 1223, 1318, 1332, 1335, 1377, 1398
teachers' comments, 0808, 0818, 0834, 0944, 0983, 1342, 1377
teaching models/philosophies, 0884, 1433
teamwork, 0627, 1090, 1140
technical writing, 0165, 0174, 0189, 0197, 0320 , 0623, 0657, 0669, 0990, 1336
technical writing labs, 0126, 0189, 0193, 0197, 0320
technocracy, 0340
technophobia, 0715, 0720, 0732, 1313
text linguistics, 0371
textual spaces, 0307
Theory Z management, 0367. *See also* management
theory-practice dichotomy, 0009, 0260, 0275, 0312, 0313, 0377, 0775
theses/dissertations. *See* graduate students, tutoring of
thesis statements, 0772, 1035, 1084, 1102, 1245, 1341, 1351
threats/dangers to writing centers, 0070, 0296, 0365, 0383, 0465, 0538, 0563, 0568, 0605, 0610, 0797, 1373. *See also* professional concerns
Test of English as a Foreign Language (TOEFL), 1325
"Three Laws of Robotics," 1391. *See also* Asimov, Isaac
Title IV-c, 0574
*topoi*, 0056
transactional theories, 0333, 0870
transactional writing, 0355, 0645
Transactional Analysis, 0926
triage tutoring, 1169
Trimbur, John, 0858
Troy State University (AL), 0156, 0224
Tulane University (LA), 0110
Turabian style, 0500
tutor attitudes, 0323, 0349, 0387, 0460, 0556, 0813, 0841, 0888, 0948, 1013,

1100, 1168, 1287, 1350, 1362, 1371, 1379, 1385, 1389, 1395. *See also* interpersonal dynamics
tutor credibility, 0795, 0834, 1130, 1132
tutor involvement in program design, 0963, 1020, 1035
tutor morale, 0233, 0957, 1121
tutor qualities/qualifications, 0420, 1112, 1194, 1249
tutor selection, 0005, 0166, 0188, 0384, 0389, 0400, 0411, 0412, 0420, 0452, 0471, 0479, 0498, 0511, 0513, 0536, 0655, 0659, 0666, 0933, 0976, 0988, 1002, 1004, 1005, 1011, 1012, 1025, 1036, 1194
tutor training, 0006, 0008, 0016, 0017, 0043, 0048, 0080, 0084, 0115, 0137, 0156, 0165, 0166, 0188, 0200, 0211, 0217, 0231, 0236, 0240, 0244, 0280, 0379, 0384, 0389, 0395, 0400, 0412, 0414, 0419, 0442, 0454, 0462, 0477, 0489, 0495, 0512, 0523, 0531, 0541, 0542, 0557, 0580, 0587, 0600, 0614, 0625, 0641, 0650, 0657, 0659, 0666, 0672, 0678, 0705, 0720, 0751, 0754, 0762, 0770, 0789, 0821, 0822, 0827, 0833, 0853, 0854, 0858, 0860, 0861, 0865, 0871, 0873, 0874, 0875, 0876, 0877, 0889, 0911, 0916, 0922, 0933, 0935, 1129, 1229, 1235, 1244, 1321, 1325, 1397, 1445. *See also* Tutor Training 0946-1042
tutor-student relationship, 0773, 0808, 0837, 0856, 0867, 0871, 0880, 0892, 0903, 0917, 1045. *See also* interpersonal dimensions
tutor-teacher communication, 0421, 0472
tutoring anxiety, 0543, 0914, 0990, 1222, 1237, 1317
tutoring faculty members, 0119, 0135, 0153, 0696, 1207
tutoring graduate students, 0082, 0124, 0138, 0259, 0374, 0382, 0500, 0561, 0799, 0890

tutoring in specific disciplines, 0031, 0066, 0082, 0108, 0116, 0126, 0129, 0141, 0172, 0175, 0184, 0193, 0197, 0320, 0358, 0505, 0561, 0593, 0613, 0614, 0623, 0624, 0633, 0635, 0640, 0648, 0650, 0656, 0667, 0669, 0700, 0990, 0997, 1024, 1086, 1120, 1126, 1138, 1164, 1216, 1238, 1246, 1251, 1264, 1273, 1336. *See also* writing across the curriculum
tutoring roles, 0013, 0769, 0794, 0796, 0798, 0808, 0825, 0830, 0928, 0953, 0965, 0984, 1010, 1166, 1190
tutoring strategies, 0633, 0758, 0768, 0825, 0886, 0951, 0960, 0966, 0999, 1007, 1009, 1010, 1024, 1026, 1030, 1033, 1034, 1041, 1056, 1060, 1173, 1189, 1191, 1192, 1202, 1208, 1215, 1220, 1234, 1235, 1236, 1244, 1245, 1247, 1257, 1261, 1268, 1277, 1288, 1289, 1292, 1293, 1300, 1318, 1320, 1323, 1324, 1325, 1329, 1331, 1332, 1338, 1340, 1341, 1346, 1351, 1357. *See also* tutoring techniques
tutoring styles, 0707, 0778, 0825, 0873, 0933, 1045, 1068, 1100
tutoring techniques, 0769, 0861, 0891, 0951, 0952, 0966, 0981, 0998, 1049, 1078, 1084, 1087, 1146, 1151, 1293, 1324, 1331, 1332, 1346. *See also* tutoring strategies
tutoring, evaluation of, 0029, 0384, 0411, 0412, 0419, 0424, 0487, 0497, 0509, 0517, 0823, 0865, 0947, 0956, 0959, 0960, 0962, 0977, 0978, 0979, 1001, 1003, 1014, 1015, 1038, 1042
tutoring, models of, 0008, 0769, 0773, 0781, 0806, 0853, 0894, 0904, 0935, 0966, 1010, 1026, 1061, 1333
tutoring, personal enrichment, 0037, 0620, 1051, 1064, 1117, 1124, 1133, 1140, 1159, 1177, 1180, 1198, 1199, 1206, 1221, 1272, 1291, 1297, 1305, 1321, 1343, 1354
tutoring, politics of 0286, 0375, 0487, 0697, 0821, 0845, 0853, 0875, 0895, 0937

## About the Compilers

CHRISTINA MURPHY is Professor of English and Chair of the English Department at the University of Memphis. She was previously the Director of the William L. Adams Writing Center and Co-Director of the University Writing Program at Texas Christian University. She is the President of the National Writing Centers Association and former editor of three scholarly journals: *Composition Studies, Studies in Psychoanalytic Theory*, and *English in Texas*. Her books include *Writing Center Perspectives* (1995), *Landmark Essays on Writing Centers* (1995), *The St. Martin's Sourcebook for Writing Tutors* (1995), *Critical Thinking Skills Journal* (1995), and *Ann Beattie* (1986).

JOE LAW is Associate Professor of English and Coordinator of the Writing Across the Curriculum Program at Wright State University in Dayton, Ohio. He was previously Assistant Director of the William L. Adams Writing Center at Texas Christian University. With Christina Murphy he co-edited *Landmark Essays on Writing Centers* (1995). He has published numerous essays on writing instruction, literature, and the arts. He was Associate Editor of *English in Texas* and *Composition Studies* as well as a reviewer for *English Journal*.

STEVE SHERWOOD is the Coordinator of Peer Tutor Training at the William L. Adams Writing Center at Texas Christian University. He has published essays or fiction in *Writing Lab Newsletter, The Writing Center Journal, Northern Lights, Outside, New Texas, RiverSedge, Weber Studies*, and other journals. He is Vice President of the South Central Writing Centers Association and co-editor of *Descant*, a journal of fiction and poetry. With Christina Murphy, he co-edited *The St. Martin's Sourcebook for Writing Tutors* (1995).